lassics.

THE
DOG CRUSOE

R.M. Ballantyne—

ABBEY CLASSICS
CRESTA HOUSE, LONDON

EDITED EDITION 1970
REPRINTED 1971

© Murray's Sales and Service Co.,
146/152, Holloway Road, London. N. 7

ISBN 0 7196 0015 4

THE DOG CRUSOE

———

CHAPTER I

The backwoods settlement—Crusoe's parentage and early history—The agonizing pains and sorrows of his puppyhood, and other interesting matters.

The dog Crusoe was once a pup. Now do not, courteous reader, toss your head contemptuously and exclaim, " Of course he was; I could have told *you* that." You know very well that you have often seen a man above six feet high, broad and powerful as a lion, with a bronzed shaggy visage and the stern glance of an eagle, of whom you have said, or thought, or heard others say, " It is scarcely possible to believe that such a man was once a squalling baby." If you had seen our hero in all the strength and majesty of full-grown doghood, you would have experienced a vague sort of surprise had we told you—as we now repeat—that the dog Crusoe was once a pup—a soft, round, sprawling, squeaking pup, as fat as a tallow candle, and as blind as a bat.

But we draw particular attention to the fact of Crusoe's having once been a pup, because in connexion with the days of his puppyhood there hangs a tale. This peculiar dog may thus be said to have had two tails—one in connexion with his body, the other with his career. This tale, though short, is very harrowing, and as it is intimately connected with Crusoe's subsequent history we will relate it here. But before doing so we must beg our reader to accompany us beyond the civilized portions of the United States of America—beyond the frontier settlements of the " far west ",

into those wild prairies which are watered by the great
Missouri River—the Father of Waters—and his numerous
tributaries.

Here dwell the Pawnees, the Sioux, the Delawarers, the
Crows, the Blackfeet, and many other tribes of Red Indians,
who are gradually retreating step by step towards the Rocky
Mountains, as the advancing white man cuts down their
trees and ploughs up their prairies. Here, too, dwell the
wild horse and the wild ass, the deer, the buffalo, and the
badger; all, men and brutes alike, wild as the power of
untamed and ungovernable passion can make them, and
free as the wind that sweeps over their mighty plains.

There is a romantic and exquisitely beautiful spot on the
banks of one of the tributaries above referred to—a long
stretch of mingled woodland and meadow, with a magnificent lake lying like a gem in its green bosom—which goes
by the name of the Mustang Valley. This remote vale, even
at the present day, is but thinly peopled by white men, and
is still a frontier settlement round which the wolf and the
bear prowl curiously, and from which the startled deer
bounds terrified away. At the period of which we write,
the valley had just been taken possession of by several
families of squatters, who, tired of the turmoil and the
squabbles of the *then* frontier settlements, had pushed boldly
into the far west to seek a new home for themselves, where
they could have ".elbow room", regardless alike of the
dangers they might encounter in unknown lands and of
the Redskins who dwelt there.

The squatters were well armed with axes, rifles, and
ammunition. Most of the women were used to dangers and
alarms, and placed implicit reliance in the power of their
fathers, husbands, and brothers to protect them; and well
they might, for a bolder set of stalwart men than these backwoodsmen never trod the wilderness. Each had been
trained to the use of the rifle and the axe from infancy, and
many of them had spent so much of their lives in the woods
that they were more than a match for the Indian in his
own peculiar pursuits of hunting and war. When the

squatters first issued from the woods bordering the valley, an immense herd of wild horses or mustangs were browsing on the plain. These no sooner beheld the cavalcade of white men than, uttering a wild neigh, they tossed their flowing manes in the breeze and dashed away like a whirl-wind. This incident procured the valley its name.

The new-comers gave one satisfied glance at their future home, and then set to work to erect log huts forthwith. Soon the axe was heard ringing through the forests, and tree after tree fell to the ground, while the occasional sharp ring of a rifle told that the hunters were catering successfully for the camp. In course of time the Mustang Valley began to assume the aspect of a thriving settlement, with cottages and waving fields clustered together in the midst of it.

Of course the savages soon found it out and paid it occa-sional visits. These dark-skinned tenants of the woods brought furs of wild animals with them, which they ex-changed with the white men for knives, and beads, and baubles and trinkets of brass and tin. But they hated the " Pale-faces " with bitter hatred, because their encroach-ments had at this time materially curtailed the extent of their hunting-grounds, and nothing but the numbers and known courage of the squatters prevented these savages from butchering and scalping them all.

The leader of this band of pioneers was a Major Hope, a gentleman whose love for nature in its wildest aspects deter-mined him to exchange barrack life for a life in the woods. The major was a first-rate shot, a bold, fearless man, and an enthusiastic naturalist. He was past the prime of life, and, being a bachelor, was unencumbered with a family. His first act on reaching the site of the new settlement was to commence the erection of a block-house, to which the people might retire in case of a general attack by the Indians.

In this block-house Major Hope took up his abode as the guardian of the settlement. And here the dog Crusoe was born; here he sprawled in the early morn of life; here he leaped, and yelped, and wagged his shaggy tail in the ex-cessive glee of puppyhood; and from the wooden portals of this block-house he bounded forth to the chase in all the fire, and strength, and majesty of full-grown doghood.

Crusoe's father and mother were magnificent Newfoundlanders. There was no doubt as to their being of the genuine breed, for Major Hope had received them as a parting gift from a brother officer, who had brought them both from Newfoundland itself. The father's name was Crusoe, the mother's name was Fan. Why the father had been so called no one could tell. The man from whom Major Hope's friend had obtained the pair was a poor illiterate fisherman, who had never heard of the celebrated " Robinson " in all his life. All he knew was that Fan had been named after his own wife. As for Crusoe, he had got him from a friend, who had got him from another friend, whose cousin had received him as a marriage-gift from a friend of *his*; and each had said to the other that the dog's name was Crusoe ", without reasons being asked or given on either side. On arriving at New York the major's friend, as we have said, made him a present of the dogs. Not being much of a dog fancier, he soon tired of old Crusoe, and gave him away to a gentleman, who took him down to Florida, and that was the end of him. He was never heard of more.

When Crusoe, junior, was born, he was born, of course, without a name. That was given to him afterwards in honour of his father. He was also born in company with a brother and two sisters, all of whom drowned themselves accidentally, in the first month of their existence, by falling into the river which flowed past the block-house—a calamity which occurred, doubtless, in consequence of their having gone out without their mother's leave. Little Crusoe was with his brother and sisters at the time, and fell in along with them, but was saved from sharing their fate by his mother, who, seeing what had happened, dashed with an agonized howl into the water, and, seizing him in her mouth, brought him ashore in a half-drowned condition. She afterwards brought the others ashore one by one, but the poor little things were dead.

And now we come to the harrowing part of our tale, for

the proper understanding of which the foregoing dissertation was needful.

One beautiful afternoon, in that charming season of the American year called the Indian summer, there came a family of Sioux Indians to the Mustang Valley, and pitched their tent close to the block-house. A young hunter stood leaning against the gate-post of the palisades, watching the movements of the Indians, who, having just finished a long " palaver " or talk with Major Hope, were now in the act of preparing supper. A fire had been kindled on the greensward in front of the tent, and above it stood a tripod, from which depended a large tin camp-kettle. Over this hung an ill-favoured Indian woman, or squaw, who, besides attending to the contents of the pot, bestowed sundry cuffs and kicks upon her little child, which sat near to her playing with several Indians curs that gambolled round the fire. The master of the family and his two sons reclined on buffalo robes, smoking their stone pipes, or calumets in silence. There was nothing peculiar in their appearance. Their faces were neither dignified nor coarse in expression, but wore an aspect of stupid apathy, which formed a striking contrast to the countenance of the young hunter, who seemed an amused spectator of their proceedings.

The youth referred to was very unlike, in many respects, to what we are accustomed to suppose a backwoods hunter should be. He did not possess that quiet gravity and staid demeanour which often characterize these men. True, he was tall and strongly made, but no one would have called him stalwart, and his frame indicated grace and agility rather than strength. But the point about him which rendered him different from his companions was his bounding, irrepressible flow of spirits, strangely coupled with an intense love of solitary wandering in the woods. None seemed so well fitted for social enjoyment as he; none laughed so heartily, or expressed such glee in his mischief-loving eye; yet for days together he went off alone into the forest, and wandered where his fancy led him, as grave and silent as an Indian warrior.

After all, there was nothing mysterious in this. The boy followed implicitly the dictates of nature within him. He was amiable, straightforward, sanguine, and intensely *earnest.* When he laughed, he let it out, as sailors have it, " with a will " When there was good cause to be grave, no power on earth could make him smile. We have called him boy, but in truth he was about that uncertain period of life when a youth is said to be neither a man nor a boy. His face was good-looking (*every* earnest, candid face is and masculine; his hair was reddish-brown and his eyes bright-blue. He was costumed in the deerskin cap, leggings, moccasins, and leathern shirt common to the western hunter.

" You seem tickled wi' the Injuns, Dick Varley," said a man who at that moment issued from the block-house.

" That's just what I am, Joe Blunt," replied the youth, turning with a broad grin to his companion.

" Have a care, lad; do not laugh at 'em too much. They soon take offence; an' them Redskins never forgive."

" But I'm only laughing at the baby," returned the youth, pointing to the child, which, with a mixture of boldness and timidity, was playing with a pup, wrinkling up its fat visage into a smile when its playmate rushed away in sport, and opening wide its jet-black eyes in grave anxiety as the pup returned at full gallop.

" It 'ud make an owl laugh," continued young Varley, " to see such a queer pictur' o' itself."

He paused suddenly, and a dark frown covered his face as he saw the Indian woman stoop quickly down, catch the pup by its hind-leg with one hand, seize a heavy piece of wood with the other, and strike it several violent blows on the throat. Without taking the trouble to kill the poor animal outright, the savage then held its still writhing body over the fire, in order to singe off the hair before putting it into the pot to be cooked.

The cruel act drew young Varley's attention more closely to the pup, and it flashed across his mind that this could be no other than young Crusoe, which neither he nor his

companion had before seen, although they had often heard
others speak of and describe it.

Had the little creature been one of the unfortunate
Indian curs, the two hunters would probably have turned
from the sickening sight with disgust, feeling that, however
much they might dislike such cruelty, it would be of no
use attempting to interfere with Indian usages. But the
instant the idea that it was Crusoe occurred to Varley he
uttered a yell of anger, and sprang towards the woman
with a bound that caused the three Indians to leap to their
feet and grasp their tomahawks.

Blunt did not move from the gate, but threw forward his
rifle with a careless motion, but an expressive glance, that
caused the Indians to resume their seats and pipes with an
emphatic " Wah!" of disgust at having been startled out of
their propriety by a trifle; while Dick Varley snatched poor
Crusoe from his dangerous and painful position, scowled
angrily in the woman's face, and turning on his heel,
walked up to the house, holding the pup tenderly in his arms.

Joe Blunt gazed after his friend with a grave, solemn
expression of countenance till he disappeared; then he
looked at the ground, and shook his head.

Joe was one of the regular out-and-out backwoods hunters,
both in appearance and in fact—broad, tall, massive, lion-
like; gifted with the hunting, stalking, running, and trail-
following powers of the savage, and with a superabundance
of the shooting and fighting powers, the daring, and dash
of the Anglo-Saxon. He was grave, too—seldom smiled,
and rarely laughed. His expression almost at all times was
a compound of seriousness and good-humour. With the rifle
he was a good, steady shot, but by no means a " crack "
one. His ball never failed to *hit*, but it often failed to
kill.

After meditating a few seconds, Joe Blunt again shook
his head, and muttered to himself, " The boy's bold enough,
but he's too reckless for a hunter. There was no need for
that yell, now—none at all."

Having uttered this sagacious remark, he threw his rifle

into the hollow of his left arm, turned round, and strode off with a long, slow step towards his own cottage.

Blunt was an American by birth, but of Irish extraction, and to an attentive ear there was a faint echo of the *brogue* in his tone, which seemed to have been handed down to him as a threadbare and almost worn-out heirloom.

Poor Crusoe was singed almost naked. His wretched tail seemed little better than a piece of wire filed off to a point, and he vented his misery in piteous squeaks as the sympathetic Varley confided him tenderly to the care of his mother. How Fan managed to cure him no one can tell, but cure him she did, for, in the course of a few weeks, Crusoe was as well and sleek and fat as ever.

CHAPTER II

A shooting-match and its consequences—New friends introduced to the reader—Crusoe and his mother change masters.

Shortly after the incident narrated in the last chapter, the squatters of the Mustang Valley lost their leader. Major Hope suddenly announced his intention of quitting the settlement and returning to the civilized world. Private matters, he said, required his presence there—matters which he did not choose to speak of, but which would prevent his returning again to reside among them. Go he must, and, being a man of determination, go he did; but before going he distributed all his goods and chattels among the settlers. He even gave away his rifle, and Fan and Crusoe. These last, however, he resolved should go together; and, as they were well worth having, he announced that he would give them to the best shot in the valley. He stipulated that the winner should escort him to the nearest settlement eastward, after which he might return with the rifle on his shoulder.

Accordingly, a long level piece of ground on the river's bank, with a perpendicular cliff at the end of it, was selected as the shooting-ground, and, on the appointed day, at the appointed hour, the competitors began to assemble.

"Well, lad, first as usual," exclaimed Joe Blunt, as he reached the ground and found Dick Varley there before him.

"I've bin here more than an hour lookin' for a new kind o' flower that Jack Morgan told me he'd seen. And I've found it too. Look here; did you ever see one like it before?"

Blunt leaned his rifle against a tree, and carefully examined the flower.

"Why, yes, I've seed a-many o' them up about the Rocky

Mountains, but never one here-away. It seems to have gone lost itself. The last I seed, if I remember rightly, wos near the head-waters o' the Yellowstone River, it wos—jest where I shot a grizzly bar."

" Was that the bar that gave you the wipe on the cheek?" asked Varley, forgetting the flower in his interest about the bear.

" It wos. I put six balls in that bar's carcass, and stuck my knife into its heart ten times, afore it gave out; an' it nearly ripped the shirt off my back afore I was done with it."

" I would give my rifle to get a chance at a grizzly!" exclaimed Varley, with a sudden burst of enthusiasm.

" Whoever got it wouldn't have much to brag of," remarked a burly young backwoodsman, as he joined them.

His remark was true, for poor Dick's weapon was but a sorry affair. It missed fire, and it hung fire; and even when it did fire, it remained a matter of doubt in its owner's mind whether the slight deviations from the direct line made by his bullets were the result of *his* or *its* bad shooting.

Further comment upon it was checked by the arrival of a dozen or more hunters on the scene of action. They were a sturdy set of bronzed, bold, fearless men, and one felt, on looking at them, that they would prove more than a match for several hundreds of Indians in open fight. A few minutes after, the major himself came on the ground with the prize rifle on his shoulder, and Fan and Crusoe at his heels—the latter tumbling, scrambling, and yelping after its mother, fat and clumsy, and happy as possible, having evidently quite forgotten that it had been nearly roasted alive only a few weeks before.

Immediately all eyes were on the rifle, and its merits were discussed with animation.

And well did it deserve discussion, for such a piece had never before been seen on the western frontier. It was shorter in the barrel and larger in the bore than the weapons chiefly in vogue at that time, and, besides being of beautiful workmanship, was silver-mounted. But the grand peculiarity about it, and that which afterwards rendered it the mystery of mysteries to the savages, was that it had two sets of locks—one percussion, the other flint—so that, when caps failed, by taking off the one set of locks and affixing the others, it was converted into a flint rifle. The major, however, took care never to run short of caps, so that the flint locks were merely held as a reserve in case of need.

" Now, lads," cried Major Hope, stepping up to the point whence they were to shoot, " remember the terms. He who first drives the nail obtains the rifle, Fan, and her pup, and accompanies me to the nearest settlement. Each man shoots with his own gun, and draws lots for the chance."

" Agreed," cried the men.

" Well, then, wipe your guns and draw lots. Henri will fix the nail. Here it is."

The individual who stepped, or rather plunged, forward to receive the nail was a rare and remarkable specimen of mankind. Like his comrades, he was half a farmer and half a hunter. Like them, too, he was clad in deerskin, and was tall and strong—nay, more, he was gigantic. But, unlike them, he was clumsy, awkward, loose-jointed, and a bad shot. Nevertheless Henri was an immense favourite in the settlement, for his good-humour knew no bounds. No one ever saw him frown. Even when fighting with the savages, as he was sometimes compelled to do in self-defence, he went at them with a sort of jovial rage that was almost laughable. Inconsiderate recklessness was one of his chief characteristics, so that his comrades were rather afraid of him on the war-trail or in the hunt, where caution and frequently *soundless* motion were essential to success or safety. But when Henri had a comrade at his side to check him he was safe enough, being humble-minded and obedient. Men used to say he must have been born under a lucky star, for, notwithstanding his natural inaptitude for all sorts of backwoods life, he managed to scramble through everything with safety, often with success, and sometimes with credit.

To see Henri stalk a deer was worth a long day's journey. Joe Blunt used to say he was " all jints together, from the top of his head to the sole of his moccasin ". He threw his immense form into the most inconceivable contortions, and slowly wound his way, sometimes on hands and knees, sometimes flat, through bush and brake, as if there was not a bone in his body, and without the slightest noise. This sort of work was so much against his plunging nature that he took long to learn it; but when, through hard practice and the loss of many a fine deer, he came at length to break himself in to it, he gradually progressed to perfection, and ultimately became the best stalker in the valley. This, and this alone, enabled him to procure game, for, being short-sighted, he could hit nothing beyond fifty yards, except a buffalo or a barn-door.

Yet that same lithe body, which seemed as though totally unhinged, could no more be bent, when the muscles were strung, than an iron post. No one wrestled with Henri unless he wished to have his back broken. Few could equal and none could beat him at running or leaping except Dick Varley. When Henri ran a race even Joe Blunt laughed outright, for arms and legs went like independent flails. When he leaped, he hurled himself into space with a degree of violence that seemed to ensure a somersault; yet he always came down with a crash on his feet. Plunging was Henri's forte. He generally lounged about the settlement when unoccupied, with his hands behind his back, apparently in a reverie, and when called on to act, he seemed to fancy he must have lost time, and could only make up for it by *plunging*. This habit got him into many awkward scrapes, but his herculean power as often got him out of them. He was a French-Canadian, and a particularly bad speaker of the English language.

We offer no apology for this elaborate introduction of Henri, for he was as good-hearted a fellow as ever lived, and deserves special notice.

But to return. The sort of rifle practice called " driving the nail ", by which this match was to be decided, was, and we believe still is, common among the hunters of the far west. It consisted in this: an ordinary large-headed nail was driven a short way into a plank or a tree, and the hunters, standing at a distance of fifty yards or so, fired at it until they succeeded in driving it home. On the present occasion the major resolved to test their shooting by making the distance seventy yards.

Some of the older men shook their heads.

" It's too far," said one; " ye might as well try to snuff the nose o' a mosquito."

" Jim Scraggs is the only man as'll hit that," said another.

The man referred to was a long, lank, lantern-jawed fellow, with a cross-grained expression of countenance. He used the long, heavy Kentucky rifle, which, from the ball being little larger than a pea, was called a pea-rifle. Jim was no favourite, and had been named Scraggs by his companions on account of his appearance.

In a few minutes the lots were drawn, and the shooting began. Each hunter wiped out the barrel of his piece with his ramrod as he stepped forward; then, placing a ball in the palm of his left hand, he drew the stopper of his powder-horn with his teeth, and poured out as much powder as sufficed to cover the bullet. This was the regular *measure* among them. Little time was lost in firing, for these men did not " hang " on their aim. The point of the rifle was slowly raised to the object, and the instant the sight covered it the ball sped to its mark. In a few minutes the nail was encircled by bullet holes, scarcely two of which were more than an inch distant from the mark, and one—fired by Joe Blunt—entered the tree close beside it.

" Ah, Joe!" said the major, " I thought you would have carried off the prize?"

" So did not I, sir," returned Blunt, with a shake of his head. " Had it a-bin a half-dollar at a hundred yards, I'd ha' done better, but I never *could* hit the nail. It's too small to *see*."

" That's cos ye've got no eyes," remarked Jim Scraggs, with a sneer, as he stepped forward.

All tongues were now hushed, for the expected champion

was about to fire. The sharp crack of the rifle was followed by a shout, for Jim had hit the nail-head on the edge, and part of the bullet stuck to it.

"That wins if there's no better," said the major, scarce able to conceal his disappointment. "Who comes next?"

To this question Henri answered by stepping up to the line, straddling his legs, and executing preliminary movements with his rifle, that seemed to indicate an intention on his part to throw the weapon bodily at the mark. He was received with a shout of mingled laughter and applause. After gazing steadily at the mark for a few seconds, a broad grin overspread his countenance, and looking round at his companions, he said,—

"Ha! mes boys, I can-not behold de nail at all!"

"Can ye 'behold' the *tree*?" shouted a voice, when the laugh that followed this announcement had somewhat abated.

"Oh! oui," replied Henri quite coolly; "I can see *him*, an' a goot small bit of de forest beyond."

"Fire at it, then. If ye hit the tree ye desarve the rifle—leastways ye ought to get the pup."

Henri grinned again, and fired instantly, without taking aim.

The shot was followed by an exclamation of surprise, for the bullet was found close beside the nail.

"It's more be good luck than good shootin'," remarked Jim Scraggs.

"Possiblement," answered Henri modestly, as he retreated to the rear and wiped out his rifle; "mais I have kill most of my deer by dat same goot luck."

"Bravo, Henri!" said Major Hope as he passed; "you *deserve* to win, anyhow. Who's next?"

"Dick Varley," cried several voices; "where's Varley? Come on, youngster, an' take yer shot."

The youth came forward with evident reluctance. "It's of no manner o' use," he whispered to Joe Blunt as he passed; "I can't depend on my old gun."

"Never give in," whispered Blunt, encouragingly.

Poor Varley's want of confidence in his rifle was merited, for, on pulling the trigger, the faithless lock missed fire.

" Lend him another gun," cried several voices.

" 'Gainst rules laid down by Major Hope," said Scraggs.

" Well, so it is; try again."

Varley did try again, and so successfully, too, that the ball hit the nail on the head, leaving a portion of the lead sticking to its edge.

Of course this was greeted with a cheer, and a loud dispute began as to which was the better shot of the two.

" There are others to shoot yet," cried the major. " Make way. Look out."

The men fell back, and the few hunters who had not yet fired took their shots, but without coming nearer the mark.

It was now agreed that Jim Scraggs and Dick Varley, being the two best shots, should try over again, and it was also agreed that Dick should have the use of Blunt's rifle. Lots were again drawn for the first shot, and it fell to Dick, who immediately stepped out, aimed somewhat hastily, and fired.

" Hit again!" shouted those who had run forward to examine the mark. " *Half* the bullet cut off by the nail head!"

Some of the more enthusiastic of Dick's friends cheered lustily, but the most of the hunters were grave and silent, for they knew Jim's powers, and felt that he would certainly do his best. Jim now stepped up to the line, and, looking earnestly at the mark, threw forward his rifle.

At that moment our friend Crusoe, tired of tormenting his mother, waddled stupidly and innocently into the midst of the crowd of men, and in so doing received Henri's heel and the full weight of his elephantine body on its fore paw. The horrible and electric yell that instantly issued from his agonized throat could only be compared, as Joe Blunt expressed it, " to the last dyin' screech o' a bustin' steam biler!" We cannot say that the effect was startling, for these backwoodsmen had been born and bred in the midst of alarms, and were so used to them that a " bustin' steam biler " itself, unless it had blown them fairly off their legs, would not have startled them. But the effect, such as it was, was sufficient to disconcert the aim of Jim Scraggs, who fired at the same instant, and missed the nail by a hair's-breadth.

Turning round in towering wrath, Scraggs aimed a kick at the poor pup, which, had it taken effect, would certainly have terminated the innocent existence of that remarkable dog on the spot; but quick as lightning Henri interposed the butt of his rifle, and Jim's shin met it with a violence that caused him to howl with rage and pain.

" Oh! pardon me, broder," cried Henri, shrinking back, with the drollest expression of mingled pity and glee.

Jim's discretion, on this occasion, was superior to his valour; he turned away with a coarse expression of anger and left the ground.

Meanwhile the major handed the silver rifle to young Varley. " It couldn't have fallen into better hands," he said. " You'll do it credit, lad; I know that full well; and let me assure you it will never play you false. Only keep it clean, don't overcharge it, aim true, and it will never miss the mark."

While the hunters crowded round Dick to congratulate him and examine the piece, he stood with a mingled feeling of bashfulness and delight at his unexpected good fortune. Recovering himself suddenly, he seized his old rifle, and dropping quietly to the outskirts of the crowd, while the men were still busy handling and discussing the merits of the prize, went up, unobserved, to a boy of about thirteen years of age, and touched him on the shoulder.

" Here, Marston; you know I often said ye should have the old rifle when I was rich enough to get a new one. Take it *now*, lad. It's come to ye sooner than either o' us expected."

" Dick," said the boy, grasping his friend's hand warmly, " ye're true as heart of oak. It's good of 'ee, that's a fact."

" Not a bit, boy; it costs me nothin' to give away an old gun that I've no use for, an's worth little, but it makes me right glad to have the chance to do it."

Marston had longed for a rifle ever since he could walk; but his prospects of obtaining one were very poor indeed at that time, and it is a question whether he did not at that moment experience as much joy in handling the old piece as his friend felt in shouldering the prize.

A difficulty now occurred which had not before been thought of. This was no less than the absolute refusal of Dick Varley's canine property to follow him. Fan had no idea of changing masters without her consent being asked or her inclination being consulted.

" You'll have to tie her up for a while, I fear," said the major.

" No fear," answered the youth. " Dog natur's like human natur' !"

Saying this he seized Crusoe by the neck, stuffed him comfortably into the bosom of his hunting-shirt, and walked rapidly away with the prize rifle on his shoulder.

Fan had not bargained for this. She stood irresolute, gazing now to the right and now to the left, as the major retired in one direction and Dick with Crusoe in another. Suddenly Crusoe, who, although comfortable in body, was ill at ease in spirit, gave utterance to a melancholy howl. The mother's love instantly prevailed. For one moment she pricked up her ears at the sound, and then, lowering them, trotted quietly after her new master, and followed him to his cottage on the margin of the lake.

CHAPTER III

It is pleasant to look upon a serene, quiet, humble face.
On such a face did Richard Varley look every night when
he entered his mother's cottage. Mrs. Varley was a widow,
and she had followed the fortunes of her brother, Daniel
Hood, ever since the death of her husband. Love for her
only brother induced her to forsake the peaceful village of
Maryland and enter upon the wild life of a backwoods
settlement. Dick's mother was thin, and old, and wrinkled,
but her face was stamped with a species of beauty which
never fades—the beauty of a loving look. Ah! the brow of
snow and the peach-bloom cheek may snare the heart of
man for a time, but the *loving look* alone can forge that
adamantine chain that time, age, eternity shall never break.

Mistake us not, reader, and bear with us if we attempt to
analyse this look which characterized Mrs. Varley. A rare
diamond is worth stopping to glance at, even when one is
in a hurry. The brightest jewel in the human heart is worth
a thought or two. By *a loving look* we do not mean a look
of love bestowed on a beloved object. *That* is common
enough; and thankful should we be that it is so common
in a world that's overfull of hatred. Still less do we mean
that smile and look of intense affection with which some
people—good people too—greet friend and foe alike, and
by which effort to work out their *beau ideal* of the expression
of Christian love they do signally damage their cause, by
saddening the serious and repelling the gay. Much less do
we mean that *perpetual* smile of good-will which argues
more of personal comfort and self-love than anything else.

No; the loving look we speak of is as often grave as gay. Its character depends very much on the face through which it beams. And it cannot be counterfeited. Its *ring* defies imitation. Like the clouded sun of April, it can pierce through tears of sorrow; like the noontide sun of summer, it can blaze in warm smiles; like the northern lights of winter, it can gleam in depths of woe;—but it is always the same, modified, doubtless, and rendered more or less patent to others, according to the natural amiability of him or her who bestows it. No one can put it on; still less can any one put it off. Its range is universal; it embraces all mankind, though, *of course*, it is intensified on a few favoured objects; its seat is in the depths of a renewed heart, and its foundation lies in love to God.

Young Varley's mother lived in a cottage which was of the smallest possible dimensions consistent with comfort. It was made of logs, as, indeed, were all the other cottages in the valley. The door was in the centre, and a passage from it to the back of the dwelling divided it into two rooms. One of these was sub-divided by a thin partition, the inner room being Mrs. Varley's bedroom, the outer Dick's. Daniel Hood's dormitory was a corner of the kitchen, which apartment served also as a parlour.

The rooms were lighted by two windows, one on each side of the door, which gave to the house the appearance of having a nose and two eyes. Houses of this kind have literally got a sort of *expression* on—if we may use the word— their countenances. *Square* windows give the appearance of easy-going placidity; *longish* ones, that of surprise. Mrs. Varley's was a surprise cottage; and this was in keeping with the scene in which it stood, for the clear lake in front, studded with islands, and the distant hills beyond, composed a scene so surprisingly beautiful that it never failed to call forth an expression of astonished admiration from every new visitor to the Mustang Valley.

" My boy," exclaimed Mrs. Varley, as her son entered the cottage with a bound, " why so hurried to-day? Deary me! where got you the grand gun?"

" Won it, mother!"

" Won it, my son?"

" Ay, won it, mother. Druve the nail *almost*, and would ha' druve it *altogether* had I bin more used to Joe Blunt's rifle."

Mrs. Varley's heart beat high, and her face flushed with pride as she gazed at her son, who laid the rifle on the table for her inspection, while he rattled off an animated and somewhat disjointed account of the match.

" Deary me! now that was good, that was cliver. But what's that scraping at the door?"

" Oh! that's Fan; I forgot her. Here! here! Fan! Come in, good dog," he cried, rising and opening the door.

Fan entered and stopped short, evidently uncomfortable.

" My boy, what do ye with the major's dog?"

" Won her too, mother!"

" Won her, my son?"

" Ay, won her, and the pup too; see, here it is!" and he plucked Crusoe from his bosom.

Crusoe having found his position to be one of great comfort had fallen into a profound slumber, and on being thus unceremoniously awakened he gave forth a yelp of discontent that brought Fan in a state of frantic sympathy to his side.

" There you are, Fan; take it to a corner and make yourself at home. Ay, that's right, mother, give her somethin' to eat; she's hungry, I know by the look o' her eye."

" Deary me, Dick!" said Mrs. Varley, who now proceeded to spread the youth's mid-day meal before him, " did ye drive the nail three times?"

" No, only once, and that not parfetly. Brought 'em all down at one shot—rifle, Fan, an' pup!"

" Well, well, now that was cliver but—" Here the old woman paused and looked grave.

" But what, mother?"

" You'll be wantin' to go off to the mountains now, I fear me, boy."

" Wantin' *now*!" exclaimed the youth earnestly; " I'm

always wantin'. I've bin wantin' ever since I could walk; but I won't go till you let me, mother, that I won't!" And he struck the table with his fist so forcibly that the platters rung again.

" You're a good boy, Dick; but you're too young yit to ventur' among the Redskins."

" An' yit, if I don't ventur' young, I'd better not ventur' at all. You know, mother dear, I don't want to leave you; but I was born to be a hunter, and everybody in them parts is a hunter, and I can't hunt in the kitchen you know, mother!"

At this point the conversation was interrupted by a sound that caused young Varley to spring up and seize his rifle, and Fan to show her teeth and growl.

" Hist, mother! that's like horses' hoofs," he whispered, opening the door and gazing intently in the direction whence the sound came.

Louder and louder it came, until an opening in the forest showed the advancing cavalcade to be a party of white men. In another moment they were in full view—a band of about thirty horsemen, clad in the leathern costume and armed with the long rifle of the far west. Some wore portions of the gaudy Indian dress, which gave to them a brilliant, dashing look. They came on straight for the block-house, and saluted the Varleys with a jovial cheer as they swept past at full speed. Dick returned the cheer with compound interest, and calling out, " They're trappers, mother; I'll be back in an hour," bounded off like a deer through the woods, taking a short cut in order to reach the block-house before them. He succeeded, for, just as he arrived at the house, the cavalcade wheeled round the bend in the river, dashed up the slope, and came to a sudden halt on the green. Vaulting from their foaming steeds they tied them to the stockades of the little fortress, which they entered in a body.

Hot haste was in every motion of these men. They were trappers, they said, on their way to the Rocky Mountains to hunt and trade furs. But one of their number had been treacherously murdered and scalped by a Pawnee chief, and they resolved to revenge his death by an attack on one of the Pawnee villages. They would teach these " red reptiles " to respect white men—they would, come of it what might; and they had turned aside here to procure an additional supply of powder and lead.

In vain did the major endeavour to dissuade these reckless men from their purpose. They scoffed at the idea of returning good for evil, and insisted on being supplied. The log hut was a store as well as a place of defence, and as they offered to pay for it there was no refusing their request—at least so the major thought. The ammunition was therefore given to them, and in half-an-hour they were away again at full gallop over the plains on their mission of vengeance. " Vengeance is mine; I will repay, saith the Lord." But these men knew not what God said, because they never read His Word and did not own His sway.

Young Varley's enthusiasm was considerably damped when he learned the errand on which the trappers were bent. From that time forward he gave up all desire to visit the mountains in company with such men, but he still retained an intense longing to roam at large among their rocky fastnesses and gallop out upon the wide prairies.

Meanwhile he dutifully tended his mother's cattle and sheep, and contented himself with an occasional deer-hunt in the neighbouring forests. He devoted himself also to the training of his dog Crusoe—an operation which at first cost him many a deep sigh.

Every one has heard of the sagacity and almost reasoning capabilities of the Newfoundland dog. Indeed, some have even gone the length of saying that what is called instinct in these animals is neither more nor less than reason. And in truth many of the noble, heroic, and sagacious deeds that have actually been performed by Newfoundland dogs incline us almost to believe that, like man, they are gifted with reasoning powers.

But every one does not know the trouble and patience that is required in order to get a juvenile dog to understand what its master means when he is endeavouring to instruct it.

Crusoe's first lesson was an interesting but not a very successful one. We may remark here that Dick Varley had presented Fan to his mother to be her watch-dog, resolving to devote all his powers to the training of the pup. We may also remark, in reference to Crusoe's appearance (and we did not remark it sooner, chiefly because up to this period in his eventful history he was little better than a ball of fat and hair), that his coat was mingled jet-black and pure white, and remarkably glossy, curly, and thick.

A week after the shooting-match Crusoe's education began. Having fed him for that period with his own hand, in order to gain his affection, Dick took him out one sunny forenoon to the margin of the lake to give him his first lesson.

And here again we must pause to remark that, although a dog's heart is generally gained in the first instance through his mouth, yet, after it is thoroughly gained, his affection is noble and disinterested. He can scarcely be driven from his master's side by blows; and even when thus harshly repelled, is always ready, on the shortest notice and with the slightest encouragement, to make it up again.

Well, Dick Varley began by calling out, "Crusoe! Crusoe! come here, pup."

Of course Crusoe knew his name by this time, for it had been so often used as a prelude to his meals that he naturally expected a feed whenever he heard it. This portal to his brain had already been open for some days; but all the other doors were fast locked, and it required a great deal of careful picking to open them.

"Now, Crusoe, come here."

Crusoe bounded clumsily to his master's side, cocked his ears, and wagged his tail,—so far his education was perfect. We say he bounded *clumsily*, for it must be remembered that he was still a very young pup, with soft, flabby muscles.

"Now, I'm goin' to begin yer edication, pup; think o' that."

Whether Crusoe thought of that or not we cannot say, but he looked up in his master's face as he spoke, cocked his ears very high, and turned his head slowly to one side, until it could not turn any farther in that direction; then he turned it as much to the other side; whereat his master burst into an uncontrollable fit of laughter, and Crusoe immediately began barking vociferously.

"Come, come," said Dick, suddenly checking his mirth, we mustn't play, pup. we must work."

Drawing a leathern mitten from his belt, the youth held it to Crusoe's nose, and then threw it a yard away, at the same time exclaiming in a loud, distinct tone, "Fetch it."

Crusoe entered at once into the spirit of this part of his training; he dashed gleefully at the mitten, and proceeded to worry it with intense gratification. As for "Fetch it" he neither understood the words nor cared a straw about them

Dick Varley rose immediately, and rescuing the mitten, resumed his seat on a rock.

"Come here, Crusoe," he repeated.

"Oh! certainly, by all means," said Crusoe—no! he didn't exactly *say* it, but really he *looked* these words so evidently that we think it right to let them stand as they are written. If he could have finished the sentence, he would certainly have said, "Go on with that game over again, old boy; it's quite to my taste—the jolliest thing in life, I assure you!" At least, if we may not positively assert that he would have said that, no one else can absolutely affirm that he wouldn't.

Well, Dick Varley did do it over again, and Crusoe worried the mitten over again, utterly regardless of "Fetch it"

Then they did it again, and again, and again, but without the slightest apparent advancement in the path of canine knowledge; and then they went home.

During all this trying operation Dick Varley never once betrayed the slightest feeling of irritability or impatience. He did not expect success at first; he was not therefore disappointed at failure.

Next day he had him out again—and the next—and the next—and the next again, with the like unfavourable result.

In short, it seemed at last as if Crusoe's mind had been deeply imbued with the idea that he had been born expressly for the purpose of worrying that mitten, and he meant to fulfil his destiny to the letter.

Young Varley had taken several small pieces of meat in his pocket each day, with the intention of rewarding Crusoe when he should at length be prevailed on to fetch the mitten; but as Crusoe was not aware of the treat that awaited him, of course the mitten never was " fetched ".

At last Dick Varley saw that this system would never do, so he changed his tactics, and the next morning gave Crusoe no breakfast, but took him out at the usual hour to go through his lesson. This new course of conduct seemed to perplex Crusoe not a little, for on his way down to the beach he paused frequently and looked back at the cottage, and then expressively up at his master's face. But the master was inexorable; he went on, and Crusoe followed, for *true* love had now taken possession of the pup's young heart, and he preferred his master's company to food.

Varley now began by letting the learner smell a piece of meat, which he eagerly sought to devour, but was prevented, to his immense disgust. Then the mitten was thrown as heretofore, and Crusoe made a few steps towards it, but being in no mood for play he turned back.

" Fetch it," said the teacher.

" I won't," replied the learner mutely, by means of that expressive sign—*not doing it.*

Hereupon Dick Varley rose, took up the mitten, and put it into the pup's mouth. Then, retiring a couple of yards, he held out the piece of meat and said, " Fetch it."

Crusoe instantly spat out the glove and bounded towards the meat—once more to be disappointed.

This was done a second time, and Crusoe came forward *with the mitten in his mouth.* It seemed as if it had been done accidentally, for he dropped it before coming quite up. If so, it was a fortunate accident, for it served as the tiny fulcrum on which to place the point of that mighty lever which was destined ere long to raise him to the pinnacle of canine erudition. Dick Varley immediately lavished upon him the tenderest caresses and gave him a lump of meat. But he quickly tried it again lest he should lose the lesson. The dog evidently felt that if he did not fetch that mitten he should have no meat or caresses. In order, however, to make sure that there was no mistake, Dick laid the mitten down beside the pup, instead of putting it into his mouth, and, retiring a few paces, cried, " Fetch it."

Crusoe looked uncertain for a moment, then he picked up the mitten and laid it at his master's feet. The lesson was learned at last! Dick Varley tumbled all the meat out of his pocket on the ground, and, while Crusoe made a hearty breakfast, he sat down on a rock and whistled with glee at having fairly picked the lock, and opened *another* door into one of the many chambers of his dog's intellect.

CHAPTER IV

Our hero enlarged upon—Grumps.

Two years passed away. The Mustang Valley settlement advanced prosperously, despite one or two attacks made upon it by the savages, who were, however, firmly repelled. Dick Varley had now become a man, and his pup Crusoe had become a full-grown dog. The " silver rifle ", as Dick's weapon had come to be named, was well known among the hunters and the Redskins of the border-lands, and in Dick's hands its bullets were as deadly as its owner's eye was quick and true.

Crusoe's education, too, had been completed. Faithfully and patiently had his young master trained his mind, until he fitted him to be a meet companion in the hunt. To " carry " and " fetch " were now but trifling portions of the dog's accomplishments. He could dive a fathom deep in the lake and bring up any article that might have been dropped or thrown in. His swimming powers were marvellous, and so powerful were his muscles that he seemed to spurn the water while passing through it, with his broad chest high out of the curling wave, at a speed that neither man nor beast could keep up with for a moment. His intellect now was sharp and quick as a needle; he never required a second bidding. When Dick went out hunting, he used frequently to drop a mitten or a powder-horn unknown to the dog, and after walking miles away from it, would stop short and look down into the mild, gentle face of his companion.

" Crusoe," he said, in the same quiet tones with which he would have addressed a human friend, " I've dropped my mitten; go fetch it, pup." Dick continued to call it " pup " from habit.

One glance of intelligence passed from Crusoe's eye, and in a moment he was away at full gallop, nor did he rest until the lost article was lying at his master's feet. Dick was loath to try how far back on his track Crusoe would run if desired. He had often gone back five and six miles at a stretch; but his powers did not stop here. He could carry articles back to the spot from which they had been taken and leave them there. He could head the game that his master was pursuing and turn it back; and he would guard any object he was desired to "watch" with unflinching constancy. But it would occupy too much space and time to enumerate all Crusoe's qualities and powers. His biography will unfold them.

In personal appearance he was majestic, having grown to an immense size even for a Newfoundland. Had his visage been at all wolfish in character, his aspect would have been terrible. But he possessed in an eminent degree that mild, humble expression of face peculiar to his race. When roused or excited, and especially when bounding through the forest with the chase in view, he was absolutely magnificent. At other times his gait was slow, and he seemed to prefer a quiet walk with Dick Varley to anything else under the sun. But when Dick was inclined to be boisterous, Crusoe's tail and ears rose at a moment's notice, and he was ready for anything. Moreover, he obeyed commands instantly and implicitly. In this respect he put to shame most of the boys of the settlement, who were by no means famed for their habits of prompt obedience.

Crusoe's eye was constantly watching the face of his master. When Dick said "Go" he went, when he said "Come" he came. If he had been in the midst of an excited bound at the throat of a stag, and Dick had called out "Down, Crusoe", he would have sunk to the earth like a stone. No doubt it took many months of training to bring the dog to this state of perfection, but Dick accomplished it by patience, perseverance, and *love*.

Besides all this, Crusoe could speak! He spoke by means of the dog's dumb alphabet in a way that defies description.

He conversed, so to speak, with his extremities—his head and his tail. But his eyes, his soft brown eyes, were the chief medium of communication. If ever the language of the eyes was carried to perfection, it was exhibited in the person of Crusoe. But, indeed, it would be difficult to say which part of his expressive face expressed most—the cocked ears of expectation, the drooped ears of sorrow; the bright, full eye of joy, the half-closed eye of contentment, and the frowning eye of indignation accompanied with a slight, a very slight pucker of the nose and a gleam of dazzling ivory —ha! no enemy ever saw this last piece of canine language without a full appreciation of what it meant. Then as to the tail—the modulations of meaning in the varied wag of that expressive member—oh! it's useless to attempt description. Mortal man cannot conceive of the delicate shades of sentiment expressible by a dog's tail, unless he has studied the subject—the wag, the waggle, the cock, the droop, the slope, the wriggle! Away with description—it is impotent and valueless here!

As we have said, Crusoe was meek and mild. He had been bitten, on the sly, by half the ill-natured curs in the settlement, and had only shown his teeth in return. He had no enmities—though several enemies—and he had a thousand friends, particularly among the ranks of the weak and the persecuted, whom he always protected and avenged when opportunity offered. A single instance of this kind will serve to show his character.

One day Dick and Crusoe were sitting on a rock beside the lake—the same identical rock near which, when a pup, the latter had received his first lesson. They were conversing as usual, for Dick had elicited such a fund of intelligence from the dog's mind, and had injected such wealth of wisdom into it, that he felt convinced it understood every word he said.

" This is capital weather, Crusoe; ain't it, pup?"

Crusoe made a motion with his head which was quite as significant as a nod.

" Ha! my pup, I wish that you and I might go and have

a slap at the grizzly bars, and a look at the Rocky Mountains. Wouldn't it be nuts, pup?"

Crusoe looked dubious.

"What, you don't agree with me! Now tell me, pup, wouldn't ye like to grip a bar?"

Still Crusoe looked dubious, but made a gentle motion with his tail, as though he would have said, "I've seen neither Rocky Mountains nor grizzly bars, and know nothin' about 'em, but I'm open to conviction."

"You're a brave pup," rejoined Dick, stroking the dog's huge head affectionately. "I wouldn't give you for ten times your weight in golden dollars—if there be sich things."

Crusoe made no reply whatever to this. He regarded it as a truism unworthy of notice; he evidently felt that a comparison between love and dollars was preposterous.

At this point in the conversation a little dog with a lame leg hobbled to the edge of the rocks in front of the spot where Dick was seated, and looked down into the water, which was deep there. Whether it did so for the purpose of admiring its very plain visage in the liquid mirror, or finding out what was going on among the fish, we cannot say, as it never told us; but at that moment a big, clumsy, savage-looking dog rushed out from the neighbouring thicket and began to worry it.

"Punish him, Crusoe," said Dick quickly.

Crusoe made one bound that a lion might have been proud of, and seizing the aggressor by the back, lifted him off his legs and held him, howling, in the air—at the same time casting a look towards his master for further instructions.

"Pitch him in," said Dick, making a sign with his hand.

Crusoe turned and quietly dropped the dog into the lake. Having regarded his struggles there for a few moments with grave severity of countenance, he walked slowly back and sat down beside his master.

The little dog made good its retreat as fast as three legs would carry it; and the surly dog, having swum ashore, retired sulkily, with his tail very much between his legs.

Little wonder, then, that Crusoe was beloved by great and small among the well-disposed of the canine tribe of the Mustang Valley.

But Crusoe was not a mere machine. When not actively engaged in Dick Varley's service, he busied himself with private little matters of his own. He undertook modest little excursions into the woods or along the margin of the lake, sometimes alone, but more frequently with a little friend, whose whole heart and being seemed to be swallowed up in admiration of his big companion. Whether Crusoe botanized or geologized on these excursions we will not venture to say. Assuredly he seemed as though he did both, for he poked his nose into every bush and tuft of moss, and turned over the stones, and dug holes in the ground—and, in short, if he did not understand these sciences, he behaved very much as if he did. Certainly he knew as much about them as many of the human species do.

In these walks he never took the slightest notice of Grumps (that was the little dog's name), but Grumps made up for this by taking excessive notice of him. When Crusoe stopped, Grumps stopped and sat down to look at him. When Crusoe trotted on, Grumps trotted on too. When Crusoe examined a bush, Grumps sat down to watch him; and when he dug a hole, Grumps looked into it to see what was there. Grumps never helped him; his sole delight was in looking on. They didn't converse much, these two dogs. To be in each other's company seemed to be happiness enough—at least Grumps thought so.

There was one point at which Grumps stopped short, however, and ceased to follow his friend, and that was when he rushed headlong into the lake and disported himself for an hour at a time in its cool waters. Crusoe was, both by nature and training, a splendid water-dog. Grumps, on the contrary, held water in abhorrence; so he sat on the shore of the lake disconsolate when his friend was bathing, and waited till he came out. The only time when Grumps was thoroughly nonplussed was when Dick Varley's whistle sounded faintly in the far distance. Then Crusoe would prick up his ears and stretch out at full gallop, clearing ditch, and fence, and brake with his strong elastic bound, and leaving Grumps to patter after him as fast as his four-inch legs would carry him. Poor Grumps usually arrived at the village to find both dog and master gone, and would betake himself to his own dwelling, there to lie down and sleep, and dream, perchance, of rambles and gambols with his gigantic friend.

CHAPTER V

One day the inhabitants of Mustang Valley were thrown into considerable excitement by the arrival of an officer of the United States army and a small escort of cavalry. They went direct to the block-house, which, since Major Hope's departure, had become the residence of Joe Blunt—that worthy having, by general consent, been deemed the fittest man in the settlement to fill the major's place.

Soon it began to be noised abroad that the strangers had been sent by Government to endeavour to bring about, if possible, a more friendly state of feeling between the Whites and the Indians by means of presents, and promises, and fair speeches.

The party remained all night in the block-house, and ere long it was reported that Joe Blunt had been requested, and had consented, to be the leader and chief of a party of three men who should visit the neighbouring tribes of Indians to the west and north of the valley as Government agents. Joe's knowledge of two or three different Indian dialects, and his well-known sagacity, rendered him a most fitting messenger on such an errand. It was also whispered that Joe was to have the choosing of his comrades in this mission, and many were the opinions expressed and guesses made as to who would be chosen.

That same evening Dick Varley was sitting in his mother's kitchen cleaning his rifle. His mother was preparing supper, and talking quietly about the obstinacy of a particular hen that had taken to laying her eggs in places where they could not be found Fan was coiled up in a corner sound asleep, and Crusoe was sitting at one side of the fire looking on at things in general.

"I wonder," remarked Mrs. Varley, as she spread the table with a pure white napkin—"I wonder what the sodgers are doin' wi' Joe Blunt."

As often happens when an individual is mentioned, the worthy referred to opened the door at that moment and stepped into the room.

"Good e'en t'ye, dame," said the stout hunter, doffing his cap, and resting his rifle in a corner, while Dick rose and placed a chair for him.

"The same to you, Master Blunt," answered the widow; "you've jist comed in good time for a cut o' venison."

"Thanks, mistress; I s'pose we're beholden to the silver rifle for that."

"To the hand that aimed it, rather," suggested the widow.

"Nay, then, say raither to the dog that turned it," said Dick Varley. "But for Crusoe, that buck would ha' bin couched in the woods this night."

"Oh! if it comes to that," retorted Joe, "I'd lay it to the door o' Fan, for if she'd niver bin born nother would Crusoe. But it's good an' tender meat, whativer ways ye got it. Howsiver, I've other things to talk about jist now. Them sodgers that are eatin' buffalo tongues up at the block-house as if they'd niver ate meat before, and didn't hope to eat again for a twelve-month——"

"Ay, what o' them?" interrupted Mrs. Varley; "I've bin wonderin' what was their errand."

"Of coorse ye wos, Dame Varley, and I've comed here a purpis to tell ye. They want me to go to the Redskins to make peace between them and us; and they've brought a lot o' goods to make them presents withal—beads, an' knives, an' lookin'-glasses, an' vermilion paint, an' sich like, jist as much as'll be a light load for one horse—for, ye see, nothin' can be done wi' the Redskins without gifts."

"'Tis a blessed mission," said the widow; ". I wish it may succeed. D'ye think ye'll go?"

" Go? ay, that will I."

" I only wish they'd made the offer to me," said Dick, with a sigh.

" An' so they do make the offer, lad. They've gin me leave to choose the two men I'm to take with me, and I've comed straight to ask *you.* Ay or no, for we must up an' away by break o' day to-morrow."

Mrs. Varley started. " So soon?" she said, with a look of anxiety.

" Ay; the Pawnees are at the Yellow Creek, jist at this time, but I've heerd they're 'bout to break up camp an' away west; so we'll need to use haste."

" May I go, mother?" asked Dick, with a look of anxiety. There was evidently a conflict in the widow's breast, but it quickly ceased.

" Yes, my boy," she said in her own low, quiet voice; " and God go with ye. I knew the time must come soon, an' I thank Him that your first visit to the Redskins will be on an errand o' peace. ' Blessed are the peace-makers: for they shall be called the children of God.' "

Dick grasped his mother's hand and pressed it to his cheek in silence. At the same moment Crusoe, seeing that the deeper feelings of his master were touched, and deeming it his duty to sympathize, rose up and thrust his nose against him.

" Ah, pup," cried the young man hastily, " you must go too. Of course Crusoe goes, Joe Blunt?"

" Hum! I don't know that. There's no dependin' on a dog to keep his tongue quiet in times o' danger."

" Believe me," exclaimed Dick, flashing with enthusiasm, " Crusoe's more trustworthy than I am myself. If ye can trust the master, ye're safe to trust the pup."

" Well, lad, ye may be right. We'll take him."

" Thanks, Joe. And who else goes with us?"

" I've bin castin' that in my mind for some time, an' I've fixed to take Henri. He's not the safest man in the valley, but he's the truest, that's a fact. And now, youngster, get yer horse an' rifle ready, and come to the block-house at day-

break to-morrow. Good luck to ye, mistress, till we meet
agin."

Joe Blunt rose, and taking up his rifle—without which he
scarcely ever moved a foot from his own door—left the
cottage with rapid strides.

Dick Varley spent that night in converse with his mother,
and next morning at daybreak he was at the place of meeting, mounted on his sturdy little horse, with the " silver
rifle " on his shoulder and Crusoe by his side.

"That's right, lad, that's right. Nothin' like keepin' yer
time," said Joe, as he led out a pack-horse from the gate
of the block-house, while his own charger was held ready
saddled by a man named Daniel Brand, who had been
appointed to the charge of the block-house in his absence.

"Where's Henri?—oh, here he comes!" exclaimed Dick,
as the hunter referred to came thundering up the slope at
a charge, on a horse that resembled its rider in size and
not a little in clumsiness of appearance.

"Ah! mes boy. Him is a goot one to go," cried Henri,
remarking Dick's smile as he pulled up. "No hoss on de
plain can beat dis one, surement."

"Now then, Henri, lend a hand to fix this pack; we've
no time to palaver."

By this time they were joined by several of the soldiers
and a few hunters who had come to see them start.

"Remember, Joe," said one, "if you don't come back
in three months we'll all come out in a band to seek you."

"If we don't come back in less than that time, what's
left o' us won't be worth seekin' for," said Joe, tightening
the girth of his saddle.

"Put a bit in yer own mouth, Henri," cried another, as
the Canadian arranged his steed's bridle; "ye'll need it
more than yer horse when ye git 'mong the red reptiles."

"Vraiment, if mon mout' needs one bit, yours will need
one padlock."

"Now, lads, mount!" cried Joe Blunt, as he vaulted into
the saddle.

Dick Varley sprang lightly on his horse, and Henri made

a rush at his steed and hurled his huge frame across its back with a violence that ought to have brought it to the ground; but the tall, raw-boned, broad-chested roan was accustomed to the eccentricities of its master, and stood the shock bravely. Being appointed to lead the pack-horse, Henri seized its halter. Then the three cavaliers shook their reins, and, waving their hands to their comrades, they sprang into the woods at full gallop, and laid their course for the " far west "

For some time they galloped side by side in silence, each occupied with his own thoughts, Crusoe keeping close beside his master's horse. The two elder hunters evidently ruminated on the object of their mission and the prospects of success, for their countenances were grave and their eyes cast on the ground. Dick Varley, too, thought upon the Red-men, but his musings were deeply tinged with the bright hues of a *first* adventure. The mountains, the plains, the Indians, the bears, the buffaloes, and a thousand other objects, danced wildly before his mind's eye, and his blood careered through his veins and flushed his forehead as he thought of what he should see and do, and felt the elastic vigour of youth respond in sympathy to the light spring of his active little steed. He was a lover of nature, too, and his flashing eyes glanced observantly from side to side as they swept along—sometimes through glades of forest trees, sometimes through belts of more open ground and shrubbery; anon by the margin of a stream or along the shores of a little lake, and often over short stretches of flowering prairie-land—while the firm, elastic turf sent up a muffled sound from the tramp of their mettlesome chargers. It was a scene of wild, luxuriant beauty, that might almost (one could fancy) have drawn involuntary homage to its bountiful Creator from the lips even of an infidel.

After a time Joe Blunt reined up, and they proceeded at an easy ambling pace. Joe and his friend Henri were so used to these beautiful scenes that they had long ceased to be enthusiastically affected by them, though they never ceased to delight in them.

"I hope," said Joe, "that them sodgers'll go their ways soon. I've no notion o' them chaps when they're left at a place wi' nothin' to do but whittle sticks."

"Why, Joe!" exclaimed Dick Varley, in a tone of surprise, "I thought you were admirin' the beautiful face o' nature all this time, and ye're only thinkin' about the sodgers. Now, that's strange!"

"Not so strange after all, lad," answered Joe. "When a man's used to a thing, he gits to admire an' enjoy it without speakin' much about it. But it *is* true, boy, that mankind gits in coorse o' time to think little o' the blissin's he's used to."

"Oui, c'est *vrai*!" murmured Henri, emphatically.

"Well, Joe Blunt, it may be so, but I'm thankful *I'm* not used to this sort o' thing yet!" exclaimed Varley. "Let's have another gallop—so ho! come along, Crusoe!" shouted the youth, as he shook his reins and flew over a long stretch of prairie on which at that moment they entered.

Joe smiled as he followed his enthusiastic companion, but after a short run he pulled up.

"Hold on, youngster," he cried; "ye must larn to do as ye're bid, lad. It's trouble enough to be among wild Injuns and wild buffaloes, as I hope soon to be, without havin' wild comrades to look after."

Dick laughed, and reined in his panting horse. "I'll be as obedient as Crusoe," he said, "and no one can beat him."

"Besides," continued Joe, "the horses won't travel far if we begin by runnin' all the wind out o' them."

"Wah!" exclaimed Henri, as the led horse became restive; "I think we must give to him de pack-hoss for to lead, eh?"

"Not a bad notion, Henri. We'll make that the penalty of runnin' off again; so look out, Master Dick."

"I'm down," replied Dick, with a modest air, "obedient as a baby, and won't run off again—till—the next time. By the way, Joe, how many days' provisions did ye bring?"

"Two. That's 'nough to carry us to the Great Prairie, which is three weeks distant from this. Our own good rifles must make up the difference, and keep us when we get there."

"And s'pose we neither find deer nor buffalo," suggested Dick.

"I s'pose we'll have to starve."

"Dat is cumfer'able to tink upon," remarked Henri.

"More comfortable to think o' than to undergo," said Dick; "but I s'pose there's little chance o' that."

"Well, not much," replied Joe Blunt, patting his horse's neck, "but d'ye see, lad, ye niver can count for sartin on anythin'. The deer and buffalo ought to be thick in them plains at this time—and when the buffalo *are* thick they covers the plains till ye can hardly see the end o' them; but, ye see, sometimes the rascally Redskins takes it into their heads to burn the prairies, and sometimes ye find the place that should ha' bin black wi' buffalo, black as a coal wi' fire for miles an' miles on end. At other times the Redskins go huntin' in 'ticlur places, and sweeps them clean o' every hoof that don't git away. Sometimes, too, the animals seems to take a scunner at a place, and keeps out o' the way. But one way or another men gin'rally manage to scramble through."

"Look yonder, Joe," exclaimed Dick, pointing to the summit of a distant ridge, where a small black object was seen moving against the sky, "that's a deer, ain't it?"

Joe shaded his eyes with his hand, and gazed earnestly at the object in question. "Ye're right, boy; and by good luck we've got the wind of him. Cut in an' take your chance now. There's a long strip o' wood as'll let ye git close to him."

Before the sentence was well finished, Dick and Crusoe were off at ful gallop. For a few hundred yards they coursed along the bottom of a hollow; then turning to the right they entered the strip of wood, and in a few minutes gained the edge of it. Here Dick dismounted.

"You can't help me here, Crusoe. Stay where you are, pup, and hold my horse."

Crusoe seized the end of the line, which was fastened to the horse's nose, in his mouth, and lay down on a hillock of moss, submissively placing his chin on his forepaws, and watching his master as he stepped noiselessly through the wood. In a few minutes Dick emerged from among the trees, and creeping from bush to bush, succeeded in getting to within six hundred yards of the deer, which was a beautiful little antelope. Beyond the bush behind which he now crouched all was bare open ground, without a shrub or a hillock large enough to conceal the hunter. There was a slight undulation in the ground, however, which enabled him to advance about fifty yards farther, by means of lying down quite flat and working himself forward like a serpent. Farther than this he could not move without being seen by the antelope, which browsed on the ridge before him in fancied security. The distance was too great even for a long shot; but Dick knew of a weak point in this little creature's nature which enabled him to accomplish his purpose—a weak point which it shares in common with animals of a higher order—namely, curiosity.

The little antelope of the North American prairies is intensely curious about everything that it does not quite understand, and will not rest satisfied until it has endeavoured to clear up the mystery. Availing himself of this propensity, Dick did what both Indians and hunters are accustomed to do on these occasions—he put a piece of rag on the end of his ramrod, and keeping his person concealed and perfectly still, waved this miniature flag in the air. The antelope noticed it at once, and, pricking up its ears, began to advance, timidly and slowly, step by step, to see what remarkable phenomenon it could be. In a few seconds the flag was lowered, a sharp crack followed, and the antelope fell dead upon the plain.

"Ha, boy! that's a good supper, anyhow," cried Joe, as he galloped up and dismounted.

"Goot! dat is better nor dried meat," added Henri. 'Give him to me; I will put him on my hoss, vich is strongar dan yourn. But ver is your hoss?"

"He'll be here in a minute," replied Dick, putting his fingers to his mouth and giving forth a shrill whistle.

The instant Crusoe heard the sound he made a savage
and apparently uncalled-for dash at the horse's heels. This
wild act, so contrary to the dog's gentle nature, was a mere
piece of acting. He knew that the horse would not advance
without getting a fright, so he gave him one in this way,
which sent him off at a gallop. Crusoe followed close at his
heels, so as to bring the line alongside of the nag's body,
and thereby prevent its getting entangled; but despite his
best efforts the horse got on one side of a tree and he on
the other, so he wisely let go his hold of the line, and waited
till more open ground enabled him to catch it again. Then
he hung heavily back, gradually checked the horse's speed,
and finally trotted him up to his master's side.

"'Tis a cliver cur, good sooth," exclaimed Joe Blunt in
surprise.

"Ah, Joe! you haven't seen much of Crusoe yet. He's
as good as a man any day. I've done little else but train
him for two years gone by, and he can do most anything
but shoot—he can't handle the rifle nohow."

"Ha! then, I tink perhaps hims could if he wos try,"
said Henri, plunging on to his horse with a laugh, and
arranging the carcass of the antelope across the pommel
of his saddle.

Thus they hunted and galloped, and trotted and ambled
on through wood and plain all day, until the sun began to
descend below the tree-tops of the bluffs on the west. Then
Joe Blunt looked about him for a place on which to camp,
and finally fixed on a spot under the shadow of a noble birch
by the margin of a little stream. The carpet of grass on its
banks was soft like green velvet, and the rippling waters of
the brook were clear as crystal—very different from the
muddy Missouri into which it flowed.

While Dick Varley felled and cut up firewood, Henri
unpacked the horses and turned them loose to graze, and
Joe kindled the fire and prepared venison steaks and hot
tea for supper.

In excursions of this kind it is customary to " hobble "
the horses—that is, to tie their fore-legs together, so that

they cannot run either fast or far, but are free enough to amble about with a clumsy sort of hop in search of food. This is deemed a sufficient check on their tendency to roam, although some of the knowing horses sometimes learn to hop so fast with their hobbles as to give their owners much trouble to recapture them. But when out in the prairies where Indians are known or supposed to be in the neighbourhood, the horses are picketed by means of a pin or stake attached to the ends of their long lariats, as well as hobbled; for Indians deem it no disgrace to steal or tell lies, though they think it disgraceful to be found out in doing either. And so expert are these dark-skinned natives of the western prairies, that they will creep into the midst of an enemy's camp, cut the lariats and hobbles of several horses, spring suddenly on their backs, and gallop away.

They not only steal from white men, but tribes that are at enmity steal from each other, and the boldness with which they do this is most remarkable. When Indians are travelling in a country where enemies are prowling, they guard their camps at night with jealous care. The horses in particular are both hobbled and picketed, and sentries are posted all round the camp. Yet, in spite of these precautions, hostile Indians manage to elude the sentries and creep into the camp. When a thief thus succeeds in effecting an entrance, his chief danger is past. He rises boldly to his feet, and wrapping his blanket or buffalo robe round him, he walks up and down as if he were a member of the tribe. At the same time he dexterously cuts the lariats of such horses as he observes are not hobbled. He dare not stoop to cut the hobbles, as the action would be observed, and suspicion would be instantly aroused. He then leaps on the best horse he can find, and uttering a terrific war-whoop darts away into the plains, driving the loosened horses before him.

No such dark thieves were supposed to be near the camp under the birch-tree, however, so Joe, and Dick, and Henri ate their supper in comfort, and let their horses browse at will on the rich pasturage.

A bright ruddy fire was soon kindled, which created, as it were, a little ball of light in the midst of surrounding darkness for the special use of our hardy hunters. Within this magic circle all was warm, comfortable, and cheery; outside all was dark, and cold, and dreary by contrast.

When the substantial part of supper was disposed of, tea and pipes were introduced, and conversation began to flow. Then the three saddles were placed in a row; each hunter wrapped himself in his blanket, and pillowing his head on his saddle, stretched his feet towards the fire and went to sleep, with his loaded rifle by his side and his hunting-knife handy in his belt. Crusoe mounted guard by stretching himself out *couchant* at Dick Varley's side. The faithful dog slept lightly, and never moved all night; but had any one observed him closely, he would have seen that every fitful flame that burst from the sinking fire, every unusual puff of wind, and every motion of the horses that fed or rested hard by, had the effect of revealing a speck of glittering white in Crusoe's watchful eye.

CHAPTER VI

The great prairies of the far west—A remarkable colony discovered
and a miserable night endured.

Of all the hours of the night or day the hour that succeeds
the dawn is the purest, the most joyous, and the best. At
least so think we, and so think hundreds and thousands of
the human family. And so thought Dick Varley, as he
sprang suddenly into a sitting posture next morning, and
threw his arms with an exulting feeling of delight round the
neck of Crusoe, who instantly sat up to greet him.

This was an unusual piece of enthusiasm on the part of
Dick; but the dog received it with marked satisfaction,
rubbed his big hairy cheek against that of his young master,
and arose from his sedentary position in order to afford
free scope for the use of his tail.

"Ho! Joe Blunt! Henri! Up, boys, up! The sun will
have the start o' us. I'll catch the nags."

So saying Dick bounded away into the woods, with
Crusoe gambolling joyously at his heels. Dick soon caught
his own horse, and Crusoe caught Joe's. Then the former
mounted and quickly brought in the other two.

Returning to the camp he found everything packed and
ready to strap on the back of the pack-horse.

"That's the way to do it, lad," cried Joe. "Here, Henri,
look alive and git yer beast ready. I do believe ye're goin'
to take another snooze!"

Henri was indeed, at that moment, indulging in a gigantic
stretch and a cavernous yawn; but he finished both hastily,
and rushed at his poor horse as if he intended to slay it on
the spot. He only threw the saddle on its back, however,
and then threw himself on the saddle.

"Now then, all ready?"

" Ay "—" Oui, yis!"

And away they went at full stretch again on their journey.
Thus day after day they travelled, and night after night
they laid them down to sleep under the trees of the forest,
until at length they reached the edge of the Great Prairie.

It was a great, a memorable day in the life of Dick
Varley, that on which he first beheld the prairie—the vast
boundless prairie. He had heard of it, talked of it, dreamed
about it, but he had never—no, he had never realized it
'Tis always thus. Our conceptions of things that we have
not seen are almost invariably wrong. Dick's eyes glittered,
and his heart swelled, and his cheeks flushed, and his breath
came thick and quick.

" There it is," he gasped, as the great rolling plain broke
suddenly on his enraptured gaze; " that's it—oh!——"

Dick uttered a yell that would have done credit to the
fiercest chief of the Pawnees, and, being unable to utter
another word, he swung his cap in the air and sprang like
an arrow from a bow over the mighty ocean of grass. The
sun had just risen to send a flood of golden glory over the
scene, the horses were fresh, so the elder hunters, gladdened
by the beauty of all around them, and inspired by the irresistible enthusiasm of their young companion, gave the reins
to the horses and flew after him. It was a glorious gallop,
that first headlong dash over the boundless prairie of the
" far west ".

The prairies have often been compared, most justly, to
the ocean. There is the same wide circle of space bounded
on all sides by the horizon; there is the same swell, or undulation, or succession of long, low, unbroken waves that
marks the ocean when it is calm; they are canopied by
the same pure sky, and swept by the same untrammelled
breezes. There are islands, too—clumps of trees and willow-
bushes—which rise out of this grassy ocean to break and
relieve its uniformity; and these vary in size and numbers
as do the isles of ocean, being numerous in some places,
while in others they are so scarce that the traveller does not
meet one in a long day's journey. Thousands of beautiful

flowers decked the greensward, and numbers of little birds hopped about among them.

" Now, lads," said Joe Blunt, reining up, " our troubles begin to-day."

" Our troubles?—our joys, you mean!" exclaimed Dick Varley.

" P'r'aps I don't mean nothin' o' the sort," retorted Joe. " Man wos never intended to swaller his joys without a strong mixtur' o' troubles. I s'pose he couldn't stand 'em pure. Ye see we've got to the prairie now——"

" One blind hoss might see dat!" interrupted Henri.

" An' we may or may not diskiver buffalo. An' water's scarce, too, so we'll need to look out for it pretty sharp, I guess, else we'll lose our horses, in which case we may as well give out at once. Besides, there's rattlesnakes about in sandy places—we'll ha' to look out for them; an' there's badger holes—we'll need to look sharp for them lest the horses put their feet in 'em; an' there's Injuns, who'll look out pretty sharp for us if they once get wind that we're in them parts."

" Oui, yis, mes boys; and there's rain, and tunder, and lightin'," added Henri, pointing to a dark cloud which was seen rising on the horizon ahead of them.

" It'll be rain," remarked Joe; " but there's no thunder in the air jist now. We'll make for yonder clump o' bushes and lay by till it's past."

Turning a little to the right of the course they had been following, the hunters galloped along one of the hollows between the prairie waves before mentioned, in the direction of a clump of willows. Before reaching it, however, they passed over a bleak and barren plain where there was neither flower nor bird. Here they were suddenly arrested by a most extraordinary sight—at least it was so to Dick Varley, who had never seen the like before. This was a colony of what Joe called " prairie-dogs ". On first beholding them Crusoe uttered a sort of half growl, half bark of surprise, cocked his tail and ears, and instantly prepared to charge; but he glanced up at his master first for permis-

sion. Observing that his finger and his look commanded
"silence", he dropped his tail at once and stepped to the
rear. He did not, however, cease to regard the prairie-
dogs with intense curiosity.

These remarkable little creatures have been egregiously
misnamed by the hunters of the west, for they bear not the
slightest resemblance to dogs, either in formation or habits.
They are, in fact, the marmot, and in size are little larger
than squirrels, which animals they resemble in some degree.
They burrow under the light soil, and throw it up in mounds
like moles.

Thousands of them were running about among their
dwellings when Dick first beheld them; but the moment
they caught sight of the horsemen rising over the ridge they
set up a tremendous hubbub of consternation. Each little
beast instantly mounted guard on the top of his house, and
prepared, as it were, " to receive cavalry ".

The most ludicrous thing about them was that, although
the most timid and cowardly creatures in the world, they
seemed the most impertinent things that ever lived! Knowing that their holes afforded them a perfectly safe retreat,
they sat close beside them; and as the hunters slowly approached, they elevated their heads, wagged their little tails,
showed their teeth, and chattered at them like monkeys.
The nearer they came the more angry and furious did the
prairie-dogs become, until Dick Varley almost fell off his
horse with suppressed laughter. They let the hunters come
come close up, waxing louder and louder in their wrath;
but the instant a hand was raised to throw a stone or point
a gun, a thousand little heads dived into a thousand holes,
and a thousand little tails wriggled for an instant in the air
—then a dead silence reigned over the deserted scene.

" Bien, them's have dive into de bo'-els of de eart',"
said Henri with a broad grin.

Presently a thousand noses appeared, and nervously disappeared, like the wink of an eye. Then they appeared
again, and a thousand pair of eyes followed. Instantly, like
Jack in the box, they were all on the top of their hillocks

again, chattering and wagging their little tails as vigorously as ever. You could not say that you *saw* them jump out of their holes. Suddenly, as if by magic, they *were* out; then Dick tossed up his arms, and suddenly, as if by magic, they were gone!

Their number was incredible, and their cities were full of riotous activity. What their occupations were the hunters could not ascertain, but it was perfectly evident that they visited a great deal and gossiped tremendously, for they ran about from house to house, and sat chatting in groups; but it was also observed that they never went far from their own houses. Each seemed to have a circle of acquaintance in the immediate neighbourhood of his own residence, to which in case of sudden danger he always fled.

But another thing about these prairie-dogs (perhaps, considering their size, we should call them prairie-doggies),— another thing about them, we say, was that each doggie lived with an owl, or, more correctly, an owl lived with each doggie! This is such an extraordinary *fact* that we could scarce hope that men would believe us, were our statement not supported by dozens of trustworthy travellers who have visited and written about these regions. The whole plain was covered with these owls. Each hole seemed to be the residence of an owl and a doggie, and these incongruous couples lived together apparently in perfect harmony.

We have not been able to ascertain from travellers *why* the owls have gone to live with these doggies, so we beg humbly to offer our own private opinion to the reader. We assume, then, that owls find it absolutely needful to have holes. Probably prairie-owls cannot dig holes for themselves. Having discovered, however, a race of little creatures that could, they very likely determined to take forcible possession of the holes made by them. Finding, no doubt, that when they did so the doggies were too timid to object, and discovering, moreover, that they were sweet, innocent little creatures, the owls resolved to take them into partnership, and so the thing was settled—that's how it came about, no doubt of it!

There is a report that rattlesnakes live in these holes also; but we cannot certify our reader of the truth of this. Still it is well to be acquainted with a report that is current among the men of the backwoods. If it be true, we are of opinion that the doggie's family is the most miscellaneous and remarkable on the face of—or, as Henri said, in the bo'-els of the earth.

Dick and his friends were so deeply absorbed in watching these curious little creatures that they did not observe the rapid spread of the black clouds over the sky. A few heavy drops of rain now warned them to seek shelter, so wheeling round they dashed off at full speed for the clump of willows, which they gained just as the rain began to descend in torrents.

" Now, lads, do it slick. Off packs and saddles," cried Joe Blunt, jumping from his horse. " I'll make a hut for ye, right off."

" A hut, Joe! what sort o' hut can ye make here?" inquired Dick.

" Ye'll see, boy, in a minute."

" Ach! lend me a hand here, Dick; de bockle am tight as de hoss's own skin. Ah! dere all right."

" Hollo! what's this?" exclaimed Dick, as Crusoe advanced with something in his mouth. " I declare, it's a bird o' some sort."

" A prairie-hen," remarked Joe, as Crusoe laid the bird at Dick's feet; " capital for supper."

" Ah! dat chien is superb! goot dog. Come here, I vill clap you."

But Crusoe refused to be caressed. Meanwhile, Joe and Dick formed a sort of beehive-looking hut by bending down the stems of a tall bush and thrusting their points into the ground. Over this they threw the largest buffalo robe, and placed another on the ground below it, on which they laid their packs of goods. These they further secured against wet by placing several robes over them and a skin of parchment. Then they sat down on this pile to rest, and consider what should be done next.

" 'Tis a bad look-out," said Joe, shaking his head

" I fear it is," replied Dick in a melancholy tone.

Henri said nothing, but he sighed deeply on looking up at the sky, which was now of a uniform watery grey, while black clouds drove athwart it The rain was pouring in torrents, and the wind began to sweep it in broad sheets over the plains, and under their slight covering, so that in a short time they were wet to the skin The horses stood meekly beside them, with their tails and heads equally pendulous; and Crusoe sat before his master looking at him with an expression that seemed to say, " Couldn't you put a stop to this if you were to try?"

" This'll never do. I'll try to git up a fire," said Dick, jumping up in desperation.

." Ye may save yerself the trouble," remarked Joe dryly— at least as dryly as was possible in the circumstances.

However, Dick did try, but he failed signally. Everything was soaked and saturated. There were no large trees; most of the bushes were green, and the dead ones were soaked The coverings were slobbery, the skins they sat on were slobbery, the earth itself was slobbery; so Dick threw his blanket (which was also slobbery) round his shoulders, and sat down beside his companions to grin and bear it As for Joe and Henri, they were old hands and accustomed to such circumstances. From the first they had resigned themselves to their fate, and wrapping their wet blankets round them sat down, side by side, wisely to endure the evils that they could not cure.

There is an old rhyme, by whom composed we know not, and it matters little, which runs thus—

> " For every evil under the sun
> There is a remedy—or there's none
> If there is—try and find it;
> If there isn't—never mind it!"

There is deep wisdom here in small compass The principle involved deserves to be heartily recommended Dick never heard of the lines, but he knew the principle well so he began to " never mind it " by sitting down beside his companions and whistling vociferously. As the wind rendered this a difficult feat, he took to singing instead. After that he said, " Let's eat a bite, Joe, and then go to bed."

" Be all means," said Joe, who produced a mass of dried deer's meat from a wallet.

" It's cold grub," said Dick, " and tough."

But the hunters' teeth were sharp and strong, so they ate a hearty supper and washed it down with a drink of rain-water collected from a pool on the top of their hut. They now tried to sleep, for the night was advancing, and it was so dark that they could scarce see their hands when held up before their faces. They sat back to back, and thus, in the form of a tripod, began to snooze. Joe's and Henri's seasoned frames would have remained stiff as posts till morning; but Dick's body was young and pliant, so he hadn't been asleep a few seconds when he fell forward into the mud and effectually awakened the others. Joe gave a grunt, and Henri exclaimed, " Hah!" but Dick was too sleepy and miserable to say anything. Crusoe, however, rose up to show his sympathy, and laid his wet head on his master's knee as he resumed his place. This catastrophe happened three times in the space of an hour, and by the third time they were all awakened up so thoroughly that they gave up the attempt to sleep, and amused each other by recounting their hunting experiences and telling stories. So engrossed did they become that day broke sooner than they had expected, and just in proportion as the grey light of dawn rose higher into the eastern sky did the spirits of these weary men rise within their soaking bodies.

CHAPTER VII

The " wallering " peculiarities of buffalo bulls—The first buffalo hunt and its consequences—Crusoe comes to the rescue—Pawnees discovered—A monster buffalo hunt—Joe acts the part of ambassador

Fortunately the day that succeeded the dreary night described in the last chapter was warm and magnificent The sun rose in a blaze of splendour, and filled the atmosphere with steam from the moist earth.

The unfortunates in the wet camp were not slow to avail themselves of his cheering rays. They hung up everything on the bushes to dry, and by dint of extreme patience and cutting out the comparatively dry hearts of several pieces of wood, they lighted a fire and boiled some rain-water, which was soon converted into soup. This, and the exercise necessary for the performance of these several duties, warmed and partially dried them; so that when they once more mounted their steeds and rode away, they were in a state of comparative comfort and in excellent spirits The only annoyance was the clouds of mosquitoes and large flies that assailed men and horses whenever they checked their speed.

" I tell ye wot it is," said Joe Blunt, one fine morning about a week after they had begun to cross the prairie, " it's my 'pinion that we'll come on buffaloes soon. Them tracks are fresh, an' yonder's one o' their wallers that's bin used not long agone."

" I'll go have a look at it," cried Dick, trotting away as he spoke.

Everything in these vast prairies was new to Dick Varley, and he was kept in a constant state of excitement during the first week or two of his journey. It is true he was quite familiar with the names and habits of all the animals that dwelt there; for many a time and oft had he listened to the "yarns" of the hunters and trappers of the Mustang Valley, when they returned laden with rich furs from their periodical hunting expeditions. But this knowledge of his only served to whet his curiosity and his desire to *see* the denizens of the prairies with his own eyes; and now that his wish was accomplished, it greatly increased the pleasures of his journey.

Dick had just reached the "wallow" referred to by Joe Blunt, and had reined up his steed to observe it leisurely, when a faint hissing sound reached his ear. Looking quickly back, he observed his two companions crouching on the necks of their horses, and slowly descending into a hollow of the prairie in front of them, as if they wished to bring the rising ground between them and some object in advance. Dick instantly followed their example, and was soon at their heels.

"Ye needn't look at the waller," whispered Joe, "for a' t'other side o' the ridge there's a bull *wallerin'*."

"Ye don't mean it!" exclaimed Dick, as they all dismounted and picketed their horses to the plain.

"Oui," said Henri, tumbling off his horse, while a broad grin overspread his good-natured countenance, "it is one fact! One buffalo bull be wollerin' like an enormous hog. Also, dere be t'ousands o' buffaloes farder on."

"Can ye trust yer dog keepin' back?" inquired Joe, with a dubious glance at Crusoe.

"Trust him! Ay, I wish I was as sure o' myself."

"Look to yer primin', then, an' we'll have tongues and marrow bones for supper to-night, I'se warrant. Hist! down on yer knees and go softly. We might ha' run them down on horseback, but it's bad to wind yer beasts on a trip like this, if ye can help it; an' it's about as easy to stalk them. Leastways, we'll try. Lift yer head slowly, Dick, an' don't show more nor the half o't above the ridge."

Dick elevated his head as directed, and the scene that met his view was indeed well calculated to send an electric shock to the heart of an ardent sportsman. The vast plain beyond was absolutely blackened with countless herds of buffaloes, which were browsing on the rich grass. They were still so far distant that their bellowing, and the trampling of their myriad hoofs, only reached the hunters like a faint murmur on the breeze. In the immediate foreground, however, there was a group of about half-a-dozen buffalo cows feeding quietly, and in the midst of them an enormous old bull was enjoying himself in his wallow. The animals, towards which our hunters now crept with murderous intent, are the fiercest and the most ponderous of the ruminating inhabitants of the western wilderness. The name of *buffalo*, however, is not correct. The animal is the *bison*, and bears no resemblance whatever to the buffalo proper; but as the hunters of the far west, and, indeed, travellers generally, have adopted the misnomer, we bow to the authority of custom and adopt it too.

Buffaloes roam in countless thousands all over the North American prairies, from the Hudson Bay Territories, north of Canada, to the shores of the Gulf of Mexico.

The advance of white men to the west has driven them to the prairies between the Missouri and the Rocky Mountains, and has somewhat diminished their numbers; but even thus diminished, they are still innumerable in the more distant plains. Their colour is dark brown, but it varies a good deal with the seasons. The hair or fur, from its great length in winter and spring and exposure to the weather, turns quite light; but when the winter coat is shed off, the new growth is a beautiful dark brown, almost approaching to jet-black. In form the buffalo somewhat resembles the ox, but its head and shoulders are much larger, and are covered with a profusion of long shaggy hair which adds greatly to the fierce aspect of the animals. It has a large hump on the shoulders, and its fore-quarters are much larger, in proportion, than the hind-quarters. The horns are short and thick, the hoofs are cloven, and the tail is short, with a tuft of hair at the extremity.

It is scarcely possible to conceive a wilder or more ferocious and terrible monster than a buffalo bull. He often grows to the enormous weight of two thousand pounds. His lion-like mane falls in shaggy confusion quite over his head and shoulders, down to the ground. When he is wounded he becomes imbued with the spirit of a tiger: he stamps, bellows, roars, and foams forth his rage with glaring eyes and steaming nostrils, and charges furiously at man and horse with utter recklessness. Fortunately, however, he is not naturally pugnacious, and can be easily thrown into a sudden panic. Moreover, the peculiar position of his eye renders this creature not so terrible as he would otherwise be to the hunter. Owing to the stiff structure of the neck, and the sunken, downward-looking eyeball, the buffalo cannot, without an effort, see beyond the direct line of vision presented to the habitual carriage of his head. When, therefore, he is wounded, and charges, he does so in a straight line, so that his pursuer can leap easily out of his way. The pace of the buffalo is clumsy, and *apparently* slow, yet when chased he dashes away over the plains in blind blundering terror, at a rate that leaves all but good horses far behind. He cannot keep the pace up, however, and is usually soon overtaken. Were the buffalo capable of the same alert and agile motions of head and eye peculiar to the deer or wild horse, in addition to his " bovine rage ", he would be the most formidable brute on earth. There is no object, perhaps, so terrible as the headlong advance of a herd of these animals when thoroughly aroused by terror. They care not for their necks. All danger in front is forgotten, or not seen, in the terror of that from which they fly. No thundering cataract is more tremendously irresistible than the black bellowing torrent which sometimes pours through the narrow defiles of the Rocky Mountains, or sweeps like a roaring flood over the trembling plains.

The wallowing, to which we have referred, is a luxury usually indulged in during the hot months of summer, when the buffaloes are tormented by flies, and heat, and drought. At this season they seek the low grounds in the prairies where there is a little stagnant water lying amongst the grass, and the ground underneath, being saturated, is soft. The leader of the herd, a shaggy old bull, usually takes upon himself to prepare the wallow.

It was a rugged monster of the largest size that did so on the present occasion, to the intense delight of Dick Varley, who begged Joe to lie still and watch the operation before trying to shoot one of the buffalo cows. Joe consented with a nod, and the four spectators—for Crusoe was as much taken up with the proceedings as any of them—crouched in the grass, and looked on.

Coming up to the swampy spot, the old bull gave a grunt of satisfaction, and going down on one knee, plunged his short thick horns into the mud, tore it up, and cast it aside. Having repeated this several times he plunged his head in, and brought it forth saturated with dirty water and be-daubed with lumps of mud, through which his fierce eyes gazed, with a ludicrous expression of astonishment, straight in the direction of the hunters, as if he meant to say, " I've done it that time, and no mistake!" The other buffaloes seemed to think so too, for they came up and looked on with an expression that seemed to say, " Well done, old fellow; try that again!"

The old fellow did try it again, and again, and again, plunging, and ramming and tearing up the earth, until he formed an excavation large enough to contain his huge body. In this bath he laid himself comfortably down, and began to roll and wallow about until he mixed up a trough full of thin soft mud, which completely covered him. When he came out of the hole there was scarcely an atom of his former self visible!

The coat of mud thus put on by bulls is usually permitted by them to dry, and is not finally got rid of until long after, when oft-repeated rollings on the grass and washings by rain at length clear it away.

When the old bull vacated this delectable bath, another bull, scarcely if at all less ferocious-looking, stepped forward to take his turn; but he was interrupted by a volley from the hunters, which scattered the animals right and left, and sent the mighty herds in the distance flying over the prairie in wild terror. The very turmoil of their own mad flight added to their panic, and the continuous thunder of their hoofs was heard until the last of them disappeared on the horizon. The family party which had been fired at, however, did not escape so well. Joe's rifle wounded a fat young cow, and Dick Varley brought it down. Henri had done his best, but as the animals were too far distant for his limited vision, he missed the cow he fired at, and hit the young bull whose bath had been interrupted. The others scattered and fled.

" Well done, Dick," exclaimed Joe Blunt, as they all ran up to the cow that had fallen. " Your first shot at the buffalo was a good un. Come, now, an' I'll show ye how to cut it up an' carry off the tit-bits."

" Ah, mon dear ole bull!" exclaimed Henri, gazing after the animal which he had wounded, and which was now limping slowly away. " You is not worth goin' after. Farewell—adieu."

" He'll be tough enough, I warrant," said Joe; " an' we've more meat here nor we can lift."

"But wouldn't it be as well to put the poor brute out o' pain?" suggested Dick.

" Oh, he'll die soon enough," replied Joe, tucking up his sleeves and drawing his long hunting-knife.

Dick, however, was not satisfied with this way of looking at it. Saying that he would be back in a few minutes, he reloaded his rifle, and calling Crusoe to his side, walked quickly after the wounded bull, which was now hid from view in a hollow of the plain.

In a few minutes he came in sight of it, and ran forward with his rifle in readiness.

" Down, Crusoe," he whispered; " wait for me here."

Crusoe crouched in the grass instantly, and Dick advanced. As he came on, the bull observed him, and turned round bellowing with rage and pain to receive him. The aspect of the brute on a near view was so terrible that Dick involuntarily stopped too, and gazed with a mingled feeling of wonder and awe, while it bristled with passion, and

blood-streaked foam dropped from its open jaws, and its
eyes glared furiously. Seeing that Dick did not advance,
the bull charged him with a terrific roar; but the youth
had firm nerves, and although the rush of such a savage
creature at full speed was calculated to try the courage of
any man, especially one who had never seen a buffalo bull
before, Dick did not lose presence of mind. He remembered
the many stories he had listened to of this very thing that
was now happening; so, crushing down his excitement as
well as he could, he cocked his rifle and awaited the charge.
He knew that it was of no use to fire at the head of the
advancing foe, as the thickness of the skull, together with
the matted hair on the forehead, rendered it impervious
to a bullet.

When the bull was within a yard of him he leaped lightly
to one side and it passed. Just as it did so, Dick aimed at
its heart and fired, but his knowledge of the creature's
anatomy was not yet correct. The ball entered the shoulder
too high, and the bull, checking himself as well as he could
in his headlong rush, turned round and made at Dick
again.

The failure, coupled with the excitement, proved too
much for Dick; he could not resist discharging his second
barrel at the brute's head as it came on. He might as well
have fired at a brick wall. It shook its shaggy front, and
with a hideous bellow thundered forward. Again Dick
sprang to one side, but in doing so a tuft of grass or stone
caught his foot, and he fell heavily to the ground.

Up to this point Crusoe's admirable training had nailed
him to the spot where he had been left; although the
twitching of every fibre in his body and a low continuous
whine showed how gladly he would have hailed permission
to join the combat; but the instant he saw his master down,
and the buffalo turning to charge again, he sprang forward
with a roar that would have done credit to his bovine
enemy, and seized him by the nose. So vigorous was the
rush that he well-nigh pulled the bull down on its side.
One toss of its head, however, sent Crusoe high into the

air; but it accomplished this feat at the expense of its nose, which was torn and lacerated by the dog's teeth.

Scarcely had Crusoe touched the ground, which he did with a sounding thump, than he sprang up and flew at his adversary again. This time, however, he adopted the plan of barking furiously and biting by rapid yet terrible snaps as he found opportunity, thus keeping the bull entirely engrossed, and affording Dick an opportunity of reloading his rifle, which he was not slow to do. Dick then stepped close up, and while the two combatants were roaring in each other's faces, he shot the buffalo through the heart. It fell to the earth with a deep groan.

Crusoe's rage instantly vanished on beholding this, and he seemed to be filled with tumultuous joy at his master's escape, for he gambolled round him, and whined and fawned upon him in a manner that could not be misunderstood.

"Good dog; thank'ee, my pup," said Dick, patting Crusoe's head as he stooped to brush the dust from his leggings. "I don't know what would ha' become o' me but for your help, Crusoe."

Crusoe turned his head a little to one side, wagged his tail, and looked at Dick with an expression that said quite plainly, "I'd die for you, I would—not once, or twice, but ten times, fifty times if need be—and that not merely to save your life, but even to please you."

There is no doubt whatever that Crusoe felt something of this sort. The love of a Newfoundland dog to its master is beyond calculation or expression. He who once gains such love carries the dog's life in his hand. But let him who reads note well, and remember that there is only one coin that can purchase such love, and that is *kindness*. The coin, too, must be genuine. Kindness merely *expressed* will not do: it must be *felt*.

"Hollo, boy, ye've bin i' the wars!" exclaimed Joe, raising himself from his task as Dick and Crusoe returned.

"You look more like it than I do," retorted Dick, laughing.

This was true, for cutting up a buffalo carcass with no other instrument than a large knife is no easy matter. Yet western hunters and Indians can do it without cleaver or saw in a way that would surprise a civilized butcher not a little. Joe was covered with blood up to the elbows. His hair, happening to have a knack of getting into his eyes, had been so often brushed off with bloody hands, that his whole visage was speckled with gore, and his dress was by no means immaculate.

While Dick related his adventure, or *mis*-adventure, with the bull, Joe and Henri completed the cutting out of the most delicate portions of the buffalo, namely, the hump on its shoulder—which is a choice piece, much finer than the best beef—and the tongue, and a few other parts. The tongues of buffaloes are superior to those of domestic cattle. When all was ready the meat was slung across the back of the pack-horse; and the party, remounting their horses, continued their journey, having first cleansed themselves as well as they could in the rather dirty waters of an old wallow.

" See," said Henri, turning to Dick and pointing to a circular spot of green as they rode along, " that is one old *dry* waller."

" Ay," remarked Joe; " after the waller dries, it becomes a ring o' greener grass than the rest o' the plain, as ye see. 'Tis said the first hunters used to wonder greatly at these myster'ous circles, and they invented all sorts o' stories to account for 'em. Some said they wos fairy-rings, but at last they comed to know they wos nothin' more nor less than places where buffaloes wos used to waller in. It's often seemed to me that if we knowed the *raisons* o' things, we wouldn't be so much puzzled wi' them as we are."

The truth of this last remark was so self-evident and incontrovertible that it elicited no reply, and the three friends rode on for a considerable time in silence.

It was now past noon, and they were thinking of calling a halt for a short rest to the horses and a pipe to themselves, when Joe was heard to give vent to one of those peculiar hisses that always accompanied either a surprise or a caution. In the present case it indicated both.

" What now, Joe?"

" Injuns!" ejaculated Joe.

" Eh! fat you say? Ou is dey?"

Crusoe at this moment uttered a low growl. Ever since the day he had been partially roasted he had maintained a rooted antipathy to Red-men. Joe immediately dismounted, and placing his ear to the ground listened intently. It is a curious fact that by placing the ear close to the ground sounds can be heard distinctly which could not be heard at all if the listener were to maintain an erect position.

" They're arter the buffalo," said Joe, rising, " an' I think it's likely they're a band o' Pawnees. Listen an' ye'll hear their shouts quite plain."

Dick and Henri immediately lay down and placed their ears to the ground.

" Now, me hear noting," said Henri, jumping up, " but me ear is like me eyes—ver' short-sighted."

" I do hear something," said Dick as he got up, " but the beating o' my heart makes row enough to spoil my hearin'."

Joe Blunt smiled " Ah! lad, ye're young, an' yer blood's too hot yet; but bide a bit—you'll cool down soon. I wos like you once. Now, lads, what think ye we should do?"

" You know best, Joe."

" Oui, nodoubtedly."

" Then wot I advise is that we gallop to the broken sand hillocks ye see yonder, get behind them, an' take a peep at the Redskins. If they are Pawnees, we'll go up to them at once; if not, we'll hold a council o' war on the spot."

Having arranged this, they mounted and hastened towards the hillocks in question, which they reached after ten minutes' gallop at full stretch. The sandy mounds afforded them concealment, and enabled them to watch the proceedings of the savages in the plain below. The scene was the most curious and exciting that can be conceived. The centre of the plain before them was crowded with hundreds of buffaloes, which were dashing about in the most frantic state of alarm. To whatever point they galloped they were met by yelling savages on horseback, who could

not have been fewer in numbers than a thousand, all being
armed with lance, bow, and quiver, and mounted on active
little horses. The Indians had completely surrounded the
herd of buffaloes, and were now advancing steadily towards
them, gradually narrowing the circle, and whenever the
terrified animals endeavoured to break through the line,
they rushed to that particular spot in a body, and scared
them back again into the centre.

Thus they advanced until they closed in on their prey
and formed an unbroken circle round them, whilst the
poor brutes kept eddying and surging to and fro in a con-
fused mass, hooking and climbing upon each other, and
bellowing furiously. Suddenly the horsemen made a rush,
and the work of destruction began. The tremendous turmoil
raised a cloud of dust that obscured the field in some places,
and hid it from our hunters' view. Some of the Indians
galloped round and round the circle, sending their arrows
whizzing up to the feathers in the sides of the fattest cows.
Others dashed fearlessly into the midst of the black heaving
mass, and, with their long lances, pierced dozens of them
to the heart. In many instances the buffaloes, infuriated
by wounds, turned fiercely on their assailants and gored
the horses to death, in which cases the men had to trust to
their nimble legs for safety. Sometimes a horse got jammed
in the centre of the swaying mass, and could neither advance nor retreat. Then the savage rider leaped upon the
buffaloes' backs, and springing from one to another, like
an acrobat, gained the outer edge of the circle; not failing,
however, in his strange flight, to pierce with his lance several
of the fattest of his stepping-stones as he sped along.

A few of the herd succeeded in escaping from the blood
and dust of this desperate battle, and made off over the
plains; but they were quickly overtaken, and the lance or
the arrow brought them down on the green turf. Many
of the dismounted riders were chased by bulls; but they
stepped lightly to one side, and, as the animals passed, drove
their arrows deep into their sides. Thus the tumultuous
war went on, amid thundering tread, and yell, and bellow,

till the green plain was transformed into a sea of blood and mire, and every buffalo of the herd was laid low.

It is not to be supposed that such reckless warfare is invariably waged without damage to the savages. Many were the wounds and bruises received that day, and not a few bones were broken, but happily no lives were lost.

"Now, lads, now's our time. A bold and fearless look's the best at all times. Don't look as if ye doubted their friendship; and mind, wotever ye do, don't use yer arms. Follow me."

Saying this, Joe Blunt leaped on his horse, and bounding over the ridge at full speed, galloped headlong across the plain.

The savages observed the strangers instantly, and a loud yell announced the fact as they assembled from all parts of the field brandishing their bows and spears. Joe's quick eye soon distinguished their chief, towards whom he galloped, still at full speed, till within a yard or two of his horse's head; then he reined up suddenly. So rapidly did Joe and his comrades approach, and so instantaneously did they pull up, that their steeds were thrown almost on their haunches.

The Indian chief did not move a muscle. He was a tall, powerful savage, almost naked, and mounted on a coal-black charger, which he sat with the ease of a man accustomed to ride from infancy. He was, indeed, a splendid-looking savage, but his face wore a dark frown, for, although he and his band had visited the settlements and trafficked with the fur-traders on the Missouri, he did not love the "Pale-faces", whom he regarded as intruders on the hunting-grounds of his fathers, and the peace that existed between them at that time was of a very fragile character. Indeed, it was deemed by the traders impossible to travel through the Indian country at that period except in strong force, and it was the very boldness of the present attempt that secured to our hunters anything like a civil reception.

Joe, who could speak the Pawnee tongue fluently, began by explaining the object of his visit, and spoke of the presents which he had brought for the great chief; but it was evident that his words made little impression. As he discoursed to them the savages crowded round the little party, and began to handle and examine their dresses and weapons with a degree of rudeness that caused Joe considerable anxiety.

" Mahtawa believes that the heart of the Pale-face is true," said the savage, when Joe paused, " but he does not choose to make peace. The Pale-faces are grasping. They never rest. They turn their eyes to the great mountains and say, ' There we will stop.' But even there they will not stop. They are never satisfied; Mahtawa knows them well."

This speech sank like a death-knell into the hearts of the hunters, for they knew that if the savages refused to make peace, they would scalp them all and appropriate their goods. To make things worse, a dark-visaged Indian suddenly caught hold of Henri's rifle, and, ere he was aware, had plucked it from his hand. The blood rushed to the gigantic hunter's forehead, and he was on the point of springing at the man, when Joe said in a deep quiet voice,—

" Be still, Henri. You will but hasten death."

At this moment there was a movement in the outskirts of the circle of horsemen, and another chief rode into the midst of them.

He was evidently higher in rank than Mahtawa, for he spoke authoritatively to the crowd, and stepped in before him. The hunters drew little comfort from the appearance of his face, however, for it scowled upon them. He was not so powerful a man as Mahtawa, but he was more gracefully formed, and had a more noble and commanding countenance.

" Have the Pale-faces no wigwams on the great river that they should come to spy out the lands of the Pawnee?" he demanded.

" We have not come to spy your country," answered Joe, raising himself proudly as he spoke, and taking off his cap. " We have come with a message from the great chief of the Pale-faces, who lives in the village far beyond the great river where the sun rises. He says, Why should the Pale-face and the Red-man fight? They are brothers. The same Manitou [1] watches over both. The Pale-faces have more beads, and guns, and blankets, and knives, and vermilion than they require; they wish to give some of these things for the skins and furs which the Red-man does not know what to do with. The great chief of the Pale-faces has sent me to say, Why should we fight? let us smoke the pipe of peace."

At the mention of beads and blankets the face of the wily chief brightened for a moment. Then he said sternly—

"The heart of the Pale-face is not true. He has come here to trade for himself. San-it-sa-rish has eyes that can see; they are not shut. Are not these your goods?" The chief pointed to the pack-horse as he spoke.

"Trappers do not take their goods into the heart of an enemy's camp," returned Joe. "San-it-sa-rish is wise, and will understand this. These are gifts to the chief of the Pawnees. There are more awaiting him when the pipe of peace is smoked. I have said. What message shall we take back to the great chief of the Pale-faces?"

San-it-sa-rish was evidently mollified.

"The hunting-field is not the council tent," he said. "The Pale-faces will go with us to our village."

Of course Joe was too glad to agree to this proposal, but he now deemed it politic to display a little firmness.

"We cannot go till our rifle is restored. It will not do to go back and tell the great chief of the Pale-faces that the Pawnees are thieves."

The chief frowned angrily.

"The Pawnees are true; they are not thieves. They choose to *look* at the rifle of the Pale-face. It shall be returned."

The rifle was instantly restored, and then our hunters rode off with the Indians towards their camp. On the way they met hundreds of women and children going to the scene of the great hunt, for it was their special duty to cut

[1] The Indian name for God.

up the meat and carry it into camp. The men, considering that they had done quite enough in killing it, returned to smoke and eat away the fatigues of the chase.

As they rode along Dick Varley observed that some of the " braves ", as Indian warriors are styled, were eating pieces of the bloody livers of the buffaloes in a raw state, at which he expressed not a little disgust.

" Ah, boy! you're green yet," remarked Joe Blunt in an undertone. " Mayhap ye'll be thankful to do that same yerself some day."

" Well, I'll not refuse to try when it is needful," said Dick with a laugh; " meanwhile I'm content to see the Redskins do it, Joe Blunt."

CHAPTER VIII

Dick and his friends visit the Indians and see many wonders—Crusoe,
too, experiences a few surprises, and teaches Indian dogs a lesson—
An Indian dandy—A foot-race.

The Pawnee village, at which they soon arrived, was
situated in the midst of a most interesting and picturesque
scene.

It occupied an extensive plain which sloped gently down
to a creek,[1] whose winding course was marked by a broken
line of wood, here and there interspersed with a fine clump
of trees, between the trunks of which the blue waters of a
lake sparkled in the distance. Hundreds of tents or " lodges "
of buffalo-skins covered the ground, and thousands of
Indians—men, women, and children—moved about the
busy scene. Some were sitting in their lodges, lazily smoking
their pipes. But these were chiefly old and infirm veterans,
for all the young men had gone to the hunt which we have
just described. The women were stooping over their fires,
busily preparing maize and meat for their husbands and
brothers; while myriads of little brown and naked children
romped about everywhere, filling the air with their yells
and screams, which were only equalled, if not surpassed,
by the yelping dogs that seemed innumerable.

Far as the eye could reach were seen scattered herds of
horses. These were tended by little boys who were totally
destitute of clothing, and who seemed to enjoy with infinite
zest the pastime of shooting-practice with little bows and
arrows. No wonder that these Indians become expert
bowmen. There were urchins there, scarce two feet high,
with round bullets of bodies and short spindle-shanks, who
could knock blackbirds off the trees at every shot, and .

[1] In America small rivers or rivulets are termed " creeks ".

cut the heads off the taller flowers with perfect certainty! There was much need, too, for the atmost proficiency they could attain, for the very existence of the Indian tribes of the prairies depends on their success in hunting the buffalo.

There are hundreds and thousands of North American savages who would undoubtedly perish, and their tribes become extinct, if the buffaloes were to leave the prairies or die out. Yet, although animals are absolutely essential to their existence, they pursue and slay them with improvident recklessness, sometimes killing hundreds of them merely for the sake of the sport, the tongues, and the marrow bones. In the bloody hunt described in the last chapter, however, the slaughter of so many was not wanton, because the village that had to be supplied with food was large, and, just previous to the hunt, they had been living on somewhat reduced allowance. Even the blackbirds shot by the brown-bodied urchins before mentioned had been thankfully put into the pot. Thus precarious is the supply of food among the Red-men, who on one day are starving, and the next are revelling in superabundance.

But to return to our story. At one end of this village the creek sprang over a ledge of rock in a low cascade and opened out into a beautiful lake, the bosom of which was studded with small islands. Here were thousands of those smaller species of wild water fowl which were either too brave or too foolish to be scared away by the noise of the camp. And here, too, dozens of children were sporting on the beach, or paddling about in their light bark canoes.

"Isn't it strange," remarked Dick to Henri, as they passed among the tents towards the centre of the village— "isn't it strange that them Injuns should be so fond o' fightin', when they've got all they can want—a fine country, lots o' buffalo, an', as far as I can see, happy homes?"

"Oui, it is remarkiabel, vraiment. Bot dey do more love war to peace. Dey loves to be excit-ed, I s'pose."

"Humph! One would think the hunt we seed a little agone would be excitement enough. But, I say, that must be the chief's tent, by the look o't."

Dick was right. The horsemen pulled up and dismounted opposite the principal chief's tent, which was a larger and more elegant structure than the others. Meantime an immense concourse of women, children, and dogs gathered round the strangers, and while the latter yelped their dislike to white men, the former chattered continuously, as they discussed the appearance of the strangers and their errand, which latter soon became known. An end was put to this by San-it-sa-rish desiring the hunters to enter the tent, and spreading a buffalo robe for them to sit on. Two braves carried in their packs, and then led away their horses.

All this time Crusoe had kept as close as possible to his master's side, feeling extremely uncomfortable in the midst of such a strange crowd, the more especially that the ill-looking Indian curs gave him expressive looks of hatred, and exhibited some desire to rush upon him in a body, so that he had to keep a sharp look-out all round him. When therefore Dick entered the tent, Crusoe endeavoured to do so along with him; but he was met by a blow on the nose from an old squaw, who scolded him in a shrill voice and bade him begone.

Either our hero's knowledge of the Indian language was insufficient to enable him to understand the order, or he had resolved not to obey it, for instead of retreating, he drew a deep gurgling breath, curled his nose, and displayed a row of teeth that caused the old woman to draw back in alarm. Crusoe's was a forgiving spirit. The instant that opposition ceased he forgot the injury, and was meekly advancing, when Dick held up his finger.

"Go outside, pup, and wait."

Crusoe's tail drooped; with a deep sigh he turned and left the tent. He took up a position near the entrance, how-ever, and sat down resignedly. So meek, indeed, did the poor dog look that six mangy-looking curs felt their dastardly hearts emboldened to make a rush at him with boisterous yells.

Crusoe did not rise. He did not even condescend to turn his head toward them; but he looked at them out of the corner of his dark eye, wrinkled—very slightly—the skin of his nose, exhibited two beautiful fangs, and gave utterance to a soft remark, that might be described as quiet, deep-toned gurgling. It wasn't much, but it was more than enough for the valiant six, who paused and snarled violently.

It was a peculiar trait of Crusoe's gentle nature that, the moment any danger ceased, he resumed his expression of nonchalant gravity. The expression on this occasion was misunderstood, however; and as about two dozen additional yelping dogs had joined the ranks of the enemy, they advanced in close order to the attack.

Crusoe still sat quiet, and kept his head high; but he *looked* at them again, and exhibited four fangs for their inspection. Among the pack there was one Indian dog of large size—almost as large as Crusoe himself—which kept well in the rear, and apparently urged the lesser dogs on. The little dogs didn't object, for little dogs are generally the most pugnacious. At this big dog Crusoe directed a pointed glance, but said nothing. Meanwhile a particularly small and vicious cur, with a mere rag of a tail, crept round by the back of the tent, and coming upon Crusoe in rear, snapped at his tail sharply, and then fled shrieking with terror and surprise, no doubt, at its own temerity.

Crusoe did not bark; he seldom barked; he usually either said nothing, or gave utterance to a prolonged roar of indignation of the most terrible character, with barks, as it were, mingled through it. It somewhat resembled that peculiar and well-known species of thunder, the prolonged roll of which is marked at short intervals in its course by cannon-like cracks. It was a continuous, but, so to speak, *knotted* roar.

On receiving the snap, Crusoe gave forth *the* roar with a majesty and power that scattered the pugnacious front rank of the enemy to the winds. Those that still remained, half stupefied, he leaped over with a huge bound, and alighted, fangs first, on the back of the big dog. There was one hideous yell, a muffled scramble of an instant's duration, and the big dog lay lay dead upon the plain!

It was an awful thing to do, but Crusoe evidently felt that the peculiar circumstances of the case required that an example should be made; and to say truth, all things considered, we cannot blame him. The news must have been carried at once through the canine portion of the camp, for Crusoe was never interfered with again after that.

Dick witnessed this little incident; but he observed that the Indian chief cared not a straw about it, and as his dog returned quietly and sat down in its old place he took no notice of it either, but continued to listen to the explanations which Joe gave to the chief, of the desire of the Pale-faces to be friends with the Red-men.

Joe's eloquence would have done little for him on this occasion had his hands been empty, but he followed it up by opening one of his packs and displaying the glittering contents before the equally glittering eyes of the chief and his squaws.

"These," said Joe, "are the gifts that the great chief of the Pale-faces sends to the great chief of the Pawnees. And he bids me say that there are many more things in his stores which will be traded for skins with the Red-men, when they visit him; and he also says that if the Pawnees will not steal horses any more from the Pale-faces, they shall receive gifts of knives, and guns, and powder, and blankets every year."

"Wah!" grunted the chief; "it is good. The great chief is wise. We will smoke the pipe of peace."

The things that afforded so much satisfaction to San-it-sa-rish were the veriest trifles. Penny looking-glasses in yellow gilt tin frames, beads of various colours, needles, cheap scissors and knives, vermilion paint, and coarse scarlet cloth, etc. They were of priceless value, however, in the estimation of the savages, who delighted to adorn them-selves with leggings made from the cloth, beautifully worked with beads by their own ingenious women. They were thankful, too, for knives even of the commonest description, having none but bone ones of their own; and they gloried in daubing their faces with intermingled streaks of charcoal and vermilion. To gaze at their visages, when thus treated, in the little penny looking-glasses is their summit of delight!

Joe presented the chief with a portion of these coveted goods, and tied up the remainder. We may remark here that the only thing which prevented the savages from taking possession of the whole at once, without asking permission, was the promise of the annual gifts, which they knew would not be forthcoming were any evil to befall the deputies of the Pale-faces. Nevertheless, it cost them a severe struggle to restrain their hands on this occasion, and Joe and his companions felt that they would have to play their part well in order to fulfil their mission with safety and credit.

"The Pale-faces may go now and talk with the braves," said San-it-sa-rish, after carefully examining everything that was given to him; "a council will be called soon, and we will smoke the pipe of peace."

Accepting this permission to retire, the hunters immediately left the tent; and being now at liberty to do what they pleased, they amused themselves by wandering about the village.

"He's a cute chap that," remarked Joe, with a sarcastic smile; "I don't feel quite easy about gettin' away. He'll bother the life out o' us to get all the goods we've got, and, ye see, as we've other tribes to visit, we must give away as little as we can here."

"Ha! you is right," said Henri; "dat fellow's eyes twinkle at de knives and tings like two stars."

"Fire-flies, ye should say. Stars are too soft an' beautiful to compare to the eyes o' yon savage," said Dick, laughing. "I wish we were well away from them.. That rascal Mahtawa is an ugly customer."

"True, lad," returned Joe; "had *he* bin the great chief our scalps had bin dryin' in the smoke o' a Pawnee wigwam afore now. What now, lad?"

Joe's question was put in consequence of a gleeful smile that overspread the countenance of Dick Varley, who replied by pointing to a wigwam towards which they were approaching.

"Oh! that's only a dandy," exclaimed Joe. "There's lots o' them in every Injun camp. They're fit for nothin' but dress, poor contemptible critters."

Joe accompanied his remark with a sneer, for of all pitiable objects he regarded an unmanly man as the most despicable. He consented, however, to sit down on a grassy bank and watch the proceedings of this Indian dandy, who had just seated himself in front of his wigwam for the purpose of making his toilet.

He began it by greasing his whole person carefully and smoothly over with buffalo fat, until he shone like a patent leather boot; then he rubbed himself almost dry, leaving the skin sleek and glossy. Having proceeded thus far, he took up a small mirror, a few inches in diameter, which he or some other member of the tribe must have procured during one of their few excursions to the trading-forts of the Pale-faces, and examined himself, as well as he could, in so limited a space. Next, he took a little vermilion from a small parcel and rubbed it over his face until it presented the somewhat demoniac appearance of a fiery red. He also drew a broad red score along the crown of his head, which was closely shaved, with the exception of the usual tuft or scalplock on the top. This scalplock stood bristling straight up a few inches, and then curved over and hung down his back about two feet. Immense care and attention was bestowed on this lock. He smoothed it, greased it, and plaited it into the form of a pigtail. Another application was here made to the glass, and the result was evidently satisfactory, to judge from the beaming smile that played on his features. But, not content with the general effect, he tried the effect of expression—frowned portentously, scowled savagely, gaped hideously, and grinned horribly a ghastly smile.

Then our dandy fitted into his ears, which were bored in several places, sundry ornaments, such as rings, wampum, etc., and hung several strings of beads round his neck.

Besides these he affixed one or two ornaments to his arms, wrists, and ankles, and touched in a few effects with vermilion on the shoulders and breast. After this, and a few more glances at the glass, he put on a pair of beautiful moccasins, which, besides being richly wrought with beads, were soft as chamois leather and fitted his feet like gloves. A pair of leggings of scarlet cloth were drawn on, attached to a waist belt, and bound below the knee with broad garters of variegated bead-work.

It was some time before this Adonis was quite satisfied with himself. He retouched the paint on his shoulders several times, and modified the glare of that on his wide-mouthed, high-cheek-boned visage, before he could tear himself away; but at last he did so, and throwing a large piece of scarlet cloth over his shoulders, he thrust his looking-glass under his belt, and proceeded to mount his palfrey, which was held in readiness near to the tent door by one of his wives. The horse was really a fine animal, and seemed worthy of a more warlike master. His shoulders, too, were striped with red paint, and feathers were intertwined with his mane and tail, while the bridle was decorated with various jingling ornaments.

Vaulting upon his steed, with a large fan of wild-goose and turkey feathers in one hand, and a whip dangling at the wrist of the other, this incomparable dandy sallied forth for a promenade—that being his chief delight when there was no buffalo hunting to be done. Other men who were not dandies sharpened their knives, smoked, feasted, and mended their spears and arrows at such seasons of leisure, or played at athletic games.

" Let's follow my buck," said Joe Blunt.

" Oui. Come 'long," replied Henri, striding after the rider at a pace that almost compelled his comrades to run.

" Hold on!" cried Dick, laughing; " we don't want to keep him company. A distant view is quite enough o' sich a chap as that."

" Mais you forgit I cannot see far."

"So much the better," remarked Joe; "it's my opinion we've seen enough o' him. Ah! he's goin' to look on at the games. Them's worth lookin' at."

The games to which Joe referred were taking place on a green level plain close to the creek, and a little above the waterfall before referred to. Some of the Indians were horse-racing, some jumping, and others wrestling; but the game which proved most attractive was throwing the javelin, in which several of the young braves were engaged.

This game is played by two competitors, each armed with a dart, in an arena about fifty yards long. One of the players has a hoop of six inches in diameter. At a signal they start off on foot at full speed, and on reaching the middle of the arena the Indian with the hoop rolls it along before them, and each does his best to send a javelin through the hoop before the other. He who succeeds counts so many points; if both miss, the nearest to the hoop is allowed to count, but not so much as if he had "ringed" it. The Indians are very fond of this game, and will play at it under a broiling sun for hours together. But a good deal of the interest attaching to it is owing to the fact that they make it a means of gambling. Indians are inveterate gamblers, and will sometimes go on until they lose horses, bows, blankets, robes, and, in short, their whole personal property. The consequences are, as might be expected, that fierce and bloody quarrels sometimes arise in which life is often lost.

"Try your hand at that," said Henri to Dick.

"By all means," cried Dick, handing his rifle to his friend, and springing into the ring enthusiastically.

A general shout of applause greeted the Pale-face, who threw off his coat and tightened his belt, while a young Indian presented him with a dart.

"Now, see that ye do us credit, lad," said Joe.

"I'll try," answered Dick.

In a moment they were off. The young Indian rolled away the hoop, and Dick threw his dart with such vigour that it went deep into the ground, but missed the hoop by a foot at least. The young Indian's first dart went through the centre.

"Ha!" exclaimed Joe Blunt to the Indians near him, "the lad's not used to that game; try him at a race. Bring out your best brave—he whose bound is like the hunted deer."

We need scarcely remind the reader that Joe spoke in the Indian language, and that the above is a correct rendering of the sense of what he said.

The name of Tarwicadia, or the little chief, immediately passed from lip to lip, and in a few minutes an Indian, a little below the medium size, bounded into the arena with an indiarubber-like elasticity that caused a shade of anxiety to pass over Joe's face.

"Ah, boy!" he whispered, "I'm afeard you'll find him a tough customer."

"That's just what I want," replied Dick. "He's supple enough, but he wants muscle in the thigh. We'll make it a long heat."

"Right, lad; ye're right."

Joe now proceeded to arrange the conditions of the race with the chiefs around him. It was fixed that the distance to be run should be a mile, so that the race would be one of two miles, out and back. Moreover, the competitors were to run without any clothes, except a belt and a small piece of cloth round the loins. This to the Indians was nothing, for they seldom wore more in warm weather; but Dick would have preferred to keep on part of his dress. The laws of the course, however, would not permit of this, so he stripped and stood forth, the *beau-ideal* of a well-formed, agile man. He was greatly superior in size to his antagonist, and more muscular, the savage being slender and extremely lithe and springy.

"Ha! I will run too," shouted Henri, bouncing forward with clumsy energy, and throwing off his coat just as they were going to start.

The savages smiled at this unexpected burst, and made no objection, considering the thing in the light of a joke.

The signal was given, and away they went. Oh! it would have done you good to have seen the way in which Henri manœuvred his limbs on this celebrated occasion! He went over the ground with huge elephantine bounds, runs, and jumps. He could not have been said to have one style of running; he had a dozen styles, all of which came into play in the course of half as many minutes. The other two ran like the wind; yet although Henri *appeared* to be going heavily over the ground, he kept up with them to the turning-point. As for Dick, it became evident in the first few minutes that he could outstrip his antagonist with ease, and was hanging back a little all the time. He shot ahead like an arrow when they came about half-way back, and it was clear that the real interest of the race was to lie in the competition between Henri and Tarwicadia.

Before they were two-thirds of the way back, Dick walked in to the winning-point, and turned to watch the others. Henri's wind was about gone, for he exerted himself with such violence that he wasted half his strength. The Indian, on the contrary, was comparatively fresh, but he was not so fleet as his antagonist, whose tremendous strides carried him over the ground at an incredible pace. On they came neck and neck, till close on the score that marked the winning-point. Here the value of enthusiasm came out strongly in the case of Henri. He *felt* that he could not gain an inch on Tarwicadia to save his life, but just as he came up he observed the anxious faces of his comrades and the half-sneering countenances of the savages. His heart thumped against his ribs, every muscle thrilled with a gush of conflicting feelings, and he *hurled* himself over the score like a cannon shot, full six inches ahead of the little chief!

But the thing did not by any means end here. Tarwicadia pulled up the instant he had passed. Not so our Canadian. Such a clumsy and colossal frame was not to be checked in a moment. The crowd of Indians opened up to let him pass, but unfortunately a small tent that stood in the way was not so obliging. Into it he went, head fore-most, like a shell, carried away the corner post with his shoulder, and brought the whole affair down about his own ears and those of its inmates, among whom were several children and two or three dogs. It required some time to extricate them all from the ruins, but when this was effected it was found that no serious damage had been done to life or limb.

CHAPTER IX

Crusoe acts a conspicuous and humane part—A friend gained—
A great feast.

When the foot-race was concluded the three hunters
hung about looking on at the various games for some time,
and then strolled towards the lake.

" Ye may be thankful yer neck's whole," said Joe, grinning, as Henri rubbed his shoulder with a rueful look.
" An' we'll have to send that Injun and his family a knife
and some beads to make up for the fright they got."

" Ha! an' fat is to be give to me for my broke shoulder?"

" Credit, man, credit," said Dick Varley, laughing.

" Credit! fat is dat?"

" Honour and glory, lad, and the praises of them
savages."

" Ha! de praise? more probeebale de ill-vill of de
rascale. I seed dem scowl at me not ver' pritty."

" That's true, Henri; but sich as it is it's all ye'll git."

" I vish," remarked Henri after a pause—" I vish I could
git de vampum belt de leetle chief had on. It vas superb.
Fat place do vampums come from?"

" They're shells——"

" Oui," interrupted Henri; " I know fat dey is. Dey
is shells, and de Injuns tink them goot monish; mais I ask
you fat place de come from."

" They are thought to be gathered on the shores o' the
Pacific," said Joe. " The Injuns on the west o' the Rocky
Mountains picks them up and exchanges them wi' the
fellows hereaway for horses and skins—so I'm told."

At this moment there was a wild cry of terror heard a
short distance ahead of them. Rushing forward they observed an Indian woman flying fractically down the river's

bank towards the waterfall, a hundred yards above which an object was seen struggling in the water.

" 'Tis her child," cried Joe, as the mother's frantic cry reached his ear. " It'll be over the fall in a minute! Run, Dick, you're quickest."

They had all started forward at speed, but Dick and Crusoe were far ahead, and abreast of the spot in a few seconds.

" Save it, pup," cried Dick, pointing to the child, which had been caught in an eddy, and was for a few moments hovering on the edge of the stream that rushed impetuously towards the fall.

The noble Newfoundland did not require to be told what to do. It seems a natural instinct in this sagacious species of dog to save man or beast that chances to be struggling in the water, and many are the authentic stories related of Newfoundland dogs saving life in cases of shipwreck. Indeed, they are regularly trained to the work in some countries; and nobly, fearlessly, disinterestedly do they discharge their trust, often in the midst of appalling dangers. Crusoe sprang from the bank with such impetus that his broad chest ploughed up the water like the bow of a boat, and the energetic workings of his muscles were indicated by the force of each successive propulsion as he shot ahead.

In a few seconds he reached the child and caught it by the hair. Then he turned to swim back, but the stream had got hold of him. Bravely he struggled, and lifted the child breast-high out of the water in his powerful efforts to stem the current. In vain. Each moment he was carried inch by inch down until he was on the brink of the fall, which, though not high, was a large body of water and fell with a heavy roar. He raised himself high out of the stream with the vigour of his last struggle, and then fell back into the abyss.

By this time the poor mother was in a canoe as close to the fall as she could with safety approach, and the little bark danced like a cockle-shell on the turmoil of waters as she stood with uplifted paddle and staring eyeballs awaiting the rising of the child.

Crusoe came up almost instantly, but *alone*, for the dash over the fall had wrenched the child from his teeth. He raised himself high up, and looked anxiously round for a moment. Then he caught sight of a little hand raised above the boiling flood. In one moment he had the child again by the hair, and just as the prow of the Indian woman's canoe touched the shore he brought the child to land.

Springing towards him, the mother snatched her child from the flood, and gazed at its death-like face with eyeballs staring from their sockets. Then she laid her cheek on its cold breast, and stood like a statue of despair. There was one slight pulsation of the heart and a gentle motion of the hand! The child still lived. Opening up her blanket she laid her little one against her naked, warm bosom, drew the covering close around it, and sitting down on the bank, wept aloud for joy.

" Come—come 'way quick," cried Henri, hurrying off to hide the emotion which he could not crush down.

" Ay, she don't need our help now," said Joe, following his comrade.

As for Crusoe, he walked along by his master's side with his usual quiet, serene look of good-will towards all mankind. Doubtless a feeling of gladness at having saved a human life filled his shaggy breast, for he wagged his tail gently after each shake of his dripping sides; but his meek eyes were downcast, save when raised to receive the welcome and unusually fervent caress. Crusoe did not know that those three men loved him as though he had been a brother.

On their way back to the village the hunters were met by a little boy, who said that a council was to be held immediately, and their presence was requested.

The council was held in the tent of the principal chief, towards which all the other chiefs and many of the noted braves hurried. Like all Indian councils, it was preceded by smoking the " medicine pipe ", and was followed by speeches from several of the best orators. The substance of the discourse differed little from what has been already related in reference to the treaty between the Pale-faces.

and upon the whole it was satisfactory. But Joe Blunt could not fail to notice that Mahtawa maintained sullen silence during the whole course of the meeting.

He observed also that there was a considerable change in the tone of the meeting when he informed them that he was bound on a similar errand of peace to several of the other tribes, especially to one or two tribes which were the Pawnees' bitter enemies at that time. These grasping savages, having quite made up their minds that they were to obtain the entire contents of the two bales of goods, were much mortified on hearing that part was to go to other Indian tribes. Some of them even hinted that this would not be allowed, and Joe feared at one time that things were going to take an unfavourable turn. The hair of his scalp, as he afterwards said, " began to lift a little and feel oneasy ". But San-it-sa-rish stood honestly to his word, said that it would be well that the Pale-faces and the Pawnees should be brothers, and hoped that they would not forget the promise of annual presents from the hand of the great chief who lived in the big village near the rising sun.

Having settled this matter amicably, Joe distributed among the Indians the proportion of his goods designed for them; and then they all adjourned to another tent, where a great feast was prepared for them.

" Are ye hungry?" inquired Joe of Dick as they walked along.

" Ay, that I am. I feel as if I could eat a buffalo alive. Why, it's my 'pinion we've tasted nothin' since daybreak this mornin'."

" Well, I've often told ye that them Redskins think it a disgrace to give in eatin' till all that's set before them at a feast is bolted. We'll ha' to stretch oursel's, we will."

" I'se got a plenty room," remarked Henri.

" Ye have, but ye'll wish ye had more in a little."

" Bien, I not care!"

In quarter of an hour all the guests invited to this great " medicine feast " were assembled. No women were admitted. They never are at Indian feasts.

We may remark in passing that the word "medicine",
as used among the North-American Indians, has a very
much wider signification than it has with us. It is an almost
inexplicable word. When asked, they cannot give a full
or satisfactory explanation of it themselves. In the general,
we may say that whatever is mysterious is "medicine".
Jugglery and conjuring, of a noisy, mysterious, and, we
must add, rather silly nature, is "medicine", and the
juggler is a "medicine man". These medicine men undertake cures; but they are regular charlatans, and know
nothing whatever of the diseases they pretend to cure, or
their remedies. They carry bags containing sundry relics;
these are "medicine bags". Every brave has his own
private medicine bag. Everything that is incomprehensible,
or supposed to be supernatural, religious, or medical, is
"medicine". This feast, being an unusual one, in honour
of strangers, and in connexion with a peculiar and unexpected event, was "medicine". Even Crusoe, since his
gallant conduct in saving the Indian child, was "medicine"; and Dick Varley's double-barrelled rifle, which had
been an object of wonder ever since his arrival at the village,
was tremendous "medicine"!

Of course the Indians were arrayed in their best. Several
wore necklaces of the claws of the grizzly bear, of which
they are extremely proud; and a gaudily picturesque group
they were. The chief, however, had undergone a trans-
formation that well-nigh upset the gravity of our hunters,
and rendered Dick's efforts to look solemn quite abortive.
San-it-sa-rish had once been to the trading-forts of the Pale-
faces, and while there had received the customary gift of a
blue surtout with brass buttons, and an ordinary hat, such
as gentlemen wear at home. As the coat was a good deal
too small for him, a terrible length of dark, bony wrist
appeared below the cuffs. The waist was too high, and it
was with great difficulty that he managed to button the
garment across his broad chest. Being ignorant of the
nature of a hat, the worthy savage had allowed the paper
and string with which it had been originally covered to

remain on, supposing them to be part and parcel of the hat; and this, together with the high collar of the coat, which gave him a crushed-up appearance, the long black naked legs, and the painted visage, gave to him a *tout en-semble* which we can compare to nothing, as there was nothing in nature comparable to it.

Those guests who assembled first passed their time in smoking the medicine pipe until the others should arrive, for so long as a single invited guest is absent the feast cannot begin. Dignified silence was maintained while the pipe thus circulated from hand to hand. When the last guest arrived they began.

The men were seated in two rows, face to face. Feasts of this kind usually consist of but one species of food, and on the present occasion it was an enormous cauldron full of maize which had to be devoured. About fifty sat down to eat a quantity of what may be termed thick porridge that would have been ample allowance for a hundred ordinary men. Before commencing, San-it-sa-rish desired an aged medicine man to make an oration, which he did fluently and poetically. Its subject was the praise of the giver of the feast. At the end of each period there was a general "hou! hou!" of assent—equivalent to the "hear! hear!" of civilized men.

Other orators then followed, all of whom spoke with great ease and fluency, and some in the most impassioned strains, working themselves and their audience up to the highest pitch of excitement, now shouting with frenzied violence till their eyes glared from their sockets and the veins of their foreheads swelled almost to bursting as they spoke of war and chase, anon breaking into soft modulated and pleasing tones while they dilated upon the pleasures of peace and hospitality.

After these had finished, a number of wooden bowls full of maize porridge were put down between the guests—one bowl to each couple facing each other. But before commencing, a portion was laid aside and dedicated to their gods, with various mysterious ceremonies; for here, as in other places where the gospel is not known, the poor savages fancied that they could propitiate God with sacrifices. They had never heard of the " sacrifice of a broken spirit and a contrite heart ". This offering being made, the feast began in earnest. Not only was it a rule in this feast that every mouthful should be swallowed by each guest, however unwilling and unable he should be to do so, but he who could dispose of it with greatest speed was deemed the greatest man—at least on that occasion—while the last to conclude his supper was looked upon with some degree of contempt!

It seems strange that such a custom should ever have arisen, and one is not a little puzzled in endeavouring to guess at the origin of it. There is one fact that occurs to us as the probable cause. The Indian is, as we have before hinted, frequently reduced to a state bordering on starvation, and in a day after he may be burdened with superabundance of food. He oftentimes therefore eats as much as he can stuff into his body when he is blessed with plenty, so as to be the better able to withstand the attacks of hunger that may possibly be in store for him. The amount that an Indian will thus eat at a single meal is incredible. He seems to have the power of distending himself for the reception of a quantity that would kill a civilized man. Children in particular become like tightly inflated little balloons after a feast, and as they wear no clothing, the extraordinary rotundity is very obvious, not to say ridiculous. We conclude, therefore, that unusual powers of gormandizing, being useful, come at last to be cultivated as praiseworthy.

By good fortune Dick and Joe Blunt happened to have such enormous gluttons as *vis-à-vis* that the portions of their respective bowls which they could not devour were gobbled up for them. By good capacity and digestion, with no small amount of effort, Henri managed to dispose of his own share; but he was last of being done, and fell in the savages' esteem greatly. The way in which that sticky compost of boiled maize went down was absolutely amazing. The man opposite Dick, in particular, was a human boa-constrictor. He well-nigh suffocated Dick with suppressed laughter. He was a great raw-boned savage, with a throat of indiarubber, and went quickly and quietly on swallowing mass after mass with the solemn gravity of an owl. It mattered not a straw to him that Dick took comparatively small mouthfuls, and nearly choked on them too for want of liquid to wash them down. Had Dick eaten none at all, he would have uncomplainingly disposed of the whole. Jack the Giant-Killer's feats were nothing to his; and when at last the bowl was empty, he stopped short like a machine from which the steam had been suddenly cut off, and laid down his buffalo horn-spoon *without* a sigh.

Dick sighed, though with relief and gratitude, when his bowl was empty.

" I hope I may never have to do it again," said Joe that night, as they wended their way back to the chief's tent after supper. " I wouldn't be fit for anything for a week arter it."

Dick could only laugh, for any allusion to the feast instantly brought back that owl-like gourmand to whom he was so deeply indebted.

Henri groaned. " Oh! mes boy, I am speechless! I am ready for bust! Oui—hah! I veesh it vas to-morrow."

Many a time that night did Henri " veesh it vas to-morrow ", as he lay helpless on his back, looking up through the roof of the chief's tent at the stars, and listening enviously to the plethoric snoring of Joe Blunt.

He was entertained, however, during those waking hours with a serenade such as few civilized ears ever listen to. This was nothing else than a vocal concert performed by all the dogs of the village, and as they amounted to nearly two thousand the orchestra was a pretty full one.

These wretches howled as if they had all gone mad. Yet there was " method in their madness "; for they congregated in a crowd before beginning, and sat down on their haunches. Then one, which seemed to be the conductor, raised his snout to the sky and uttered a long, low, melancholy wail. The others took it up by twos and threes, until the whole pack had their noses pointing to the stars and their throats distended to the uttermost, while a prolonged yell filled the air. Then it sank gradually, one or two (bad performers probably) making a yelping attempt to get it up again at the wrong time. Again the conductor raised his nose, and out it came—full swing. There was no vociferous barking. It was simple wolfish howling increased in fervour to an electric yell, with slight barks running continuously through it like an obligato accompaniment.

When Crusoe first heard the unwonted sound he sprang to his feet, bristled up like a hyena, showed all his teeth, and bounded out of the tent blazing with indignation and astonishment. When he found out what it was he returned quite sleek, and with a look of profound contempt on his countenance, as he resumed his place by his master's side and went to sleep.

CHAPTER X

Dick Varley sat before the fire ruminating. We do not
mean to assert that Dick had been previously eating grass.
By no means. For several days past he had been mentally
subsisting on the remarkable things that he heard and saw
in the Pawnee village, and wondering how he was to get
away without being scalped. He was now chewing the cud
of this intellectual fare. We therefore repeat emphatically
—in case any reader should have presumed to contradict
us—that Dick Varley sat before the fire *ruminating*!

Joe Blunt likewise sat by the fire along with him, ruminating too, and smoking besides. Henri also sat there smoking,
and looking a little the worse of his late supper.

"I don't like the look o' things," said Joe, blowing a
whiff of smoke slowly from his lips, and watching it as it
ascended into the still air. "That blackguard Mahtawa is
determined not to let us off till he gits all our goods; an' if
he gits them, he may as well take our scalps too, for we
would come poor speed in the prairies without guns,
horses, or goods."

Dick looked at his friend with an expression of concern.
"What's to be done?" said he.

"Ve must escape," answered Henri; but his tone was
not a hopeful one, for he knew the danger of their position
better than Dick.

"Ay, we must escape—at least we must try," said Joe.
"But I'll make one more effort to smooth over San-it-sa-
rish, an' git him to snub that villain Mahtawa."

Just as he spoke the villain in question entered the tent
with a bold, haughty air, and sat down before the fire in

sullen silence. For some minutes no one spoke, and Henri, who happened at the time to be examining the locks of Dick's rifle, continued to inspect them with an appearance of careless indifference that he was far from feeling.

Now, this rifle of Dick's had become a source of unceasing wonder to the Indians—wonder which was greatly increased by the fact that no one could discharge it but himself. Dick had, during his short stay at the Pawnee village, amused himself and the savages by exhibiting his marvellous powers with the "silver rifle". Since it had been won by him at the memorable match in the Mustang Valley, it had scarce ever been out of his hand, so that he had become decidedly the best shot in the settlement, could "bark" squirrels (that is, hit the bark of the branch on which a squirrel happened to be standing, and so kill it by the concussion alone), and could "drive the nail" every shot. The silver rifle, as we have said, became "great medicine" to the Red-men when they saw it kill at a distance which the few wretched guns they had obtained from the fur-traders could not even send a spent ball to. The double shot, too, filled them with wonder and admiration; but that which they regarded with an almost supernatural feeling of curiosity was the percussion cap, which, in Dick's hands, always exploded, but in theirs was utterly useless!

This result was simply owing to the fact that Dick, after firing, handed the rifle to the Indians without renewing the cap; so that when they loaded and attempted to fire, of course it merely snapped. When he wished again to fire, he adroitly exchanged the old cap for a new one. He was immensely tickled by the solemn looks of the Indians at this most incomprehensible of all "medicines", and kept them for some days in ignorance of the true cause, intending to reveal it before he left. But circumstances now arose which banished all trifling thoughts from his mind.

Mahtawa raised his head suddenly, and said, pointing to the silver rifle, "Mahtawa wishes to have the two-shotted medicine gun. He will give his best horse in exchange."

"Mahtawa is liberal," answered Joe; "but the pale-faced youth cannot part with it. He has far to travel, and must shoot buffaloes by the way."

"The pale-faced youth shall have a bow and arrows to shoot the buffalo," rejoined the Indian.

"He cannot use the bow and arrow," answered Joe "He has not been trained like the Red-man."

Mahtawa was silent for a few seconds, and his dark brows frowned more heavily than ever over his eyes.

"The Pale-faces are too bold," he exclaimed, working himself into a passion. "They are in the power of Mahtawa. If they will not give the gun he will take it."

He sprang suddenly to his feet as he spoke, and snatched the rifle from Henri's hand.

Henri, being ignorant of the language, had not been able to understand the foregoing conversation, although he saw well enough that it was not an agreeable one; but no sooner did he find himself thus rudely and unexpectedly deprived of the rifle than he jumped up, wrenched it in a twinkling from the Indian's grasp, and hurled him violently out of the tent.

In a moment Mahtawa drew his knife, uttered a savage yell, and sprang on the reckless hunter, who, however, caught his wrist, and held it as if in a vice. The yell brought a dozen warriors instantly to the spot, and before Dick had time to recover from his astonishment, Henri was surrounded and pinioned despite his herculean struggles.

Before Dick could move, Joe Blunt grasped his arm, and whispered quickly, "Don't rise. You can't help him. They daren't kill him till San-it-sa-rish agrees."

Though much surprised, Dick obeyed, but it required all his efforts, both of voice and hand, to control Crusoe, whose mind was much too honest and straightforward to understand such subtle pieces of diplomacy, and who strove to rush to the rescue of his ill-used friend.

When the tumult had partly subsided, Joe Blunt rose and said,—

"Have the Pawnee braves turned traitors that they draw the knife against those who have smoked with them the pipe of peace and eaten their maize? The Pale-faces are three; the Pawnees are thousands. If evil has been done, let it be laid before the chief. Mahtawa wishes to have the medicine gun. Although we said, No, we could not part with it, he tried to take it by force. Are we to go back to the great chief of the Pale-faces and say that the Pawnees are thieves? Are the Pale-faces henceforth to tell their children when they steal, 'That is bad; that is like the Pawnee?' No; this must not be. The rifle shall be restored, and we will forget this disagreement. Is it not so?"

There was an evident disposition on the part of many of the Indians, with whom Mahtawa was no favourite, to applaud this speech; but the wily chief sprang forward, and, with flashing eyes, sought to turn the tables.

"The Pale-face speaks with soft words, but his heart is false. Is he not going to make peace with the enemies of the Pawnee? Is he not going to take goods to them, and make them gifts and promises? The Pale-faces are spies. They come to see the weakness of the Pawnee camp; but they have found that it is strong. Shall we suffer the false hearts to escape? Shall they live? No; we will hang their scalps in our wigwams, for they have *struck a chief*, and we will keep all their goods for our squaws—wah!"

This allusion to keeping all the goods had more effect on the minds of the vacillating savages than the chief's eloquence. But a new turn was given to their thoughts by Joe Blunt remarking in a quiet, almost contemptuous tone—

"Mahtawa is not the *great* chief."

"True, true," they cried, and immediately hurried to the tent of San-it-sa-rish.

Once again this chief stood between the hunters and the savages, who wanted but a signal to fall on them. There was a long palaver, which ended in Henri being set at liberty and the rifle being restored.

That evening, as the three friends sat beside their fire eating their supper of boiled maize and buffalo meat, they laughed and talked as carelessly as ever; but the gaiety was assumed, for they were at the time planning their escape from a tribe which, they foresaw, would not long refrain from carrying out their wishes, and robbing, perhaps murdering them.

"Ye see," said Joe with a perplexed air, while he drew a piece of live charcoal from the fire with his fingers and lighted his pipe—"ye see, there's more difficulties in the way o' gettin' off than ye think——"

"Oh, nivare mind de difficulties," interrupted Henri, whose wrath at the treatment he had received had not yet cooled down. "Ve must jump on de best horses ve can git hold, shake our fists at de reptiles, and go away fast as ve can. De best hoss *must* vin de race."

Joe shook his head. "A hundred arrows would be in our backs before we got twenty yards from the camp. Besides, we can't tell which are the best horses. Our own are the best in my 'pinion, but how are we to git 'em?"

"I know who has charge o' them," said Dick. "I saw them grazing near the tent o' that poor squaw whose baby was saved by Crusoe. Either her husband looks after them, or some neighbours."

"That's well," said Joe. "That's one o' my difficulties gone."

"What are the others?"

"Well, d'ye see, they're troublesome. We can't git the horses out o' camp without bein' seen, for the red rascals would see what we were at in a jiffy. Then, if we do git 'em out, we can't go off without our bales, an' we needn't think to take 'em from under the nose o' the chief and his squaws without bein' axed questions. To go off without them would niver do at all."

"Joe," said Dick earnestly, "I've hit on a plan."

"Have ye, Dick—what is't?"

"Come and I'll let ye see," answered Dick, rising hastily and quitting the tent, followed by his comrades and his faithful dog.

It may be as well to remark here, that no restraint whatever had yet been put on the movements of our hunters as long as they kept to their legs, for it was well known that

any attempt by men on foot to escape from mounted
Indians on the plains would be hopeless. Moreover, the
savages thought that as long as there was a prospect of their
being allowed to depart peaceably with their goods, they
would not be so mad as to fly from the camp, and, by so
doing, risk their lives and declare war with their enter-
tainers. They had therefore been permitted to wander
unchecked, as yet, far beyond the outskirts of the camp, and
amuse themselves in paddling about the lake in the small
Indian canoes and shooting wild-fowl.

Dick now led the way through the labyrinth of tents in
the direction of the lake, and they talked and laughed
loudly, and whistled to Crusoe as they went, in order to
prevent their purpose being suspected. For the purpose of
further disarming suspicion, they went without their rifles.
Dick explained his plan by the way, and it was at once
warmly approved of by his comrades.

On reaching the lake they launched a small canoe, into
which Crusoe was ordered to jump; then, embarking, they
paddled swiftly to the opposite shore, singing a canoe song
as they dipped their paddles in the moonlit waters of the
lake. Arrived at the other side, they hauled the canoe up
and hurried through the thin belt of wood and willows that
intervened between the lake and the prairie. Here they
paused.

" Is that the bluff, Joe?"

" No, Dick; that's too near. T'other one'll be best—far
away to the right. It's a little one, and there's others near
it. The sharp eyes o' the Red-skins won't be so likely to be
prowlin' there."

" Come on, then; but we'll have to take down by the
lake first."

In a few minutes the hunters were threading their way
through the outskirts of the wood at a rapid trot, in the
opposite direction from the bluff, or wooded knoll, which
they wished to reach. This they did lest prying eyes should
have followed them. In quarter of an hour they turned at
right angles to their track, and struck straight out into the

prairie, and after a long run they edged round and came in upon the bluff from behind. It was merely a collection of stunted but thick-growing willows.

Forcing their way into the centre of this they began to examine it.

"It'll do," said Joe.

"De very ting," remarked Henri.

"Come here, Crusoe."

Crusoe bounded to his master's side, and looked up in his face.

"Look at this place, pup; smell it well."

Crusoe instantly set off all round among the willows, in and out, snuffing everywhere, and whining with excitement.

"Come here, good pup; that will do. Now, lads, we'll go back." So saying, Dick and his friends left the bluff, and retraced their steps to the camp. Before they had gone far, however, Joe halted and said,—

"D'ye know, Dick, I doubt if the pup's so cliver as ye think. What if he don't quite onderstand ye?"

Dick replied by taking off his cap and throwing it down, at the same time exclaiming, "Take it yonder, pup," and pointing with his hand towards the bluff. The dog seized the cap, and went off with it at full speed towards the willows, where it left it, and came galloping back for the expected reward—not now, as in days of old, a bit of meat, but a gentle stroke of its head and a hearty clap on its shaggy side.

"Good pup! go now an' fetch it."

Away he went with a bound, and in a few seconds came back and deposited the cap at his master's feet.

"Will that do?" asked Dick, triumphantly.

"Ay, lad, it will. The pup's worth its weight in goold."

"Oui, I have said, and I say it agen, de dog is *human*, so him is. If not, fat am he?"

Without pausing to reply to this perplexing question, Dick stepped forward again, and in half an hour or so they were back in the camp.

"Now for *your* part of the work, Joe. Yonder's the

squaw that owns the half-drowned baby. Everything depends on her."

Dick pointed to the Indian woman as he spoke. She was sitting beside her tent, and playing at her knee was the identical youngster who had been saved by Crusoe.

" I'll manage it," said Joe, and walked towards her, while Dick and Henri returned to the chief's tent:

" Does the Pawnee woman thank the Great Spirit that her child is saved?" began Joe as he came up.

" She does," answered the woman, looking up at the hunter. " And her heart is warm to the Pale-faces."

After a short silence Joe continued—

" The Pawnee chiefs do not love the Pale-faces. Some of them hate them."

" The Dark Flower knows it," answered the woman; " she is sorry. She would help the Pale-faces if she could."

This was uttered in a low tone, and with a meaning glance of the eye.

Joe hesitated again—could he trust her? Yes; the feelings that filled her breast and prompted her words were not those of the Indian just now—they were those of a *mother*, whose gratitude was too full for utterance.

" Will the Dark Flower," said Joe, catching the name she had given herself, " help the Pale-face if he opens his heart to her? Will she risk the anger of her nation?"

" She will," replied the woman: " she will do what she can."

Joe and his dark friend now dropped their high-sounding style of speech, and spoke for some minutes rapidly in an undertone. It was finally arranged that on a given day, at a certain hour, the woman should take the four horses down the shores of the lake to its lower end, as if she were going for firewood, there cross the creek at the ford, and drive them to the willow bluff, and guard them till the hunters should arrive.

Having settled this, Joe returned to the tent and informed his comrades of his success.

During the next three days Joe kept the Indians in good

humour by giving them one or two trinkets, and speaking in glowing terms of the riches of the white men, and the readiness with which they would part with them to the savages if they would only make peace.

Meanwhile, during the dark hours of each night, Dick managed to abstract small quantities of goods from their pack, in room of which he stuffed in pieces of leather to keep up the size and appearance. The goods thus taken out he concealed about his person, and went off with a careless swagger to the outskirts of the village, with Crusoe at his heels. Arrived there, he tied the goods in a small piece of deerskin, and gave the bundle to the dog, with the injunction, " Take it yonder, pup."

Crusoe took it up at once, darted off at full speed with the bundle in his mouth, down the shore of the lake towards the ford of the river, and was soon lost to view. In this way, little by little, the goods were conveyed by the faithful dog to the willow bluff and left there, while the stuffed pack still remained in safe keeping in the chief's tent.

Joe did not at first like the idea of thus sneaking off from the camp, and more than once made strong efforts to induce San-it-sa-rish to let him go: but even that chief's countenance was not so favourable as it had been. It was clear that he could not make up his mind to let slip so good a chance of obtaining guns, powder and shot, horses and goods, without any trouble; so Joe made up his mind to give them the slip at once.

A dark night was chosen for the attempt, and the Indian woman went off with the horses to the place where firewood for the camp was usually cut. Unfortunately, the suspicion of that wily savage Mahtawa had been awakened, and he stuck close to the hunters all day—not knowing what was going on, but feeling convinced that something was brewing which he resolved to watch, without mentioning his suspicions to any one.

" I think that villain's away at last," whispered Joe to his comrades. " It's time to go, lads; the moon won't be up for an hour. Come along."

" Have ye got the big powder-horn, Joe?"

" Ay, ay—all right."

" Stop! stop! my knife, my couteau. Ah, here I be! Now, boy."

The three set off as usual, strolling carelessly to the out-skirts of the camp; then they quickened their pace, and, gaining the lake, pushed off in a small canoe.

At the same moment Mahtawa stepped from the bushes, leaped into another canoe, and followed them.

" Ha! he must die," muttered Henri.

" Not at all," said Joe; " we'll manage him without that."

The chief landed and strode boldly up to them, for he knew well that whatever their purpose might be they would not venture to use their rifles within sound of the camp at that hour of the night. As for their knives, he could trust to his own active limbs and the woods to escape and give the alarm if need be.

" The Pale-faces hunt very late," he said, with a malicious grin. " Do they love the dark better than the sunshine?"

" Not so," replied Joe, coolly; " but we love to walk by the light of the moon. It will be up in less than an hour, and we mean to take a long ramble to-night."

" The Pawnee chief loves to walk by the moon, too; he will go with the Pale-faces."

" Good!" ejaculated Joe. " Come along, then."

The party immediately set forward, although the savage was a little taken by surprise at the indifferent way in which Joe received his proposal to accompany them. He walked on to the edge of the prairie, however, and then stopped.

" The Pale-faces must go alone," said he; " Mahtawa will return to his tent."

Joe replied to this intimation by seizing him suddenly by the throat and choking back the yell that would otherwise have brought the Pawnee warriors rushing to the scene of action in hundreds. Mahtawa's hand was on the handle of his scalping-knife in a moment, but before he could draw it his arms were glued to his sides by the bear-like embrace of Henri, while Dick tied a handkerchief quickly yet firmly round his mouth. The whole thing was accomplished in two minutes. After taking his knife and tomahawk away, they loosened their gripe and escorted him swiftly over the prairie.

Mahtawa was perfectly submissive after the first convulsive struggle was over. He knew that the men who walked on each side of him grasping his arms were more than his match singly, so he wisely made no resistance.

Hurrying him to a clump of small trees on the plain which was so far distant from the village that a yell could not be heard, they removed the bandage from Mahtawa's mouth.

" *Must* he be kill?" inquired Henri, in a tone of commiseration.

"Not at all," answered Joe; "we'll tie him to a tree and leave him here."

"Then he vill be starved to deat'. Oh, dat is more horrobell!"

"He must take his chance o' that. I've no doubt his friends'll find him in a day or two, an' he's game to last for a week or more. But you'll have to run to the willow bluff, Dick, and bring a bit of line to tie him. We can't spare it well; but there's no help."

"But there *is* help," retorted Dick. "Just order the villain to climb into that tree."

"Why so, lad?"

"Don't ask questions, but do what I bid ye."

The hunter smiled for a moment as he turned to the Indian and ordered him to climb up a small tree near to which he stood. Mahtawa looked surprised, but there was no alternative. Joe's authoritative tone brooked no delay, so he sprang into the tree like a monkey.

"Crusoe," said Dick, " *watch him!*"

The dog sat quietly down at the foot of the tree, and fixed his eyes on the savage with a glare that spoke unutterable things. At the same time he displayed his full complement of teeth, and uttered a sound like distant thunder.

Joe almost laughed, and Henri did laugh outright.

"Come along; he's safe now," cried Dick, hurrying away in the direction of the willow bluff, which they soon reached, and found that the faithful squaw had tied their steeds to the bushes, and, moreover, had bundled up their goods into a pack, and strapped it on the back of the pack-horse; but she had not remained with them.

"Bless yer dark face!" ejaculated Joe, as he sprang into the saddle and rode out of the clump of bushes. He was followed immediately by the others, and in three minutes they were flying over the plain at full speed.

On gaining the last far-off ridge, that afforded a distant view of the woods skirting the Pawnee camp, they drew up; and Dick, putting his fingers to his mouth, drew a long, shrill whistle.

It reached the willow bluff like a faint echo. At the same moment the moon arose and more clearly revealed Crusoe's cataleptic glare at the Indian chief, who, being utterly unarmed, was at the dog's mercy. The instant the whistle fell on his ear, however, he dropped his eyes, covered his teeth, and, leaping through the bushes, flew over the plains like an arrow. At the same instant Mahtawa, descending from his tree, ran as fast as he could towards the village, uttering the terrible war-hoop when near enough to be heard. No sound sends such a thrill through an Indian camp. Every warrior flew to arms, and vaulted on his steed. So quickly was the alarm given that in less than ten minutes a thousand hoofs were thundering on the plain, and faintly reached the ears of the fugitives.

Joe smiled. "It'll puzzle them to come up wi' nags like ours. They're in prime condition, too—lots o' wind in 'em. If we only keep out o' badger holes we may laugh at the red varmints."

Joe's opinion of Indian horses was correct. In a very few minutes the sound of hoofs died away; but the fugitives did not draw bridle during the remainder of that night, for they knew not how long the pursuit might be continued. By pond, and brook, and bluff they passed, down in the grassy bottoms and over the prairie waves—nor checked their headlong course till the sun blazed over the level sweep of the eastern plain as if it arose out of the mighty ocean.

Then they sprang from the saddle, and hastily set about the preparation of their morning meal.

CHAPTER XI

Evening meditations and morning reflections—Buffaloes, badgers, antelopes, and accidents—An old bull and the wolves—" Mad tails "—Henri floored, etc.

There is nothing that prepares one so well for the enjoyment of rest, both mental and physical, as a long-protracted period of excitement and anxiety, followed up by bodily fatigue. Excitement alone banishes rest; but, united with severe physical exertion, it prepares for it. At least, courteous reader, this is our experience; and certainly this was the experience of our three hunters as they lay on their backs beneath the branches of a willow bush and gazed serenely up at the twinkling stars two days after their escape from the Indian village.

They spoke little; they were too tired for that, also they were too comfortable. Their respective suppers of fresh antelope steak, shot that day, had just been disposed of. Their feet were directed towards the small fire on which the said steaks had been cooked, and which still threw a warm, ruddy glow over the encampment. Their blankets were wrapped comfortably round them, and tucked in as only hunters and mothers know *how* to tuck them in. Their respective pipes delivered forth, at stated intervals, three richly yellow puffs of smoke, as if a three-gun battery were playing upon the sky from that particular spot of earth. The horses were picketed and hobbled in a rich grassy bottom close by, from which the quiet munch of their equine jaws sounded pleasantly, for it told of healthy appetites, and promised speed on the morrow. The fear of being overtaken during the night was now past, and the faithful Crusoe, by virtue of sight, hearing, and smell, guaranteed them against sudden attack during the hours of slumber. A perfume of wild flowers mingled with the loved odours of the "weed", and the tinkle of a tiny rivulet fell sweetly on their ears. In short, the "Pale-faces" were supremely happy, and disposed to be thankful for their recent deliverance and their present comforts.

"I wonder what the stars are," said Dick, languidly taking the pipe out of his mouth.

"Bits o' fire," suggested Joe.

"I tink dey are vorlds," muttered Henri, "an' have peepels in dem. I have hear men say dat."

A long silence followed, during which, no doubt, the star-gazers were working out various theories in their own minds.

"Wonder," said Dick again, "how far off they be."

"A mile or two, maybe," said Joe.

Henri was about to laugh sarcastically at this, but on further consideration he thought it would be more com-fortable not to, so he lay still. In another minute he said—

"Joe Blunt, you is ver' igrant. Don't you know dat de books say de stars be hondreds, tousands—oh! milleryons of mile away to here, and dat dey is more bigger dan dis vorld?"

Joe snored lightly, and his pipe fell out of his mouth at this point, so the conversation dropped. Presently Dick asked in a low tone, "I say, Henri, are ye asleep?"

"Oui," replied Henri, faintly. "Don't speak, or you vill vaken me."

"Ah, Crusoe! you're not asleep, are you, pup?" No need to ask that question. The instantaneous wag of that speaking tail and the glance of that wakeful eye, as the dog lifted his head and laid his chin on Dick's arm, showed that he had been listening to every word that was spoken. We cannot say whether he understood it, but beyond all doubt he heard it. Crusoe never presumed to think of going to sleep until his master was as sound as a top, then he ventured to indulge in that light species of slumber which is familiarly known as " sleeping with one eye open ". But, comparatively as well as figuratively speaking, Crusoe slept usually with one eye and a half open, and the other half was never very tightly shut.

Gradually Dick's pipe fell out of his mouth—an event which the dog, with an exercise of instinct almost, if not quite, amounting to reason, regarded as a signal for him to go off. The camp fire went slowly out, the stars twinkled down at their reflections in the brook, and a deep breathing of wearied men was the only sound that rose in harmony with the purling stream.

Before the sun rose next morning, and while many of the brighter stars were still struggling for existence with the approaching day, Joe was up and buckling on the saddle-bags, while he shouted to his unwilling companions to rise.

" If it depended on you," he said, " the Pawnees wouldn't be long afore they got our scalps. Jump, ye dogs, an' lend a hand, will ye?"

A snore from Dick and a deep sigh from Henri was the answer to this pathetic appeal. It so happened, however, that Henri's pipe, in falling from his lips, had emptied the ashes just under his nose, so that the sigh referred to drew a quantity thereof into his throat and almost choked him. Nothing could have been a more effective awakener. He was up in a moment coughing vociferously. Most men have a tendency to vent ill-humour on some one, and they generally do it on one whom they deem to be worse than themselves. Henri, therefore, instead of growling at Joe for rousing him, scolded Dick for not rising.

" Ha, mauvais dog! bad chien! vill you dare to look to me?"

Crusoe did look with amiable placidity, as though to say, " Howl away, old boy, I won't budge till Dick does."

With a mighty effort Giant Sleep was thrown off at last, and the hunters were once more on their journey, cantering lightly over the soft turf.

" Ho, let's have a run!" cried Dick, unable to repress the feelings aroused by the exhilarating morning air.

" Have a care, boy," cried Joe, as they stretched out at full gallop. " Keep off the ridge; it's riddled wi' badger—— Ha! I thought so."

At that moment Dick's horse put its foot into a badger-hole and turned completely over, sending its rider through the air in a curve that an East Indian acrobat would have envied. For a few seconds Dick lay flat on his back, then he jumped up and laughed, while his comrades hurried up anxiously to his assistance.

"No bones broke?" inquired Joe.

Dick gave a hysterical gasp. "I—I think not."

"Let's have a look. No, nothin' to speak o', be good luck. Ye should niver go slap through a badger country like that, boy; always keep i' the bottoms, where the grass is short. Now then, up ye go. That's it!"

Dick remounted, though not with quite so elastic a spring as usual, and they pushed forward at a more reasonable pace.

Accidents of this kind are of common occurrence in the prairies. Some horses, however, are so well trained that they look sharp out for these holes, which are generally found to be most numerous on the high and dry grounds. But in spite of all the caution both of man and horse many ugly falls take place, and sometimes bones are broken.

They had not gone far after this accident when an antelope leaped from a clump of willows, and made for a belt of woodland that lay along the margin of a stream not half-a-mile off.

"Hurrah!" cried Dick, forgetting his recent fall. "Come along, Crusoe." And away they went again full tilt, for the horse had not been injured by its somersault.

The antelope which Dick was thus wildly pursuing was of the same species as the one he had shot some time before—namely, the prong-horned antelope. These graceful creatures have long, slender limbs, delicately formed heads, and large, beautiful eyes. The horns are black, and rather short; they have no branches, like the antlers of the red-deer, but have a single projection on each horn, near the head, and the extreme points of the horns curve suddenly inwards, forming the hook or prong from which the name of the animal is derived. Their colour is dark-yellowish brown. They are so fleet that not one horse in a hundred can overtake them; and their sight and sense of smell are so acute that it would be next to impossible to kill them, were it not for the inordinate curiosity which we have before referred to. The Indians manage to attract these simple little creatures by merely lying down on their backs and kicking their heels in the air, or by waving any white object on the point of an arrow, while the hunter keeps concealed by lying flat in the grass. By these means a herd of antelopes may be induced to wheel round and round an object in timid but intense surprise, gradually approaching until they come near enough to enable the hunter to make sure of his mark. Thus the animals, which of all others *ought* to be the most difficult to slay, are, in consequence of their insatiable curiosity, more easily shot than any other deer of the plains.

May we not gently suggest to the reader for his or her consideration that there are human antelopes, so to speak, whose case bears a striking resemblance to the prong-horn of the North American prairie?

Dick's horse was no match for the antelope, neither was Crusoe; so they pulled up shortly and returned to their companions, to be laughed at.

"It's no manner o' use to wind yer horse, lad, after sich game. They're not much worth, an', if I mistake not, we'll be among the buffalo soon. There's fresh tracks everywhere, and the herds are scattered now. Ye see, when they keep together in bands o' thousands ye don't so often fall in wi' them. But when they scatters about in twos, an' threes, an' sixes, ye may shoot them every day as much as ye please."

Several groups of buffalo had already been seen on the horizon, but as a red-deer had been shot in a belt of woodland the day before they did not pursue them. The red-deer is very much larger than the prong-horned antelope, and is highly esteemed both for its flesh and its skin, which latter becomes almost like chamois leather when dressed. Notwithstanding this supply of food, the hunters could not resist the temptation to give chase to a herd of about nine buffaloes that suddenly came into view as they overtopped an undulation in the plain.

"It's no use," cried Dick, "I *must* go at them!"

Joe himself caught fire from the spirit of his young friend, so calling to Henri to come on and let the pack-horse remain to feed, he dashed away in pursuit. The buffaloes gave one stare of surprise, and then fled as fast as possible. At first it seemed as if such huge, unwieldy carcasses could not run very fast; but in a few minutes they managed to get up a pace that put the horses to their mettle. Indeed, at first it seemed as if the hunters did not gain an inch; but by degrees they closed with them, for buffaloes are not long winded.

On nearing the herd, the three men diverged from each other and selected their animals. Henri, being short-sighted, naturally singled out the largest; and the largest—also naturally—was a tough old bull. Joe brought down a fat young cow at the first shot, and Dick was equally fortunate. But he well-nigh shot Crusoe, who, just as he was about to fire, rushed in unexpectedly and sprang at the animal's throat, for which piece of recklessness he was ordered back to watch the pack-horse.

Meanwhile, Henri, by dint of yelling, throwing his arms wildly about, and digging his heels into the sides of his long-legged horse, succeeded in coming close up with the bull, which once or twice turned his clumsy body half round and glared furiously at its pursuer with its small black eyes. Suddenly it stuck out its tail, stopped short, and turned full round. Henri stopped short also. Now, the sticking out of a buffalo's tail has a peculiar significance which it is well to point out. It serves, in a sense, the same purpose to the hunter that the compass does to the mariner—it points out where to go and what to do. When galloping away in ordinary flight, the buffalo carries his tail like ordinary cattle, which indicates that you may push on. When wounded, he lashes it from side to side, or carries it over his back, up in the air; this indicates, "Look out! haul off a bit!" But when he carries it stiff and horizontal,

with a *slight curve* in the middle of it, it says plainly, " Keep
back, or kill me as quick as you can", for that is what
Indians call the *mad tail*, and is a sign that mischief is
brewing.

Henri's bull displayed the mad tail just before turning,
but he didn't observe it, and, accordingly, waited for the
bull to move and show his shoulder for a favourable shot.
But instead of doing this he put his head down, and, foaming
with rage, went at him full tilt. The big horse never stirred;
it seemed to be petrified. Henri had just time to fire at
the monster's neck, and the next moment was sprawling
on his back, with the horse rolling over four or five yards
beyond him. It was a most effective tableau—Henri rub-
bing his shins and grinning with pain, the horse gazing in
affright as he rose trembling from the plain, and the buffalo
bull looking on half stunned, and evidently very much
surprised at the result of his charge.

Fortunately, before he could repeat the experiment, Dick
galloped up and put a ball through his heart.

Joe and his comrades felt a little ashamed of their exploit
on this occasion, for there was no need to have killed three
animals—they could not have carried with them more than
a small portion of one—and they upbraided themselves
several times during the operation of cutting out the tongues
and other choice portions of the two victims. As for the
bull, he was almost totally useless, so they left him as a
gift to the wolves.

Now that they had come among the buffalo, wolves were
often seen sneaking about and licking their hungry jaws;
but although they approached pretty near to the camp at
nights, they did not give the hunters any concern. Even
Crusoe became accustomed to them at last, and ceased to
notice them. These creatures are very dangerous sometimes, however, and when hard pressed by hunger will even
attack man. The day after this hunt the travellers came
upon a wounded old buffalo which had evidently escaped
from the Indians (for a couple of arrows were sticking in its
side), only to fall a prey to his deadly enemies, the white

wolves. These savage brutes hang on the skirts of the herds of buffaloes to attack and devour any one that may chance, from old age or from being wounded, to linger behind the rest. The buffalo is tough and fierce, however, and fights so desperately that, although surrounded by fifty or a hundred wolves, he keeps up the unequal combat for several days before he finally succumbs.

The old bull that our travellers discovered had evidently been long engaged with his ferocious adversaries, for his limbs and flesh were torn in shreds in many places, and blood was streaming from his sides. Yet he had fought so gallantly that he had tossed and stamped to death dozens of the enemy. There could not have been fewer than fifty wolves round him; and they had just concluded another of many futile attacks when the hunters came up, for they were ranged in a circle round their huge adversary—some lying down, some sitting on their haunches to rest, and others sneaking about, lolling out their red tongues and licking their chops as if impatient to renew the combat. The poor buffalo was nearly spent, and it was clear that a few hours more would see him torn to shreds and his bones picked clean.

" Ugh! de brutes," ejaculated Henri.

" They don't seem to mind us a bit," remarked Dick, as they rode up to within pistol shot.

" It'll be merciful to give the old fellow a shot," said Joe. " Them varmints are sure to finish him at last."

Joe raised his rifle as he spoke, and fired. The old bull gave his last groan and fell, while the wolves, alarmed by the shot, fled in all directions; but they did not run far. They knew well that some portion, at least, of the carcass would fall to their share; so they sat down at various distances all round, to wait as patiently as they might for the hunters to retire. Dick left the scene with a feeling of regret that the villainous wolves should have their feast so much sooner than they expected.

Yet, after all, why should we call these wolves villainous? They did nothing wrong—nothing contrary to the laws of their peculiar nature. Nay, if we come to reason upon it, they rank higher in this matter than man; for while the wolf does no violence to the laws of its instincts, man often deliberately silences the voice of conscience, and violates the laws of his own nature. But we will not insist on the term, good reader, if you object strongly to it. We are willing to admit that the wolves are *not* villainous, but, *assuredly*, they are unlovable.

In the course of the afternoon the three horsemen reached a small creek, the banks of which were lined with a few stunted shrubs and trees. Having eaten nothing since the night before, they dismounted here to "feed", as Joe expressed it.

"Cur'ous thing," remarked Joe, as he struck a light by means of flint, steel, and tinder-box—"cur'ous thing that we're made to need sich a lot o' grub. If we could only get on like the sarpints, now, wot can breakfast on a rabbit, and then wait a month or two for dinner! Ain't it cur'ous?"

Dick admitted that it was, and stooped to blow the fire into a blaze.

Here Henri uttered a cry of consternation, and stood speechless, with his mouth open.

"What's the matter? what is't?" cried Dick and Joe, seizing their rifles instinctively.

"De—grub—him—be—forgat!"

There was a look of blank horror, and then a burst of laughter from Dick Varley. "Well, well," cried he, "we've got lots o' tea an' sugar, an' some flour; we can git on wi' that till we shoot another buffalo, or a—ha!"

Dick observed a wild turkey stalking among the willows as he spoke. It was fully a hundred yards off, and only its head was seen above the leaves. This was a matter of little moment, however, for by aiming a little lower he knew that he must hit the body. But Dick had driven the nail too often to aim at its body; he aimed at the bird's eye, and cut its head off.

"Fetch it, Crusoe."

In three minutes it was at Dick's feet, and it is not too much to say that in five minutes more it was in the pot.

As this unexpected supply made up for the loss of the meat which Henri had forgotten at their last halting-place, their equanimity was restored; and while the meal was in preparation Dick shouldered his rifle and went into the bush to try for another turkey. He did not get one, however, but he shot a couple of prairie-hens, which are excellent eating. Moreover, he found a large quantity of wild grapes and plums. These were unfortunately not nearly ripe, but Dick resolved to try his hand at a new dish, so he stuffed the breast of his coat full of them.

After the pot was emptied, Dick washed it out, and put a little clean water in it. Then he poured some flour in, and stirred it well. While this was heating, he squeezed the sour grapes and plums into what Joe called a "mush", mixed it with a spoonful of sugar, and emptied it into the pot. He also skimmed a quantity of the fat from the remains of the turkey soup and added that to the mess, which he stirred with earnest diligence till it boiled down into a sort of thick porridge.

"D'ye think it'll be good?" asked Joe gravely; "I've me doubts of it."

"We'll see. Hold the tin dish, Henri."

"Take care of de fingers. Ha! it looks magnifique—superb!"

The first spoonful produced an expression on Henri's face that needed not to be interpreted. It was as sour as vinegar.

"Ye'll ha' to eat it yerself, Dick, lad," cried Joe, throwing down his spoon, and spitting out the unsavoury mess.

"Nonsense," cried Dick, bolting two or three mouthfuls, and trying to look as if he liked it. "Try again; it's not so bad as you think."

"Ho-o-o-o-o!" cried Henri, after the second mouthful. "'Tis vinégre. All de sugare in de pack would not make more sweeter one bite of it."

Dick was obliged to confess the dish a failure, so it was

thrown out after having been offered to Crusoe, who gave it one sniff and turned away in silence. Then they mounted and resumed their journey.

At this place mosquitoes and horse-flies troubled our hunters and their steeds a good deal. The latter especially were very annoying to the poor horses. They bit them so much that the blood at last came trickling down their sides. They were troubled also, once or twice, by cock-chafers and locusts, which annoyed them, not indeed by biting, but by flying blindly against their faces, and often narrowly missed hitting them in the eyes. Once particularly they were so bad that Henri in his wrath opened his lips to pronounce a malediction on the whole race, when a cock-chafer flew into his mouth, and, to use his own forcible expression, " nearly knocked him off de hoss " But these were minor evils, and scarcely cost the hunters a thought.

CHAPTER XII

For many days the three hunters wandered over the
trackless prairie in search of a village of the Sioux Indians,
but failed to find one, for the Indians were in the habit of
shifting their ground and following the buffalo. Several
times they saw small isolated bands of Indians; but these
they carefully avoided, fearing they might turn out to be
war parties, and if they fell into their hands the white men
could not expect civil treatment, whatever nation the
Indians might belong to.

During the greater portion of this time they met with
numerous herds of buffalo and deer, and were well supplied
with food; but they had to cook it during the day, being
afraid to light a fire at night while Indians were prowling
about.

One night they halted near the bed of a stream which
was almost dry. They had travelled a day and a night
without water, and both men and horses were almost
choking, so that when they saw the trees on the horizon
which indicated the presence of a stream, they pushed forward with almost frantic haste.

"Hope it's not dry," said Joe anxiously, as they galloped
up to it. "No, there's water, lads," and they dashed forward to a pool that had not yet been dried up. They drank
long and eagerly before they noticed that the pool was
strongly impregnated with salt. Many streams in those
parts of the prairies are quite salt, but fortunately this
one was not utterly undrinkable, though it was very un-
palatable.

"We'll make it better, lads," said Joe, digging a deep

hole in the sand with his hands, a little below the pool. In a short time the water filtered through, and though not rendered fresh, it was, nevertheless, much improved.

"We may light a fire to-night, d'ye think?" inquired Dick; "we've not seed Injuns for some days."

"P'r'aps 'twould be better not," said Joe; "but I daresay we're safe enough."

A fire was therefore lighted in as sheltered a spot as could be found, and the three friends bivouacked as usual. Towards dawn they were aroused by an angry growl from Crusoe.

"It's a wolf likely," said Dick, but all three seized and cocked their rifles nevertheless.

Again Crusoe growled more angrily than before, and springing out of the camp snuffed the breeze anxiously.

"Up, lads! catch the nags! There's something in the wind, for the dog niver did that afore." o

In a few seconds the horses were saddled and the packs secured.

"Call in the dog," whispered Joe Blunt; "if he barks they'll find out our whereabouts."

"Here, Crusoe, come——"

It was too late; the dog barked loudly and savagely at the moment, and a troop of Indians came coursing over the plain. On hearing the unwonted sound they wheeled directly and made for the camp.

"It's a war party; fly, lads! nothin' 'll save our scalps now but our horses' heels," cried Joe.

In a moment they vaulted into the saddle and urged their steeds forward at the utmost speed. The savages observed them, and with an exulting yell dashed after them. Feeling that there was now no need of concealment, the three horsemen struck off into the open prairie, intending to depend entirely on the speed and stamina of their horses. As we have before remarked, they were good ones; but the Indians soon proved that they were equally well if not better mounted.

"It'll be a hard run," said Joe, in a low, muttering tone,

and looking furtively over his shoulder. "The varmints are mounted on wild horses—leastways they were wild not long agone. Them chaps can throw the lasso and trip a mustang as well as a Mexican. Mind the badger-holes, Dick. Hold in a bit, Henri; yer nag don't need drivin'; a foot in a hole just now would cost us our scalps. Keep down by the creek, lads."

"Ha! how dey yell," said Henri in a savage tone, looking back, and shaking his rifle at them, an act that caused them to yell more fiercely than ever. "Dis old pack-hoss give me moche trobel."

The pace was now tremendous. Pursuers and pursued rose and sank on the prairie billows, as they swept along, till they came to what is termed a " dividing ridge ", which is a cross wave, as it were, that cuts the others in two, thus forming a continuous level. Here they advanced more easily; but the advantage was equally shared with their pursuers, who continued the headlong pursuit with occasional yells, which served to show the fugitives that they at least did not gain ground.

A little to the right of the direction in which they were flying a blue line was seen on the horizon. This indicated the existence of trees to Joe's practised eyes, and feeling that if the horses broke down they could better make a last manful stand in the wood than on the plain, he urged his steed towards it. The savages noticed the movement at once, and uttered a yell of exultation, for they regarded it as an evidence that the fugitives doubted the strength of their horses.

"Ye haven't got us yet," muttered Joe, with a sardonic grin. "If they get near us, Dick, keep yer eyes open an' look out for yer neck, else they'll drop a noose over it, they will, afore ye know they're near, an' haul ye off like a sack."

Dick nodded in reply, but did not speak, for at that moment his eye was fixed on a small creek ahead which they must necessarily leap or dash across. It was lined with clumps of scattered shrubbery, and he glanced rapidly for the most suitable place to pass. Joe and Henri did the same, and having diverged a little to the different points chosen, they dashed through the shrubbery and were hid from each other's view. On approaching the edge of the stream, Dick found to his consternation that the bank was twenty feet high opposite him, and too wide for any horse to clear. Wheeling aside without checking speed, at the risk of throwing his steed, he rode along the margin of the stream for a few hundred yards until he found a ford—at least such a spot as might be cleared by a bold leap. The temporary check, however, had enabled an Indian to gain so close upon his heels that his exulting yell sounded close in his ear.

With a vigorous bound his gallant little horse went over. Crusoe could not take it, but he rushed down the one bank and up the other, so that he only lost a few yards. These few yards, however, were sufficient to bring the Indian close upon him as he cleared the stream at full gallop. The savage whirled his lasso swiftly round for a second, and in another moment Crusoe uttered a tremendous roar as he was tripped up violently on the plain.

Dick heard the cry of his faithful dog, and turned quickly round, just in time to see him spring at the horse's throat, and bring both steed and rider down upon him. Dick's heart leaped to his throat. Had a thousand savages been rushing on him he would have flown to the rescue of his favourite; but an unexpected obstacle came in the way. His fiery little steed, excited by the headlong race and the howls of the Indians, had taken the bit in his teeth and was now unmanageable. Dick tore at the reins like a maniac, and in the height of his frenzy even raised the butt of his rifle with the intent to strike the poor horse to the earth, but his better nature prevailed. He checked the uplifted hand, and with a groan dropped the reins and sank almost helplessly forward on the saddle; for several of the Indians had left the main body and were pursuing him alone, so that there would have been now no chance of his reaching the place where Crusoe fell, even if he could have turned his horse.

Spiritless, and utterly indifferent to what his fate might be, Dick Varley rode along with his head drooping, and keeping his seat almost mechanically, while the mettlesome little steed flew on over wave and hollow. Gradually he awakened from this state of despair to a sense of danger. Glancing round he observed that the Indians were now far behind him, though still pursuing. He also observed that his companions were galloping miles away on the horizon to the left, and that he had foolishly allowed the savages to get between him and them. The only chance that remained for him was to outride his pursuers, and circle round towards his comrades, and this he hoped to accomplish, for his little horse had now proved itself to be superior to those of the Indians, and there was good running in him still.

Urging him forward, therefore, he soon left the savages still further behind, and feeling confident that they could not now overtake him, he reined up and dismounted. The pursuers quickly drew near, but short though it was, the rest did his horse good. Vaulting into the saddle, he again stretched out, and now skirted along the margin of a wood which seemed to mark the position of a river of considerable size.

At this moment his horse put his foot into a badger-hole, and both of them came heavily to the ground. In an instant Dick rose, picked up his gun, and leaped unhurt into the saddle. But on urging his poor horse forward he found that its shoulder was badly sprained. There was no room for mercy, however—life and death were in the balance—so he plied the lash vigorously, and the noble steed warmed into something like a run, when again it stumbled, and fell with a crash on the ground, while the blood burst from its mouth and nostrils. Dick could hear the shout of triumph uttered by his pursuers.

" My poor, poor horse!" he exclaimed in a tone of the deepest commiseration, while he stooped and stroked its foam-studded neck.

The dying steed raised its head for a moment, it almost

seemed as if to acknowledge the tones of affection, then it sank down with a gurgling groan.

Dick sprang up, for the Indians were now upon him, and bounded like an antelope into the thickest of the shrubbery; which was nowhere thick enough, however, to prevent the Indians following. Still, it sufficiently retarded them to render the chase a more equal one than could have been expected. In a few minutes Dick gained a strip of open ground beyond, and found himself on the bank of a broad river, whose evidently deep waters rushed impetuously along their unobstructed channel. The bank at the spot where he reached it was a sheer precipice of between thirty and forty feet high. Glancing up and down the river he retreated a few paces, turned round and shook his clenched fist at the savages, accompanying the action with a shout of defiance, and then running to the edge of the bank, sprang far out into the boiling flood and sank.

The Indians pulled up on reaching the spot. There was no possibility of galloping down the wood-encumbered banks after the fugitive; but quick as thought each Red-man leaped to the ground, and fitting an arrow to his bow, awaited Dick's reappearance with eager gaze.

Young though he was, and unskilled in such wild warfare, Dick knew well enough what sort of reception he would meet with on coming to the surface, so he kept under water as long as he could, and struck out as vigorously as the care of his rifle would permit. At last he rose for a few seconds, and immediately half-a-dozen arrows whizzed through the air; but most of them fell short—only one passed close to his cheek, and went with a " whip " into the river. He immediately sank again, and the next time he rose to breathe he was far beyond the reach of his Indian enemies.

CHAPTER XIII

Escape from Indians—A discovery—Alone in the desert.

Dick Varley had spent so much of his boyhood in sporting about among the waters of the rivers and lakes near which he had been reared, and especially during the last two years had spent so much of his leisure time in rolling and diving with his dog Crusoe in the lake of the Mustang Valley, that he had become almost as expert in the water as a South Sea islander; so that when he found himself whirling down the rapid river, as already described, he was more impressed with a feeling of gratitude to God for his escape from the Indians than anxiety about getting ashore.

He was not altogether blind or indifferent to the danger into which he might be hurled if the channel of the river should be found lower down to be broken with rocks, or should a waterfall unexpectedly appear. After floating down a sufficient distance to render pursuit out of the question, he struck into the bank opposite to that from which he had plunged, and clambering up to the greensward above, stripped off the greater part of his clothing and hung it on the branches of a bush to dry. Then he sat down on the trunk of a fallen tree to consider what course he had best pursue in his present circumstances.

These circumstances were by no means calculated to inspire him with hope or comfort. He was in the midst of an unknown wilderness, hundreds of miles from any white man's settlement; surrounded by savages; without food or blanket; his companions gone, he knew not whither—perhaps taken and killed by the Indians; his horse dead; and his dog, the most trusty and loving of all his friends, lost to him, probably, for ever! A more veteran heart might have quailed in the midst of such accumulated evils; but

Dick Varley possessed a strong, young, and buoyant constitution, which, united with a hopefulness of disposition that almost nothing could overcome, enabled him very quickly to cast aside the gloomy view of his case and turn to its brighter aspects.

He still grasped his good rifle—that was some comfort; and as his eye fell upon it, he turned with anxiety to examine into the condition of his powder-horn and the few things that he had been fortunate enough to carry away with him about his person.

The horn in which western hunters carry their powder is usually that of an ox. It is closed up at the large end with a piece of hard wood fitted tightly into it, and the small end is closed with a wooden peg or stopper. It is therefore completely water-tight, and may be for hours immersed without the powder getting wet, unless the stopper should chance to be knocked out. Dick found, to his great satisfaction, that the stopper was fast and the powder perfectly dry. Moreover, he had by good fortune filled it full two days before from the package that contained the general stock of ammunition, so that there were only two or three charges out of it. His percussion caps, however, were completely destroyed; and even though they had not been, it would have mattered little, for he did not possess more than half-a-dozen. But this was not so great a misfortune as at first it might seem, for he had the spare flint locks and the little screw-driver necessary for fixing and unfixing them stowed away in his shot pouch.

To examine his supply of bullets was his next care, and slowly he counted them out, one by one, to the number of thirty. This was a pretty fair supply, and with careful economy would last him many days. Having relieved his mind on these all-important points, he carefully examined every pouch and corner of his dress to ascertain the exact amount and value of his wealth.

Besides the leather leggings, moccasins, deerskin hunting-shirt, cap, and belt which composed his costume, he had a short heavy hunting-knife, a piece of tinder, a little tin pannikin, which he had been in the habit of carrying at his belt, and a large cake of maple sugar. This last is a species of sugar which is procured by the Indians from the maple-tree. Several cakes of it had been carried off from the Pawnee village, and Dick usually carried one in the breast of his coat.

The sun was hot, and a warm breeze gently shook the leaves, so that Dick's garments were soon dry. A few minutes served to change the locks of his rifle, draw the wet charges, dry out the barrels, and reload. Then throwing it across his shoulder, he entered the wood and walked lightly away. And well he might, poor fellow, for at that moment he felt light enough in person if not in heart. His worldly goods were not such as to oppress him; but his thoughts had turned towards home, and he felt comforted.

Traversing the belt of woodland that marked the course of the river, Dick soon emerged on the wide prairie beyond, and here he paused in some uncertainty as to how he should proceed.

He was too good a backwoodsman, albeit so young, to feel perplexed as to the points of the compass. He knew pretty well what hour it was, so that the sun showed him the general bearings of the country, and he knew that when night came he could correct his course by the pole star. Dick's knowledge of astronomy was limited; he knew only one star by name, but that one was an inestimable treasure of knowledge. His perplexity was owing to his uncertainty as to the direction in which his companions and their pursuers had gone; for he had made up his mind to follow their trail if possible, and render all the succour his single arm might afford. To desert them, and make for the settlement, he held, would be a faithless and cowardly act.

While they were together Joe Blunt had often talked to him about the route he meant to pursue to the Rocky Mountains, so that, if they had escaped the Indians, he thought there might be some chance of finding them at last. But, to set against this, there was the probability that they had been taken and carried away in a totally different direction; or they might have taken to the river, as he had done, and gone farther down without his observing them. Then, again, if they had escaped, they would be sure to return and search the country round for him, so that if he left the spot he might miss them.

"Oh for my dear pup Crusoe!" he exclaimed aloud in this dilemma; but the faithful ear was shut now, and the deep silence that followed his cry was so oppressive that the young hunter sprang forward at a run over the plain, as if to fly from solitude. He soon became so absorbed, however, in his efforts to find the trail of his companions, that he forgot all other considerations, and ran straight forward for hours together with his eyes eagerly fixed on the ground. At last he felt so hungry, having tasted no food since supper-time the previous evening, that he halted for the purpose of eating a morsel of maple sugar. A line of bushes in the distance indicated water, so he sped on again, and was soon seated beneath a willow, drinking water from the cool stream. No game was to be found here, but there were several kinds of berries, among which wild grapes and plums grew in abundance. With these and some sugar he made a meal, though not a good one, for the berries were quite green and intensely sour.

All that day Dick Varley followed up the trail of his companions, which he discovered at a ford in the river. They had crossed, therefore, in safety, though still pursued; so he ran on at a regular trot, and with a little more hope than he had felt during the day. Towards night, however, Dick's heart sank again, for he came upon innumerable buffalo tracks, among which those of the horses soon became mingled up, so that he lost them altogether. Hoping to find them again more easily by broad daylight, he went to the nearest clump of willows he could find, and encamped for the night.

Remembering the use formerly made of the tall willows, he set to work to construct a covering to protect him from the dew. As he had no blanket or buffalo skin, he used leaves and grass instead, and found it a better shelter than he had expected, especially when the fire was lighted, and a pannikin of hot sugar and water smoked at his feet; but as no game was to be found, he was again compelled to sup off unripe berries. Before lying down to rest he remembered his resolution, and pulling out the little Bible, read a portion of it by the fitful blaze of the fire, and felt great comfort in its blessed words. It seemed to him like a friend with whom he could converse in the midst of his loneliness.

The plunge into the river having broken Dick's pipe and destroyed his tobacco, he now felt the want of that luxury very severely, and, never having wanted it before, he was greatly surprised to find how much he had become enslaved to the habit. It cost him more than an hour's rest that night, the craving for his wonted pipe.

The sagacious reader will doubtless not fail here to ask himself the question, whether it is wise in man to create in himself an unnatural and totally unnecessary appetite, which may, and often does, entail hours—ay, sometimes months—of exceeding discomfort; but we would not for a moment presume to suggest such a question to him. We have a distinct objection to the ordinary method of what is called " drawing a moral ". It is much better to leave wise men to do this for themselves.

Next morning Dick rose with the sun, and started without breakfast, preferring to take his chance of finding a bird or animal of some kind before long, to feeding again on sour berries. He was disappointed, however, in finding the tracks of his companions. The ground here was hard and sandy, so that little or no impression of a distinct kind was made on it; and as buffaloes had traversed it in all directions, he was soon utterly bewildered. He thought it possible that, by running out for several miles in a straight line, and then taking a wide circuit round, he might find the tracks emerging from the confusion made by the buffaloes. But he was again disappointed, for the buffalo tracks still continued, and the ground became less capable of showing a footprint.

Soon Dick began to feel so ill and weak from eating such

poor fare, that he gave up all hope of discovering the tracks, and was compelled to push forward at his utmost speed in order to reach a less barren district, where he might procure fresh meat; but the farther he advanced the worse and more sandy did the district become. For several days he pushed on over this arid waste without seeing bird or beast, and, to add to his misery, he failed at last to find water. For a day and a night he wandered about in a burning fever, and his throat so parched that he was almost suffocated. Towards the close of the second day he saw a slight line of bushes away down in a hollow on his right. With eager steps he staggered towards them, and, on drawing near, beheld—blessed sight!—a stream of water glancing in the beams of the setting sun.

Dick tried to shout for joy, but his parched throat refused to give utterance to the voice. It mattered not. Exerting all his remaining strength he rushed down the bank, dropped his rifle, and plunged head-foremost into the stream.

The first mouthful sent a thrill of horror to his heart; it was salt as brine!

The poor youth's cup of bitterness was now full to overflowing. Crawling out of the stream, he sank down on the bank in a species of lethargic torpor, from which he awakened next morning in a raging fever. Delirium soon rendered him insensible to his sufferings. The sun rose like a ball of fire, and shone down with scorching power on the arid plain. What mattered it to Dick? He was far away in the shady groves of the Mustang Valley, chasing the deer at times, but more frequently cooling his limbs and sporting with Crusoe in the bright blue lake. Now he was in his mother's cottage, telling her how he had thought of her when far away on the prairie, and what a bright, sweet word it was she had whispered in his ear—so unexpectedly, too. Anon he was scouring over the plains on horseback, with the savages at his heels; and at such times Dick would spring with almost supernatural strength from the ground, and run madly over the burning plain; but, as if by a species of fascination, he always returned to the salt river, and sank exhausted by its side, or plunged helplessly into its waters.

These sudden immersions usually restored him for a short time to reason, and he would crawl up the bank and gnaw a morsel of the maple sugar; but he could not eat much, for it was in a tough, compact cake, which his jaws had not power to break. All that day and the next night he lay on the banks of the salt stream, or rushed wildly over the plain. It was about noon of the second day after his attack that he crept slowly out of the water, into which he had plunged a few seconds before. His mind was restored, but he felt an indescribable sensation of weakness, that seemed to him to be the approach of death. Creeping towards the place where his rifle lay, he fell exhausted beside it.

While his eyes were closed in a dreamy sort of half-waking slumber, he felt the rough, hairy coat of an animal brush against his forehead. The idea of being torn to pieces by wolves flashed instantly across his mind, and with a shriek of terror he sprang up—to be almost overwhelmed by the caresses of his faithful dog.

Yes, there he was, bounding round his master, barking and whining, and giving vent to every possible expression of canine joy!

CHAPTER XIV

Crusoe's return, and his private adventures among the Indians—Dick at a very low ebb—Crusoe saves him.

The means by which Crusoe managed to escape from his two-legged captors, and rejoin his master, require separate and special notice.

In the struggle with the fallen horse and Indian, which Dick had seen begun but not concluded, he was almost crushed to death; and the instant the Indian gained his feet, he sent an arrow at his head with savage violence. Crusoe, however, had been so well used to dodging the blunt-headed arrows that were wont to be shot at him by the boys of the Mustang Valley, that he was quite prepared, and eluded the shaft by an active bound. Moreover, he uttered one of his own peculiar roars, flew at the Indian's throat, and dragged him down. At the same moment the other Indians came up, and one of them turned aside to the rescue. This man happened to have an old gun, of the cheap sort at that time exchanged for peltries by the fur-traders. With the butt of this he struck Crusoe a blow on the head that sent him sprawling on the grass.

The rest of the savages, as we have seen, continued in pursuit of Dick until he leaped into the river; then they returned, took the saddle and bridle off his dead horse, and rejoined their comrades. Here they held a court-martial on Crusoe, who was now bound foot and muzzle with cords. Some were for killing him; others, who admired his noble appearance, immense size, and courage, thought it would be well to carry him to their village and keep him. There was a pretty violent dispute on the subject, but at length it was agreed that they should spare his life in the mean-

(B 361)

time, and perhaps have a dog-dance round him when they got to their wigwams.

This dance, of which Crusoe was to be the chief though passive performer, is peculiar to some of the tribes east of the Rocky Mountains, and consists in killing a dog and cutting out its liver, which is afterwards sliced into shreds or strings and hung on a pole about the height of a man's head. A band of warriors then come and dance wildly round this pole, and each one in succession goes up to the raw liver and bites a piece off it, without, however, putting his hands near it. Such is the dog-dance, and to such was poor Crusoe destined by his fierce captors, especially by the one whose throat still bore very evident marks of his teeth.

But Crusoe was much too clever a dog to be disposed of in so disgusting a manner. He had privately resolved in his own mind that he would escape; but the hopelessness of his ever carrying that resolution into effect would have been apparent to anyone who could have seen the way in which his muzzle was secured, and his four paws were tied together in a bunch, as he hung suspended across the saddle of one of the savages!

This particular party of Indians who had followed Dick Varley determined not to wait for the return of their comrades who were in pursuit of the other two hunters, but to go straight home, so for several days they galloped away over the prairie. At nights, when they encamped, Crusoe was thrown on the ground like a piece of old lumber, and left to lie there with a mere scrap of food till morning, when he was again thrown across the horse of his captor and carried on. When the village was reached, he was thrown again on the ground, and would certainly have been torn to pieces in five minutes by the Indian curs which came howling round him, had not an old woman come to the rescue and driven them away. With the help of her grandson—a little naked creature, just able to walk, or rather to stagger—she dragged him to her tent, and, undoing the line that fastened his mouth, offered him a bone.

Although lying in a position that was unfavourable for
eating purposes, Crusoe opened his jaws and took it. An
awful crash was followed by two crunches—and it was gone!
and Crusoe looked up in the old squaw's face with a look
that said plainly, " Another of the same, please, and as
quick as possible ". The old woman gave him another,
and then a lump of meat, which latter went down with a
gulp; but he coughed after it! and it was well he didn't
choke. After this the squaw left him, and Crusoe spent the
remainder of that night gnawing the cords that bound him.
So diligent was he that he was free before morning and
walked deliberately out of the tent. Then he shook himself,
and with a yell that one might have fancied was intended for
defiance he bounded joyfully away, and was soon out of sight.

To a dog with a good appetite which had been on short
allowance for several days, the mouthful given to him by
the old squaw was a mere nothing. All that day he kept
bounding over the plain from bluff to bluff in search of
something to eat, but found nothing until dusk, when he
pounced suddenly and most unexpectedly on a prairie-
hen fast asleep. In one moment its life was gone. In less
than a minute its body was gone too—feathers and bones
and all—down Crusoe's ravenous throat.

On the identical spot Crusoe lay down and slept like a
top for four hours. At the end of that time he jumped up,
bolted a scrap of skin that somehow had been overlooked at
supper, and flew straight over the prairie to the spot where
he had had the scuffle with the Indian. He came to the
edge of the river, took precisely the same leap that his
master had done before him, and came out on the other
side a good deal higher up than Dick had done, for the
dog had no savages to dodge, and was, as we have said
before, a powerful swimmer.

It cost him a good deal of running about to find the trail,
and it was nearly dark before he resumed his journey; then,
putting his keen nose to the ground, he ran step by step
over Dick's track, and at last found him, as we have shown,
on the banks of the salt creek.

It is quite impossible to describe the intense joy which filled Dick's heart on again beholding his favourite. Only those who have lost and found such an one can know it. Dick seized him round the neck and hugged him as well as he could, poor fellow! in his feeble arms; then he wept, then he laughed, and then he fainted.

This was a consummation that took Crusoe quite aback. Never having seen his master in such a state before, he seemed to think at first that he was playing some trick, for he bounded round him, and barked, and wagged his tail. But as Dick lay quite still and motionless, he went forward with a look of alarm; snuffed him once or twice, and whined piteously; then he raised his nose in the air and uttered a long melancholy wail.

The cry seemed to revive Dick, for he moved, and with some difficulty sat up, to the dog's evident relief. There is no doubt whatever that Crusoe learned an erroneous lesson that day, and was firmly convinced thenceforth that the best cure for a fainting fit is a melancholy yell. So easy is it for the wisest of dogs as well as men to fall into gross error!

" Crusoe," said Dick, in a feeble voice, " dear good pup, come here." He crawled, as he spoke, down to the water's edge, where there was a level patch of dry sand.

" Dig," said Dick, pointing to the sand.

Crusoe looked at him in surprise, as well he might, for he had never heard the word " dig " in all his life before.

Dick pondered a minute; then a thought struck him. He turned up a little of the sand with his fingers, and, pointing to the hole, cried, " *Seek him out, pup!*"

Ha! Crusoe understood *that*. Many and many a time had he unhoused rabbits, and squirrels, and other creatures at that word of command; so, without a moment's delay, he commenced to dig down into the sand, every now and then stopping for a moment and shoving in his nose, and snuffing interrogatively, as if he fully expected to find a buffalo at the bottom of it. Then he would resume again, one paw after another so fast that you could scarce see them going—" hand over hand ", as sailors would have called it —while the sand flew out between his hind legs in a continuous shower. When the sand accumulated so much behind him as to impede his motions he scraped it out of his way, and set to work again with tenfold earnestness. After a good while he paused and looked up at Dick with an "it-won't-do,-I-fear,-there's-nothing-here" expression on his face.

" Seek him out, pup!" repeated Dick.

" Oh! very good," mutely answered the dog, and went at it again, tooth and nail, harder than ever.

In the course of a quarter of an hour there was a deep yawning hole in the sand, into which Dick peered with intense anxiety. The bottom appeared slightly *damp*. Hope now reanimated Dick Varley, and by various devices he succeeded in getting the dog to scrape away a sort of tunnel from the hole, into which he might roll himself and put down his lips to drink when the water should rise high enough. Impatiently and anxiously he lay watching the moisture slowly accumulate in the bottom of the hole, drop by drop, and while he gazed he fell into a troubled, restless slumber, and dreamed that Crusoe's return was a dream, and that he was alone again, perishing for want of water.

When he awakened the hole was half full of clear water, and Crusoe was lapping it greedily.

" Back, pup!" he shouted, as he crept down to the hole and put his trembling lips to the water. It was brackish, but drinkable, and as Dick drank deeply of it he esteemed it at that moment better than nectar. Here he lay for half an hour, alternately drinking and gazing in surprise at his own emaciated visage as reflected in the pool.

The same afternoon Crusoe, in a private hunting excursion of his own, discovered and caught a prairie-hen, which he quietly proceeded to devour on the spot, when Dick, who saw what had occurred, whistled to him.

Obedience was engrained in every fibre of Crusoe's mental and corporeal being. He did not merely answer at once to the call—he *sprang* to it, leaving the prairie-hen untasted.

" Fetch it, pup," cried Dick eagerly, as the dog came up.
In a few moments the hen was at his feet. Dick's circumstances could not brook the delay of cookery; he gashed
the bird with his knife and drank the blood, and then gave
the flesh to the dog, while he crept to the pool again for
another draught. Ah! think not, reader, that although
we have treated this subject in a slight vein of pleasantry,
because it ended well, that therefore our tale is pure fiction.
Not only are Indians glad to satisfy the urgent cravings of
hunger with raw flesh, but many civilized men and delicately nurtured have done the same—ay, and doubtless will
do the same again, as long as enterprising and fearless men
shall go forth to dare the dangers of flood and field in the
wild places of our wonderful world!

Crusoe had finished his share of the feast before Dick
returned from the pool. Then master and dog lay down
together side by side and fell into a long, deep, peaceful
slumber.

CHAPTER XV

Dick Varley's fears and troubles, in the meantime, were
ended. On the day following he awoke refreshed and
happy—so happy and light at heart, as he felt the glow of
returning health coursing through his veins, that he fancied
he must have dreamed it all. In fact, he was so certain that
his muscles were strong that he endeavoured to leap up,
but was powerfully convinced of his true condition by the
miserable stagger that resulted from the effort.

However, he knew he was recovering, so he rose, and
thanking God for his recovery, and for the new hope that
was raised in his heart, he went down to the pool and drank
deeply of its water. He at last fell asleep; and when he
awakened felt so much refreshed in body and mind that he
determined to attempt to pursue his journey.

He had not proceeded far when he came upon a colony
of prairie-dogs. Upon this occasion he was little inclined
to take a humorous view of the vagaries of these curious
little creatures, but he shot one, and, as before, ate part of
it raw. These creatures are so active that they are difficult
to shoot, and even when killed generally fall into their holes
and disappear. Crusoe, however, soon unearthed the dead
animal on this occasion. That night the travellers came to
a stream of fresh water, and Dick killed a turkey, so that
he determined to spend a couple of days there to recruit.
At the end of that time he again set out, but was able only
to advance five miles when he broke down. In fact, it
became evident to him that he must have a longer period
of absolute repose ere he could hope to continue his journey;
but to do so without food was impossible. Fortunately

there was plenty of water, as his course lay along the margin of a small stream, and, as the arid piece of prairie was now behind him, he hoped to fall in with birds, or perhaps deer, soon.

While he was plodding heavily and wearily along, pondering these things, he came to the brow of a wave from which he beheld a most magnificent view of green grassy plains decked with flowers, and rolling out to the horizon, with a stream meandering through it, and clumps of trees scattered everywhere far and wide. It was a glorious sight; but the most glorious object in it to Dick, at that time, was a fat buffalo which stood grazing not a hundred yards off. The wind was blowing towards him, so that the animal did not scent him, and, as he came up very slowly, and it was turned away, it did not see him.

Crusoe would have sprung forward in an instant, but his master's finger imposed silence and caution. Trembling with eagerness, Dick sank flat down in the grass, cocked both barrels of his piece, and, resting it on his left hand with his left elbow on the ground, he waited until the animal should present its side. In a few seconds it moved; Dick's eye glanced along the barrel, but it trembled—his wonted steadiness of aim was gone. He fired, and the buffalo sprang off in terror. With a groan of despair he fired again —almost recklessly—and the buffalo fell! It rose once or twice and stumbled forward a few paces, then it fell again. Meanwhile Dick reloaded with trembling hand, and advanced to give it another shot; but it was not needful— the buffalo was already dead.

" Now, Crusoe," said Dick, sitting down on the buffalo's shoulder and patting his favourite on the head, " we're all right at last. You and I shall have a jolly time o't, pup, from this time for'ard."

Dick paused for breath, and Crusoe wagged his tail and looked as if to say—pshaw! " as if!"

We tell you what it is, reader, it's of no use at all to go on writing " as if ", when we tell you what Crusoe said. If there is any language in eyes whatever—if there is language in a tail, in a cocked ear, in a mobile eyebrow, in the point of a canine nose,—if there is language in any terrestrial thing at all, apart from that which flows from the tongue, then Crusoe *spoke*! Do we not speak at this moment to *you*? and if so, then tell me wherein lies the difference between a written *letter* and a given *sign*?

Yes, Crusoe spoke. He said to Dick as plain as dog could say it, slowly and emphatically, " That's my opinion precisely, Dick. You're the dearest, most beloved, jolliest fellow that ever walked on two legs, you are; and whatever's your opinion is mine, no matter *how* absurd it may be."

Dick evidently understood him perfectly, for he laughed as he looked at him and patted him on the head, and called him a " funny dog ". Then he continued his discourse—

" Yes, pup, we'll make our camp here for a long bit, old dog, in this beautiful plain. We'll make a willow wigwam to sleep in, you and I, jist in yon clump o' trees, not a stone's-throw to our right, where we'll have a run o' pure water beside us, and be near our buffalo at the same time. For, ye see, we'll need to watch him lest the wolves take a notion to eat him—that'll be *your* duty, pup. Then I'll skin him when I get strong enough, which'll be in a day or two, I hope, and we'll put one-half of the skin below us and t'other half above us i' the camp, an' sleep, an' eat, an' take it easy for a week or two—won't we, pup?"

" Hoora-a-a-y!" shouted Crusoe, with a jovial wag of his tail, that no human arm with hat, or cap, or kerchief ever equalled.

Poor Dick Varley! He smiled to think how earnestly he had been talking to the dog; but he did not cease to do it, for although he entered into discourses the drift of which Crusoe's limited education did not permit him to follow, he found comfort in hearing the sound of his own voice, and in knowing that it fell pleasantly on another ear in that lonely wilderness.

Our hero now set about his preparations as vigorously as he could. He cut out the buffalo's tongue—a matter of great difficulty to one in his weak state—and carried it to a pleasant spot near to the stream where the turf was level and green, and decked with wild flowers. Here he resolved to make his camp.

His first care was to select a bush whose branches were long enough to form a canopy over his head when bent, and the ends thrust into the ground. The completing of this exhausted him greatly, but after a rest he resumed his labours. The next thing was to light a fire—a comfort which he had not enjoyed for many weary days. Not that he required it for warmth, for the weather was extremely warm, but he required it to cook with, and the mere *sight* of a blaze in a dark place is a most heart-cheering thing, as every one knows.

When the fire was lighted he filled his pannikin at the brook and put it on to boil, and cutting several slices of buffalo tongue, he thrust short stakes through them and set them up before the fire to roast. By this time the water was boiling, so he took it off with difficulty, nearly burning his fingers and singeing the tail of his coat in so doing. Into the pannikin he put a lump of maple sugar, and stirred it about with a stick, and tasted it. It seemed to him even better than tea or coffee. It was absolutely delicious!

Really one has no notion what he can do if he makes believe *very hard*. The human mind is a nicely balanced and extremely complex machine, and when thrown a little off the balance can be made to believe almost anything, as we see in the case of some poor monomaniacs, who have fancied that they were made of all sorts of things—glass and porcelain, and such like. No wonder then that poor Dick Varley, after so much suffering and hardship, came to regard that pannikin of hot syrup as the most delicious beverage he ever drank.

During all these operations Crusoe sat on his haunches beside him and looked. And you haven't—no, you haven't got the most distant notion of the way in which that dog manœuvred with his head and face. He opened his eyes wide, and cocked his ears, and turned his head first a little to one side, then a little to the other. After that he turned it a *good deal* to one side, and then a good deal more to the other. Then he brought it straight, and raised one eyebrow a little, and then the other a little, and then both together very much. Then, when Dick paused to rest and did nothing, Crusoe looked mild for a moment, and yawned vociferously. Presently Dick moved—up went the ears again, and Crusoe came, in military parlance, " to the position of attention "! At last supper was ready, and they began.

Dick had purposely kept the dog's supper back from him, in order that they might eat it in company. And between every bite and sup that Dick took, he gave a bite—but not a sup—to Crusoe. Thus lovingly they ate together; and when Dick lay that night under the willow branches, looking up through them at the stars, with his feet to the fire and Crusoe close along his side, he thought it the best and sweetest supper he ever ate, and the happiest evening he ever spent—so wonderfully do circumstances modify our notions of felicity.

Two weeks after this " Richard was himself again ". The muscles were springy, and the blood coursed fast and free, as was its wont. Only a slight, and, perhaps, salutary feeling of weakness remained, to remind him that young muscles might again become more helpless than those of an aged man or a child.

Dick had left his encampment a week ago, and was now advancing by rapid stages towards the Rocky Mountains, closely following the trail of his lost comrades, which he had no difficulty in finding and keeping now that Crusoe was with him. The skin of the buffalo that he had killed was now strapped to his shoulders, and the skin of another animal that he had shot a few days after was cut up into a long line and slung in a coil round his neck. Crusoe was also laden. He had a little bundle of meat slung on each side of him.

For some time past numerous herds of mustangs, or wild horses, had crossed their path, and Dick was now on the look-out for a chance to *crease* one of those magnificent creatures.

On one occasion a band of mustangs galloped close up to him before they were aware of his presence, and stopped short with a wild snort of surprise on beholding him; then, wheeling round, they dashed away at full gallop, their long tails and manes flying wildly in the air, and their hoofs thundering on the plain. Dick did not attempt to crease one upon this occasion, fearing that his recent illness might have rendered his hand too unsteady for so extremely delicate an operation.

In order to crease a wild horse the hunter requires to be a perfect shot, and it is not every man of the west who carries a rifle that can do it successfully. Creasing consists in sending a bullet through the gristle of the mustang's neck, just above the bone, so as to stun the animal. If the ball enters a hair's-breadth too low, the horse falls dead instantly. If it hits the exact spot, the horse falls as instantaneously, and dead to all appearance; but, in reality, he is only stunned, and if left for a few minutes will rise and gallop away nearly as well as ever. When hunters crease a horse successfully they put a rope, or halter, round his under jaw and hobbles round his feet, so that when he rises he is secured, and, after considerable trouble, reduced to obedience.

The mustangs which roam in wild freedom on the prairies of the far west are descended from the noble Spanish steeds that were brought over by the wealthy cavaliers who accompanied Fernando Cortez, the conqueror of Mexico, in his expedition to the New World in 1518. These bold and, we may add, lawless cavaliers were mounted on the finest horses that could be procured from Barbary and the deserts of the Old World. The poor Indians of the New World were struck with amazement and terror at these awful beings, for, never having seen horses before, they believed that horse and rider were one animal. During the wars that followed many of the Spaniards were killed, and their steeds bounded into the wilds of the new country, to enjoy a life of unrestrained freedom. These were the fore-lathers of the present race of magnificent creatures, which are found in immense droves all over the western wilderness, from the Gulf of Mexico to the confines of the snowy regions of the far north.

At first the Indians beheld these horses with awe and terror, but gradually they became accustomed to them, and finally succeeded in capturing great numbers and reducing them to a state of servitude. Net, however, to the service of the cultivated field, but to the service of the chase and war. The savages soon acquired the method of capturing wild horses by means of the lasso—as the noose at that end of a long line of raw hide is termed—which they adroitly threw over the heads of the animals and secured them, having previously run them down. At the present day many of the savage tribes of the west almost live upon horseback, and without these useful creatures they could scarcely subsist, as they are almost indispensable in the chase of the buffalo.

Mustangs are regularly taken by the Indians to the settlements of the white men for trade, but very poor specimens are these of the breed of wild horses. This arises from two causes. First, the Indian cannot overtake the finest of a drove of wild mustangs, because his own steed is inferior to the best among the wild ones, besides being weighted with a rider, so that only the weak and inferior animals are captured. And, secondly, when the Indian does succeed in lassoing a first-rate horse he keeps it for his own use. Thus, those who have not visited the far-off prairies and seen the mustang in all the glory of untrammelled freedom, can form no adequate idea of its beauty, fleetness, and strength.

The horse, however, was not the only creature imported by Cortez. There were priests in his army who rode upon asses, and although we cannot imagine that the " fathers " charged with the cavaliers and were unhorsed, or, rather, un-assed in battle, yet, somehow, the asses got rid of their riders and joined the Spanish chargers in their joyous bound into a new life of freedom. Hence wild asses also are found in the western prairies. But think not, reader, of those poor miserable wretches we see at home, which seem little better than rough door-mats sewed up and stuffed, with head, tail, and legs attached, and just enough of life infused to make them move! No, the wild ass of the prairie is a large, powerful, swift creature. He has the same long ears, it is true, and the same hideous, exasperating bray, and the same tendency to flourish his heels; but for all that he is a very fine animal, and often wages *successful* warfare with the wild horse.

But to return. The next drove of mustangs that Dick and Crusoe saw were feeding quietly and unsuspectingly in a rich green hollow in the plain. Dick's heart leaped up as his eyes suddenly fell on them, for he had almost discovered himself before he was aware of their presence.

"Down, pup!" he whispered, as he sank and disappeared among the grass, which was just long enough to cover him when lying quite flat.

Crusoe crouched immediately, and his master made his observations of the drove, and the dispositions of the ground that might favour his approach, for they were not within rifle range. Having done so he crept slowly back until the undulation of the prairie hid him from view; then he sprang to his feet, and ran a considerable distance along the bottom until he gained the extreme end of a belt of low bushes, which would effectually conceal him while he approached to within a hundred yards or less of the troop.

Here he made his arrangements. Throwing down his buffalo robe, he took the coil of line and cut off a piece of about three yards in length. On this he made a running noose. The longer line he also prepared with a running noose. These he threw in a coil over his arm.

He also made a pair of hobbles, and placed them in the breast of his coat, and then, taking up his rifle, advanced cautiously through the bushes—Crusoe following close behind him. In a few minutes he was gazing in admiration at the mustangs, which were now within easy shot, and utterly ignorant of the presence of man, for Dick had taken

care to approach in such a way that the wind did not
carry the scent of him in their direction.

And well might he admire them. The wild horse of these
regions is not very large, but it is exceedingly powerful,
with prominent eye, sharp nose, distended nostril, small
feet, and a delicate leg. Their beautiful manes hung at
great length down their arched necks, and their thick tails
swept the ground. One magnificent fellow in particular
attracted Dick's attention. He was of a rich dark-brown
colour, with black mane and tail, and seemed to be the
leader of the drove.

Although not the nearest to him, he resolved to crease
this horse. It is said that creasing generally destroys or
damages the spirit of the horse, so Dick determined to try
whether his powers of close shooting would not serve him
on this occasion. Going down on one knee he aimed at the
creature's neck, just a hair's-breadth above the spot where
he had been told that hunters usually hit them, and fired.
The effect upon the group was absolutely tremendous.
With wild cries and snorting terror they tossed their proud
heads in the air, uncertain for one moment in which direction to fly; then there was a rush as if a hurricane swept
over the place, and they were gone.

But the brown horse was down. Dick did not wait until
the others had fled. He dropped his rifle, and with the
speed of a deer sprang towards the fallen horse, and affixed
the hobbles to his legs. His aim had been true. Although
scarcely half a minute elapsed between the shot and the
fixing of the hobbles, the animal recovered, and with a
frantic exertion rose on his haunches, just as Dick had
fastened the noose of the short line in his under jaw. But
this was not enough. If the horse had gained his feet
before the longer line was placed round his neck, he would
have escaped. As the mustang made the second violent
plunge that placed it on its legs, Dick flung the noose hastily;
it caught on one ear, and would have fallen off, had not
the horse suddenly shaken its head, and unwittingly sealed
its own fate by bringing the noose round its neck.

And now the struggle began. Dick knew well enough, from hearsay, the method of "breaking down" a wild horse. He knew that the Indians choke them with the noose round the neck until they fall down exhausted and covered with foam, when they creep up, fix the hobbles, and the line in the lower jaw, and then loosen the lasso to let the horse breathe, and resume its plungings till it is almost subdued, when they gradually draw near and breathe into its nostrils. But the violence and strength of this animal rendered this an apparently hopeless task. We have already seen that the hobbles and noose in the lower jaw had been fixed, so that Dick had nothing now to do but to choke his captive, and tire him out, while Crusoe remained a quiet though excited spectator of the scene.

But there seemed to be no possibility of choking this horse. Either the muscles of his neck were too strong, or there was something wrong with the noose which prevented it from acting, for the furious creature dashed and bounded backwards and sideways in its terror for nearly an hour, dragging Dick after it, till he was almost exhausted; and yet, at the end of that time, although flecked with foam and panting with terror, it seemed as strong as ever. Dick held both lines, for the short one attached to its lower jaw gave him great power over it. At last he thought of seeking assistance from his dog.

"Crusoe," he cried; "lay hold, pup!"

The dog seized the long line in his teeth and pulled with all his might. At the same moment Dick let go the short line and threw all his weight upon the long one. The noose tightened suddenly under this strain, and the mustang, with a gasp, fell choking to the ground.

Dick had often heard of the manner in which the Mexicans "break" their horses, so he determined to abandon the method which had already almost worn him out, and adopt the other, as far as the means in his power rendered it possible. Instead, therefore, of loosening the lasso and re-commencing the struggle, he tore a branch from a neighbouring bush, cut the hobbles, strode with his legs across the fallen steed, seized the end of the short line or bridle, and then, ordering Crusoe to quit his hold, he loosened the noose which compressed the horse's neck and had already well-nigh terminated its existence.

One or two deep sobs restored it, and in a moment it leaped to its feet with Dick firmly on its back. To say that the animal leaped and kicked in its frantic efforts to throw this intolerable burden would be a tame manner of expressing what took place. Words cannot adequately describe the scene. It reared, plunged, shrieked, vaulted into the air, stood straight up on its hind legs, and then almost as straight upon its fore ones; but its rider held on like a burr. . Then the mustang raced wildly forwards a few paces, then as wildly back, and then stood still and trembled violently. But this was only a brief lull in the storm, so Dick saw that the time was now come to assert the superiority of his race.

" Stay back, Crusoe, and watch my rifle, pup," he cried, and raising his heavy switch he brought it down with a sharp cut across the horse's flank, at the same time loosening the rein which hitherto he had held tight.

The wild horse uttered a passionate cry, and sprang forward like the bolt from a cross-bow.

And now commenced a race which, if not so prolonged, was at least as furious as that of the far-famed Mazeppa. Dick was a splendid rider, however—at least as far as " sticking on " goes. He might not have come up to the precise pitch desiderated by a riding-master in regard to carriage, etc., but he rode that wild horse of the prairie with as much ease as he had formerly ridden his own good steed, whose bones had been picked by the wolves not long ago.

The pace was tremendous, for the youth's weight was nothing to that muscular frame, which bounded with cat-like agility from wave to wave of the undulating plain in ungovernable terror. In a few minutes the clump of willows where Crusoe and his rifle lay were out of sight behind; but it mattered not, for Dick had looked up at the sky and noted the position of the sun at the moment of starting. Away they went on the wings of the wind, mile after mile over the ocean-like waste—curving slightly aside now and then to avoid the bluffs that occasionally appeared on the scene for a few minutes and then swept out of sight behind them. Then they came to a little rivulet. It was a mere brook of a few feet wide, and two or three yards, perhaps, from bank to bank. Over this they flew so easily that the spring was scarcely felt, and continued the headlong course. And now a more barren country was around them. Sandy ridges and scrubby grass appeared everywhere, reminding Dick of the place where he had been so ill. Rocks, too, were scattered about, and at one place the horse dashed with clattering hoofs between a couple of rocky sand-hills which, for a few seconds, hid the prairie from view. Here the mustang suddenly shied with such violence that his rider was nearly thrown, while a rattlesnake darted from the path. Soon they emerged from this pass, and again the plains became green and verdant. Presently a distant line of trees showed that they were approaching water, and in a few minutes they were close on it. For the first time Dick felt alarm. He sought to check his steed, but no force he could exert had the smallest influence on it.

Trees and bushes flew past in bewildering confusion. The river was before him; what width, he could not tell, but he was reckless now, like his charger, which he struck with the willow rod with all his force as they came up. One tremendous bound, and they were across, but Dick had to lie flat on the mustang's back as it crashed through the bushes to avoid being scraped off by the trees. Again they were on the open plain, and the wild horse began to show signs of exhaustion.

Now was its rider's opportunity to assert his dominion. He plied the willow rod and urged the panting horse on, until it was white with foam and laboured a little in its gait. Then Dick gently drew the halter, and it broke into a trot; still tighter, and it walked, and in another minute stood still, trembling in every limb. Dick now quietly rubbed its neck, and spoke to it in soothing tones; then he wheeled it gently round, and urged it forward. It was quite subdued and docile. In a little time they came to the river and forded it, after which they went through the belt of woodland at a walk. By the time they reached the open prairie the mustang was recovered sufficiently to feel its spirit returning, so Dick gave it a gentle touch with the switch, and away they went on their return journey.

But it amazed Dick not a little to find how long that journey was. Very different was the pace, too, from the previous mad gallop, and often would the poor horse have stopped had Dick allowed him. But this might not be. The shades of night were approaching, and the camp lay a long way ahead.

At last it was reached, and Crusoe came out with great demonstrations of joy, but was sent back lest he should alarm the horse. Then Dick jumped off his back, stroked his head, put his cheek close to his mouth and whispered softly to him, after which he fastened him to a tree and rubbed him down slightly with a bunch of grass. Having done this, he left him to graze as far as his tether would permit; and, after supping with Crusoe, lay down to rest, not a little elated with his success in this first attempt at " creasing " and " breaking " a mustang.

CHAPTER XVI

Dick becomes a horse tamer—Resumes his journey—Charlie's doings—
Misfortunes which lead to, but do not terminate in, the Rocky
Mountains—A grizzly bear.

There is a proverb—or a saying—or at least somebody
or book has told us, that some Irishman once said, " Be
aisy; or, if ye can't be aisy, be as aisy as ye can."

Now, we count that good advice, and strongly recom-
mend it to all and sundry. Had we been at the side of
Dick Varley on the night after his taming of the wild horse,
we would· have strongly urged that advice upon him.
Whether he would have listened to it or not is quite another
question; we rather think not. Reader, if you wish to
know why, go and do what he did, and if you feel no
curious sensations about the· region of the loins after it,
we will tell you why Dick Varley wouldn't have listened to
that advice. Can a man feel as if his joints were wrenched
out of their sockets, and listen to advice—be that advice
good or bad? Can he feel as though these joints were trying
to re-set and re-dislocate themselves perpetually, and listen
to advice? Can he feel as if he were sitting down on red-
hot iron, when he's not sitting down at all, and listen to
advice? Can he—but no! Why pursue the subject? Poor
Dick spent that night in misery, and the greater part of
the following day in sleep, to make up for it.

When he got up to breakfast in the afternoon he felt
much better, but shaky.

" Now, pup," he said, stretching himself, " we'll go and
see our horse. *Ours*, pup; yours and mine: Didn't you help
to catch him, eh, pup?"

Crusoe acknowledged the fact with a wag and a playful

" Bow-wow—wow-oo-ow !" and followed his master to the place where the horse had been picketed. It was standing there quite quiet, but looking a little timid.

Dick went boldly up to it, and patted its head and stroked its nose, for nothing is so likely to alarm either a tame or a wild horse as any appearance of timidity or hesitation on the part of those who approach them.

After treating it thus for a short time, he stroked down its neck, and then its shoulders—the horse eyeing him all the time nervously. Gradually he stroked its back and limbs gently, and walked quietly round and round it once or twice, sometimes approaching and sometimes going away, but never either hesitating or doing anything abruptly. This done, he went down to the stream and filled his cap with water and carried it to the horse, which snuffed suspiciously and backed a little; so he laid the cap down, and went up and patted him again. Presently he took up the cap and carried it to his nose. The poor creature was almost choking with thirst, so that, the moment he understood what was in the cap, he buried his lips in it and sucked it up.

This was a great point gained: he had accepted a benefit at the hands of his new master; he had become a debtor to man, and no doubt he felt the obligation. Dick filled the cap and the horse emptied it again, and again, and again, until its burning thirst was slaked. Then Dick went up to his shoulder, patted him, undid the line that fastened him, and vaulted lightly on his back !

We say *lightly*, for it was so, but it wasn't *easily*, as Dick could have told you ! However, he was determined not to forgo the training of his steed on account of what *he* would have called a " little bit pain ".

At this unexpected act the horse plunged and reared a good deal, and seemed inclined to go through the performance of the day before over again; but Dick patted and stroked him into quiescence, and having done so, urged him into a gallop over the plains, causing the dog to gambol round in order that he might get accustomed to him. This tried his nerves a good deal, and no wonder, for if he took Crusoe for a wolf, which no doubt he did, he must have thought him a very giant of the pack.

By degrees they broke into a furious gallop, and after breathing him well, Dick returned and tied him to the tree. Then he rubbed him down again, and gave him another drink. This time the horse smelt his new master all over, and Dick felt that he had conquered him by kindness. No doubt the tremendous run of the day before could scarcely be called kindness, but without this subduing run he never could have brought the offices of kindness to bear on so wild a steed.

During all these operations Crusoe sat looking on with demure sagacity—drinking in wisdom and taking notes. We know not whether any notes made by the canine race have ever been given to the world, but certain are we that, if the notes and observations made by Crusoe on that journey were published, they would, to say the least, surprise us!

Next day Dick gave the wild horse his second lesson and his name. He called him " Charlie ", after a much-loved companion in the Mustang Valley. And long and heartily did Dick Varley laugh as he told the horse his future designation in the presence of Crusoe, for it struck him as somewhat ludicrous that a mustang which, two days ago, pawed the earth in all the pride of independent freedom, should suddenly come down so low as to carry a hunter on his back and be named Charlie.

The next piece of instruction began by Crusoe being led up under Charlie's nose, and while Dick patted the dog with his right hand he patted the horse with his left. It backed a good deal at first and snorted, but Crusoe walked slowly and quietly in front of him several times, each time coming nearer, until he again stood under his nose; then the horse smelt him nervously, and gave a sigh of relief when he found that Crusoe paid no attention to him whatever. Dick then ordered the dog to lie down at Charlie's feet, and went to the camp to fetch his rifle, and buffalo robe, and pack of meat. These and all the other things belonging to him were presented for inspection, one by one, to the horse, who arched his neck, and put forward his ears, and eyed them at first, but smelt them all over, and seemed to feel more easy in his mind.

Next, the buffalo robe was rubbed over his nose, then over his eyes and head, then down his neck and shoulder, and lastly was placed on his back. Then it was taken off and *flung* on; after that it was strapped on, and the various little items of the camp were attached to it. This done, Dick took up his rifle and let him smell it; then he put his hand on Charlie's shoulder, vaulted on to his back, and rode away.

Charlie's education was completed. And now our hero's journey began again in earnest, and with some prospect of its speedy termination.

In this course of training through which Dick put his wild horse, he had been at much greater pains and had taken far longer time than is usually the case among the Indians, who will catch, and " break ", and ride a wild horse into camp in less than *three hours*. But Dick wanted to do the thing well, which the Indians are not careful to do; besides, it must be borne in remembrance that this was his first attempt, and that his horse was one of the best and most high-spirited, while those caught by the Indians, as we have said, are generally the poorest of a drove.

Dick now followed the trail of his lost companions at a rapid pace, yet not so rapidly as he might have done; being averse to exhausting his good dog and his new companion. Each night he encamped under the shade of a tree or a bush when he could find one, or in the open prairie when there were none, and, picketing his horse to a short stake or pin which he carried with him for the purpose, lit his fire, had supper, and lay down to rest. In a few days Charlie became so tame and so accustomed to his master's voice that he seemed quite reconciled to his new life. There can be no doubt whatever that he had a great dislike to solitude; for on one occasion, when Dick and Crusoe went off a mile or so from the camp, where

Charlie was tied, and disappeared from his view, he was heard to neigh so loudly that Dick ran back, thinking the wolves must have attacked him. He was all right, however, and exhibited evident tokens of satisfaction when they returned.

On another occasion his fear of being left alone was more clearly demonstrated.

Dick had been unable to find wood or water that day, so he was obliged to encamp upon the open plain. The want of water was not seriously felt, however, for he had prepared a bladder in which he always carried enough to give him one pannikin of hot syrup, and leave a mouthful for Crusoe and Charlie. Dried buffalo dung formed a substitute for fuel. Spreading his buffalo robe, he lit his fire, put on his pannikin to boil, and stuck up a piece of meat to roast, to the great delight of Crusoe, who sat looking on with much interest.

Suddenly Charlie, who was picketed a few hundred yards off in a grassy spot, broke his halter close by the headpiece, and with a snort of delight bounded away, prancing and kicking up his heels!

Dick heaved a deep sigh, for he felt sure that his horse was gone. However, in a little Charlie stopped, and raised his nose high in the air, as if to look for his old equine companions. But they were gone; no answering neigh replied to his; and he felt, probably for the first time, that he was really alone in the world. Having no power of smell, whereby he might have traced them out as the dog would have done, he looked in a bewildered and excited state all round the horizon. Then his eye fell on Dick and Crusoe sitting by their little fire. Charlie looked hard at them, and then again at the horizon; and then, coming to the conclusion, no doubt, that the matter was quite beyond his comprehension, he quietly took to feeding.

Dick availed himself of the chance, and tried to catch him; but he spent an hour with Crusoe in the vain attempt, and at last they gave it up in disgust and returned to the fire, where they finished their supper and went to bed.

Next morning they saw Charlie feeding close at hand, so they took breakfast, and tried to catch him again. But it was of no use; he was evidently coquetting with them, and dodged about and defied their utmost efforts, for there were only a few inches of line hanging to his head. At last it occurred to Dick that he would try the experiment of forsaking him. So he packed up his things, rolled up the buffalo robe, threw it and the rifle on his shoulder, and walked deliberately away.

"Come along, Crusoe!" he cried, after walking a few paces.

But Crusoe stood by the fire with his head up, and an expression on his face that said, "Hollo, man! what's wrong? You've forgot Charlie! Hold on! Are you mad?"

"Come here, Crusoe!" cried his master in a decided tone.

Crusoe obeyed at once. Whatever mistake there might be, there was evidently none in that command; so he lowered his head and tail humbly, and trotted on with his master, but he perpetually turned his head as he went, first on this side and then on that, to look and wonder at Charlie.

When they were far away on the plain, Charlie suddenly became aware that something was wrong. He trotted to the brow of a slope, with his head and tail very high up indeed, and looked after them; then he looked at the fire, and neighed; then he trotted quickly up to it, and seeing that everything was gone he began to neigh violently, and at last started off at full speed, and overtook his friends, passing within a few feet of them, and, wheeling round a few yards off, stood trembling like an aspen leaf.

Dick called him by his name and advanced, while Charlie met him half-way, and allowed himself to be saddled, bridled, and mounted forthwith.

After this Dick had no further trouble with his wild horse.

At his next camping-place, which was in the midst of a cluster of bushes close beside a creek, Dick came un-expectedly upon a little wooden cross which marked the

head of a grave. There was no inscription on it, but the
Christian symbol told that it was the grave of a white man.
It is impossible to describe the rush of mingled feelings that
filled the soul of the young hunter as he leaned on the muzzle
of his rifle and looked at this solitary resting-place of one
who, doubtless like himself, had been a roving hunter. Had
he been young or old when he fell? had he a mother in the
distant settlement who watched and longed and waited for
the son that was never more to gladden her eyes? had he
been murdered, or had he died there and been buried by
his sorrowing comrades? These and a thousand questions
passed rapidly through his mind as he gazed at the little
cross.

Suddenly he started. "Could it be the grave of Joe or
Henri?" For an instant the idea sent a chill to his heart;
but it passed quickly, for a second glance showed that the
grave was old, and that the wooden cross had stood over
it for years.

A misfortune soon after this befell Dick Varley which
well-nigh caused him to give way to despair. For some time
past he had been approaching the eastern slopes of the
Rocky Mountains—those ragged, jagged, mighty hills which
run through the whole continent from north to south in a
continuous chain, and form, as it were, the backbone of
America. One morning, as he threw the buffalo robe off
his shoulders and sat up, he was horrified to find the whole
earth covered with a mantle of snow. We say he was
horrified, for this rendered it absolutely impossible any
further to trace his companions either by scent or sight.

For some time he sat musing bitterly on his sad fate,
while his dog came and laid his head sympathizingly on his
arm.

"Ah, pup!" he said, "I know ye'd help me if ye could!
But it's all up now; there's no chance of findin' them—
none!"

To this Crusoe replied by a low whine. He knew full
well that something distressed his master, but he hadn't
yet ascertained what it was. As something had to be done,

Dick put the buffalo robe on his steed, and mounting said, as he was in the habit of doing each morning, " Lead on, pup."

Crusoe put his nose to the ground and ran forward a few paces, then he returned and ran about snuffing and scraping up the snow. At last he looked up and uttered a long melancholy howl.

" Ah! I knowed it," said Dick, pushing forward. " Come on, pup; you'll have to *follow* now. Any way we must go on."

The snow that had fallen was not deep enough to offer the slightest obstruction to their advance. It was, indeed, only one of those occasional showers common to that part of the country in the late autumn, which season had now crept upon Dick almost before he was aware of it, and he fully expected that it would melt away in a few days. In this hope he kept steadily advancing, until he found himself in the midst of those rocky fastnesses which divide the waters that flow into the Atlantic from those that flow into the Pacific Ocean. Still the slight crust of snow lay on the ground, and he had no means of knowing whether he was going in the right direction or not.

Game was abundant, and there was no lack of wood now, so that his night bivouac was not so cold or dreary as might have been expected.

Travelling, however, had become difficult, and even dangerous, owing to the rugged nature of the ground over which he proceeded. The scenery had completely changed in its character. Dick no longer coursed over the free, open plains, but he passed through beautiful valleys filled with luxuriant trees, and hemmed in by stupendous mountains, whose rugged sides rose upward until the snow-clad peaks pierced the clouds.

There was something awful in these dark solitudes, quite overwhelming to a youth of Dick's temperament. His heart began to sink lower and lower every day, and the utter impossibility of making up his mind what to do became at length agonizing. To have turned and gone back the hundreds of miles over which he had travelled would have caused him some anxiety under any circumstances, but to do so while Joe and Henri were either wandering about there or in the power of the savages was, he felt, out of the question. Yet in which way should he go? Whatever course he took might lead him farther and farther away from them.

In this dilemma he came to the determination of remaining where he was—at least until the snow should leave the ground.

He felt great relief even when this hopeless course was decided upon, and set about making himself an encampment with some degree of cheerfulness. When he had completed this task, he took his rifle, and leaving Charlie picketed in the centre of a dell, where the long, rich grass rose high above the snow, went off to hunt.

On turning a rocky point his heart suddenly bounded into his throat, for there, not thirty yards distant, stood a huge grizzly bear!

Yes, there he was at last, the monster to meet which the young hunter had so often longed—the terrible size and fierceness of which he had heard so often spoken about by the old hunters. There it stood at last; but little did Dick Varley think that the first time he should meet with his foe should be when alone in the dark recesses of the Rocky Mountains, and with none to succour him in the event of the battle going against him. Yes, there was one. The faithful Crusoe stood by his side, with his hair bristling, all his formidable teeth exposed, and his eyes glaring in their sockets. Alas for poor Crusoe had he gone into that combat alone! One stroke of that monster's paw would have hurled him dead upon the ground.

CHAPTER XVII

Dick's first fight with a grizzly—Adventure with a deer—A surprise.

There is no animal in all the land so terrible and dangerous as the grizzly bear. Not only is he the largest of the
species in America, but he is the fiercest, the strongest, and
the most tenacious of life—facts which are so well understood that few of the western hunters like to meet him
single-handed, unless they happen to be first-rate shots;
and the Indians deem the encounter so dangerous that to
wear a collar composed of the claws of the grizzly bear of
his own killing is counted one of the highest honours to
which a young warrior can attain.

The grizzly bear resembles the brown bear of Europe, but
it is larger, and the hair is long, the points being of a paler
shade. About the head there is a considerable mixture of
grey hair, giving it the " grizzly " appearance from which
it derives its name. The claws are dirty white, arched, and
very long, and so strong that when the animal strikes with
its paw they cut like a chisel. These claws are not embedded
in the paw, as is the case with the cat, but always project
far beyond the hair, thus giving the foot a very ungainly
appearance. They are not sufficiently curved to enable the
grizzly bear to climb trees, like the black and brown bears;
and this inability on their part is often the only hope of
the pursued hunter, who, if he succeeds in ascending a tree,
is safe, for the time at least, from the bear's assaults. But
" Caleb " is a patient creature, and will often wait at the
foot of the tree for many hours for his victim.

The average length of his body is about nine feet, but he
sometimes attains to a still larger growth. Caleb is more
carnivorous in his habits than other bears; but, like them,
he does not object to indulge occasionally in vegetable diet,

being partial to the bird-cherry, the choke-berry, and various shrubs. He has a sweet tooth, too, and revels in honey—when he can get it.

The instant the grizzly bear beheld Dick Varley standing in his path, he rose on his hind legs and made a loud hissing noise, like a man breathing quick, but much harsher. To this Crusoe replied by a deep growl, and showing the utmost extent of his teeth, gums and all; and Dick cocked both barrels of his rifle.

To say that Dick Varley felt no fear would be simply to make him out that sort of hero which does not exist in nature—namely, a *perfect* hero. He *did* feel a sensation as if his bowels had suddenly melted into water! Let not our reader think the worse of Dick for this. There is not a man living who, having met with a huge grizzly bear for the first time in his life in a wild, solitary place, all alone, has not experienced some such sensation. There was no cowardice in this feeling. Fear is not cowardice. Acting in a wrong and contemptible manner because of our fear is cowardice.

It is said that Wellington or Napoleon, we forget which, once stood watching the muster of the men who were to form the forlorn hope in storming a citadel. There were many brave, strong, stalwart men there, in the prime of life, and flushed with the blood of high health and courage. There were also there a few stern-browed men of riper years, who stood perfectly silent, with lips compressed, and as pale as death. "Yonder veterans," said the general, pointing to these soldiers, "are men whose courage I can depend on; they *know* what they are going to, the others *don't*!" Yes, these young soldiers *very probably* were brave; the others *certainly* were.

Dick Varley stood for a few seconds as if thunderstruck, while the bear stood hissing at him. Then the liquefaction of his interior ceased, and he felt a glow of fire gush through his veins. Now Dick knew well enough that to fly from a grizzly bear was the sure and certain way of being torn to pieces, as when taken thus by surprise they almost invariably follow a retreating enemy. He also knew that if he stood where he was, perfectly still, the bear would get uncomfortable under his stare, and would retreat from him. But he neither intended to run away himself nor to allow the bear to do so; he intended to kill it, so he raised his rifle quickly, " drew a bead ", as the hunters express it, on the bear's heart, and fired.

It immediately dropped on its fore legs and rushed at him.

" Back, Crusoe! out of the way, pup!" shouted Dick, as his favourite was about to spring forward.

The dog retired, and Dick leaped behind a tree. As the bear passed he gave it the contents of the second barrel behind the shoulder, which brought it down; but in another moment it rose and again rushed at him. Dick had no time to load, neither had he time to spring up the thick tree beside which he stood, and the rocky nature of the ground out of which it grew rendered it impossible to dodge round it. His only resource was flight; but where was he to fly to? If he ran along the open track, the bear would overtake him in a few seconds. On the right was a sheer precipice one hundred feet high; on the left was an impenetrable thicket. In despair he thought for an instant of clubbing his rifle and meeting the monster in close conflict; but the utter hopelessness of such an effort was too apparent to be entertained for a moment. He glanced up at the overhanging cliffs. There were one or two rents and projections close above him. In the twinkling of an eye he sprang up and grasped a ledge of about an inch broad, ten or twelve feet up, to which he clung while he glanced upward. Another projection was within reach; he gained it, and in a few seconds he stood upon a ledge about twenty feet up the cliff, where he had just room to plant his feet firmly.

Without waiting to look behind, he seized his powder-horn and loaded one barrel of his rifle; and well was it for him that his early training had fitted him to do this with rapidity, for the bear dashed up the precipice after him at once. The first time it missed its hold, and fell back with a savage growl; but on the second attempt it sunk its long claws into the fissures between the rocks, and ascended steadily till within a foot of the place where Dick stood.

At this moment Crusoe's obedience gave way before a sense of Dick's danger. Uttering one of his lion-like roars, he rushed up the precipice with such violence that, although naturally unable to climb, he reached and seized the bear's flank, despite his master's stern order to " keep back ", and in a moment the two rolled down the face of the rock together, just as Dick completed loading.

Knowing that one stroke of the bear's paw would be certain death to his poor dog, Dick leaped from his perch, and with one bound reached the ground at the same moment with the struggling animals, and close beside them, and, before they had ceased rolling, he placed the muzzle of his rifle into the bear's ear, and blew out its brains.

Crusoe, strange to say, escaped with only one scratch on the side. It was a deep one, but not dangerous, and gave him but little pain at the time, although it caused him many a smart for some weeks after.

Thus happily ended Dick's encounter with a grizzly bear; and although, in the course of his wild life, he shot many specimens of " Caleb ", he used to say that " he an' pup were never so near goin' under as on the day he dropped *that* bar !"

Having refreshed himself with a long draught from a neighbouring rivulet, and washed Crusoe's wound, Dick skinned the bear on the spot.

" We chawed him up that time, didn't we, pup?" said Dick, with a smile of satisfaction, as he surveyed his prize.

Crusoe looked up and assented to this.

" Gave us a hard tussle, though; very nigh sent us both under, didn't he, pup?"

Crusoe agreed entirely, and, as if the remark reminded him of honourable scars, he licked his wound.

" Ah, pup !" cried Dick, sympathetically, " does't hurt ye, eh, poor dog?"

Hurt him? such a question! No, he should think not; better ask if that leap from the precipice hurt yourself.

So Crusoe might have said, but he didn't; he took no notice of the remark whatever.

"We'll cut him up now, pup," continued Dick. "The skin'll make a splendid bed for you an' me o' nights, and a saddle for Charlie."

Dick cut out all the claws of the bear by the roots, and spent the remainder of that night in cleaning them and stringing them on a strip of leather to form a necklace. Independently of the value of these enormous claws (the largest as long as a man's middle finger) as an evidence of prowess, they formed a remarkably graceful collar, which Dick wore round his neck ever after with as much pride as if he had been a Pawnee warrior.

When it was finished he held it out at arm's-length, and said, "Crusoe, my pup, ain't ye proud of it? I'll tell ye what it is, pup, the next time you an' I floor Caleb, I'll put the claws round *your* neck, an' make ye wear em ever arter, so I will."

The dog did not seem quite to appreciate this piece of prospective good fortune. Vanity had no place in his honest breast, and, sooth to say, it had not a large place in that of his master either, as we may well grant when we consider that this first display of it was on the occasion of his hunter's soul having at last realized its brightest day-dream.

Dick's dangers and triumphs seemed to accumulate on him rather thickly at this place, for on the very next day he had a narrow escape of being killed by a deer. The way of it was this.

Having run short of meat, and not being particularly fond of grizzly bear steak, he shouldered his rifle and sallied forth in quest of game, accompanied by Crusoe, whose frequent glances towards his wounded side showed that, whatever may have been the case the day before, it "hurt" him now.

They had not gone far when they came on the track of a deer in the snow, and followed it up till they spied a magnificent buck about three hundred yards off, standing in a level patch of ground which was everywhere surrounded either by rocks or thicket. It was a long shot, but as the nature of the ground rendered it impossible for Dick to get nearer without being seen, he fired, and wounded the buck so badly that he came up with it in a few minutes. The snow had drifted in the place where it stood bolt upright, ready for a spring, so Dick went round a little way, Crusoe following, till he was in a proper position to fire again. Just as he pulled the trigger, Crusoe gave a howl behind him and disturbed his aim, so that he feared he had missed; but the deer fell, and he hurried towards it. On coming up, however, the buck sprang to its legs, rushed at him with its hair bristling, knocked him down in the snow, and deliberately commenced stamping him to death.

Dick was stunned for a moment, and lay quite still, so the deer left off pommelling him, and stood looking at him. But the instant he moved it plunged at him again and gave him another pounding, until he was content to lie still. This was done several times, and Dick felt his strength going fast. He was surprised that Crusoe did not come to his rescue, and once he cleared his mouth and whistled to him; but as the deer gave him another pounding for this, he didn't attempt it again. He now for the first time bethought him of his knife, and quietly drew it from his belt; but the deer observed the motion, and was on him again in a moment. Dick, however, sprang up on his left elbow, and making several desperate thrusts upward, succeeded in stabbing the animal to the heart.

Rising and shaking the snow from his garments, he whistled loudly to Crusoe, and, on listening, heard him whining piteously. He hurried to the place whence the sound came, and found that the poor dog had fallen into a deep pit or crevice in the rocks, which had been concealed from view by a crust of snow, and he was now making frantic but unavailing efforts to leap out.

Dick soon freed him from his prison by means of his belt, which he let down for the dog to grasp, and then returned to camp with as much deer-meat as he could carry. Dear meat it certainly was to him, for it had nearly cost him his life, and left him all black and blue for weeks after. Happily no bones were broken, so the incident only confined him a day to his encampment.

Soon after this the snow fell thicker than ever, and it became evident that an unusually early winter was about to set in among the mountains. This was a terrible calamity, for if the regular snow of winter set in, it would be impossible for him either to advance or retreat.

While he was sitting on his bearskin by the camp-fire one day, thinking anxiously what he should do, and feeling that he must either make the attempt to escape or perish miserably in that secluded spot, a strange, unwonted sound struck upon his ear, and caused both him and Crusoe to spring violently to their feet and listen. Could he be dreaming?—it seemed like the sound of human voices. For a moment he stood with his eyes riveted on the ground, his lips apart, and his nostrils distended, as he listened with the utmost intensity. Then he darted out and bounded round the edge of a rock which concealed an extensive but narrow valley from his view, and there, to his amazement, he beheld a band of about a hundred human beings advancing on horseback slowly through the snow.

CHAPTER XVIII

A surprise, and a piece of good news—The fur-traders—Crusoe
proved, and the Peigans pursued.

Dick's first and most natural impulse, on beholding this
band, was to mount his horse and fly, for his mind naturally
enough recurred to the former rough treatment he had
experienced at the hands of Indians. On second thoughts,
however, he considered it wiser to throw himself upon the
hospitality of the strangers; "for," thought he, "they can
but kill me, an' if I remain here I'm like to die at any
rate."

So Dick mounted his wild horse, grasped his rifle in his
right hand, and, followed by Crusoe, galloped full tilt down
the valley to meet them.

He had heard enough of the customs of savage tribes,
and had also of late experienced enough, to convince him
that when a man found himself in the midst of an overwhelming force, his best policy was to assume an air of
confident courage. He therefore approached them at his
utmost speed.

The effect upon the advancing band was electrical; and
little wonder, for the young hunter's appearance was very
striking. His horse, for having rested a good deal of late,
was full of spirit. Its neck was arched, its nostrils expanded,
and its mane and tail never having been checked in their
growth flew wildly around him in voluminous curls. Dick's
own hair, not having been clipped for many months,
appeared scarcely less wild, as they thundered down the
rocky pass at what happened a breakneck gallop. Add to
this the grandeur of the scene out of which they sprang,
and the gigantic dog that bounded by his side, and you

will not be surprised to hear that the Indian warriors clustered together, and prepared to receive this bold horseman as if he, in his own proper person, were a complete squadron of cavalry. It is probable, also, that they fully expected the tribe of which Dick was the chief to be at his heels.

As he drew near the excitement among the strangers seemed very great, and, from the peculiarity of the various cries that reached him, he knew that there were women and children in the band—a fact which, in such a place and at such a season, was so unnatural that it surprised him very much. He noted also that, though the men in front were Indians, their dresses were those of trappers and hunters, and he almost leaped out of his saddle when he observed that " *Pale-faces* " were among them. But he had barely time to note these facts when he was up with the band. According to Indian custom, he did not check his speed till he was within four or five yards of the advance-guard, who stood in a line before him, quite still, and with their rifles lying loosely in their left palms; then he reined his steed almost on its haunches.

One of the Indians advanced and spoke a few words in a language which was quite unintelligible to Dick, who replied, in the little Pawnee he could muster, that he didn't understand him.

" Why, you must be a trapper!" exclaimed a thick-set, middle-aged man, riding out from the group. " Can you speak English?"

" Ay, that can I," cried Dick joyfully, riding up and shaking the stranger heartily by the hand; " an' right glad am I to fall in wi' a white-skin an' a civil tongue in his head."

" Good sooth, sir," replied the stranger, with a quiet smile on his kind, weather-beaten face, " I can return you the compliment; for when I saw you come thundering down the corrie with that wonderful horse and no less wonderful dog of yours, I thought you were the wild man o' the mountain himself, and had an ambush ready to back you. But, young man, do you mean to say that you live here in the mountain all alone after this fashion?"

"No, that I don't. I've comed here in my travels, but truly this bean't my home. But, sir (for I see you are what the fur-traders call a bourgeois), how comes it that such a band as this rides i' the mountains? D'ye mean to say that *they* live here?" Dick looked round in surprise, as he spoke, upon the crowd of mounted men and women, with children and pack-horses, that now surrounded him.

" 'Tis a fair question, lad. I am a principal among the fur-traders whose chief trading-post lies near the Pacific Ocean, on the west side of these mountains; and I have come with these trappers and their families, as you see, to hunt the beaver and other animals for a season in the mountains. We've never been here before; but that's a matter of little moment, for it's not the first time I've been on what may be called a discovery-trading expedition. We are somewhat entangled, however, just now among these wild passes, and if you can guide us out of our difficulties to the east side of the mountains, I'll thank you heartily and pay you well. But first tell me who and what you are, if it's a fair question."

"My name is Dick Varley, and my home's in the Mustang Valley, near the Missouri River. As to *what* I am—I'm nothin' yet, but I hope to desarve the name o' a hunter some day. I can guide you to the east side o' the mountains, for I've comed from there; but more than that I can't do, for I'm a stranger to the country here, like yourself. But you're on the east side o' the mountains already, if I mistake not; only these mountains are so rugged and jumbled up, that it's not easy tellin' where ye are. And what," continued Dick, "may be the name o' the bourgeois who speaks to me?"

"My name is Cameron—Walter Cameron—a well-known name among the Scottish hills, although it sounds a little strange here. And now, young man, will you join my party as guide, and afterwards remain as trapper? It will pay you better, I think, than roving about alone."

Dick shook his head and looked grave. "I'll guide you," said he, "as far as my knowledge 'll help me; but after that I must return to look for two comrades whom I have lost. They have been driven into the mountains by a band of Injuns. God grant they may not have bin scalped!"

The trader's face looked troubled, and he spoke with one of his Indians for a few minutes in earnest, hurried tones.

"What were they like, young man?"

Dick described them.

"The same," continued the trader. "They've been seen, lad, not more than two days ago, by this Indian here, when he was out hunting alone some miles away from our camp. He came suddenly on a band of Indians who had two prisoners with them, such as you describe. They were stout, said you?"

"Yes, both of them," cried Dick, listening with intense eagerness.

"Ay. They were tied to their horses, an' from what I know of these fellows I'm sure they're doomed. But I'll help you, my friend, as well as I can. They can't be far from this. I treated my Indian's story about them as a mere fabrication, for he's the most notorious liar in my company; but he seems to have spoken truth for once."

"Thanks, thanks, good sir," cried Dick. "Had we not best turn back and follow them at once?"

"Nay, friend, not quite so fast," replied Cameron, pointing to his people. "These must be provided for first, but I shall be ready before the sun goes down. And now, as I presume you don't bivouac in the snow, will you kindly conduct us to your encampment, if it be not far hence?"

Although burning with impatience to fly to the rescue of his friends, Dick felt constrained to comply with so reasonable a request, so he led the way to his camping-place, where the band of fur-traders immediately began to pitch their tents, cut down wood, kindle fires, fill their kettles with water, cook their food, and, in fact, make themselves comfortable. The wild spot which, an hour before, had been so still, and grand, and gloomy, was now, as if by magic, transformed into a bustling village, with bright fires blazing among the rocks and bushes, and merry voices of men, women, and children ringing in the air. It seemed almost incredible, and no wonder Dick, in his bewilderment, had difficulty in believing it was not all a dream.

In days long gone by the fur-trade in that country was carried on in a very different way from the manner in which it is now conducted. These wild regions, indeed, are still as lonesome and untenanted (save by wild beasts and wandering tribes of Indians) as they were then; but the Indians of the present day have become accustomed to the " Pale-face " trader, whose little wooden forts or trading-posts are dotted here and there, at wide intervals, all over the land. But in the days of which we write it was not so. The fur-traders at that time went forth in armed bands into the heart of the Indians' country, and he who went forth did so " with his life in his hand ". As in the case of the soldier who went out to battle, there was great probability that he might never return.

The band of which Walter Cameron was the chief had, many months before, started from one of the distant posts of Oregon on a hunting expedition into the then totally unknown lands of the Snake Indians. It consisted of about sixty men, thirty women, and as many children of various ages—about a hundred and twenty souls in all. Many of the boys were capable of using the gun and setting a beaver-trap. The men were a most motley set. There were Canadians, half-breeds, Iroquois, and Scotchmen. Most of the women had Indian blood in their veins, and a few were pure Indians.

The equipment of this strange band consisted of upwards of two hundred beaver-traps—which are similar to our rat-traps, with this difference, that they have two springs and no teeth—seventy guns, a few articles for trade with the Indians, and a large supply of powder and ball; the whole—men, women, children, goods and chattels—being carried on the backs of nearly four hundred horses. Many of these horses, at starting, were not laden, being designed for the transport of furs that were to be taken in the course of the season.

For food this adventurous party depended entirely on their guns, and during the march hunters were kept constantly out ahead. As a matter of course, their living was precarious. Sometimes their kettles were overflowing; at others they scarce refrained from eating their horses. But during the months they had already spent in the wilderness good living had been the rule, starvation the exception. They had already collected a large quantity of beaver skins, which at that time were among the most valuable in the market, although they are now scarcely saleable.

Having shot two wild horses, seven elks, six small deer, and four big-horned sheep the day before they met Dick Varley, the camp kettles were full, and the people consequently happy.

"Now, Master Dick Varley," said Cameron, touching the young hunter on the shoulder as he stood ready equipped by one of the camp-fires, "I'm at your service. The people won't need any more looking after to-night. I'll divide my men—thirty shall go after this rascally band of Peigans, for such I believe they are, and thirty shall remain to guard the camp. Are you ready?"

"Ready! ay, this hour past."

"Mount then, lad; the men have already been told off, and are mustering down yonder where the deer gave you such a licking."

Dick needed no second bidding. He vaulted on Charlie's back, and along with their commander joined the men, who were thirty as fine, hardy, reckless-looking fellows as one could desire for a forlorn hope. They were chatting and laughing while they examined their guns and saddle-girths. Their horses were sorry-looking animals compared with the magnificent creature that Dick bestrode, but they were hardy, nevertheless, and well fitted for their peculiar work.

"My! wot a blazer!" exclaimed a trapper as Dick rode up.

"Where you git him?" inquired a half-breed.

" I caught him," answered Dick.

" Baw!" cried the first speaker.

Dick took no notice of this last remark.

" No, did ye, though?" he asked again.

" I did," answered Dick quietly. " I creased him in the prairie; you can see the mark on his neck if you look."

The men began to feel that the young hunter was perhaps a little beyond them at their own trade, and regarded him with increased respect.

" Look sharp now, lads," said Cameron, impatiently, to several dilatory members of the band. " Night will be on us ere long."

" Who sold ye the bear-claw collar?" inquired another man of Dick.

" I didn't buy it. I killed the bear and made it."

" Did ye, though, all be yer lone?"

" Ay; that wasn't much, was it?"

" You've begun well, yonker," said a tall, middle-aged hunter, whose general appearance was not unlike that of Joe Blunt. " Jest keep clear o' the Injuns an' the grog bottle, an' ye've a glor'ous life before ye."

At this point the conversation was interrupted by the order being given to move on, which was obeyed in silence, and the cavalcade, descending the valley, entered one of the gorges in the mountains.

For the first half-mile Cameron rode a little ahead of his men, then he turned to speak to one of them, and for the first time observed Crusoe trotting close beside his master's horse.

" Ah! Master Dick," he exclaimed with a troubled expression, " that won't do. It would never do to take a dog on an expedition like this."

" Why not?" asked Dick; " the pup's quiet and peaceable."

" I doubt it not; but he will betray our presence to the Indians, which might be inconvenient."

" I have travelled more than a thousand miles through prairie and forest, among game an' among Injuns, an' the pup never betrayed me yet," said Dick, with suppressed vehemence. "He has saved my life more than once, though."

"You seem to have perfect confidence in your dog, but as this is a serious matter you must not expect me to share in it without proof of his trustworthiness."

"The pup may be useful to us; how would you have it proved?" inquired Dick.

"Any way you like."

"You forgot your belt at starting, I think I heerd ye say."

"Yes, I did," replied the trader, smiling.

Dick immediately took hold of Cameron's coat, and bade Crusoe smell it, which the dog did very carefully. Then he showed him his own belt and said, "Go back to the camp and fetch it, pup."

Crusoe was off in a moment, and in less than twenty minutes returned with Cameron's belt in his mouth.

"Well, I'll trust him," said Cameron, patting Crusoe's head. "Forward, lads!" and away they went at a brisk trot along the bottom of a beautiful valley on each side of which the mountains towered in dark masses. Soon the moon rose and afforded light sufficient to enable them to travel all night in the track of the Indian hunter who said he had seen the Peigans, and who was constituted guide to the party. Hour after hour the horsemen pressed on without check, now galloping over a level plain, now bounding by the banks of a rivulet, or bending their heads to escape the boughs of overhanging trees, and anon toiling slowly up among the rocks of some narrow defile. At last the moon set, and the order was given to halt in a little plain where there were wood and water.

The horses were picketed, a fire kindled, a mouthful of dried meat hastily eaten, the watch was set, and then each man scraped away the snow, spread some branches on the ground, and wrapping himself in his blanket, went to sleep with his feet presented towards the fire.

Two hours were allowed for rest; then they were awakened, and in a few minutes were off again by the gray light

of dawn. In this way they travelled two nights and a day
At the end of that time they came suddenly on a small
party of nine Indians, who were seated on the ground with
their snow-shoes and blankets by their sides. They had
evidently been taken by surprise, but they made no attempt
to escape, knowing that it was useless. Each sat still with
his bow and arrows between his legs on the ground ready
for instant use.

As soon as Cameron spoke, however, in their own language they felt relieved, and began to talk.

"Where do you come from, and what are you doing
here?" asked the trader.

"We have come to trade with the white men," one of
them replied, "and to hunt. We have come from the
Missouri. Our country is far away."

"Do Peigans hunt with *war-arrows*?" asked Cameron,
pointing to their weapons.

This question seemed to perplex them, for they saw that
their interrogator knew the difference between a war and
a hunting arrow—the former being barbed in order to
render its extraction from the wound difficult, while the
head of the latter is round, and can be drawn out of game
that has been killed, and used again.

"And do Peigans," continued Cameron, "come from a
far country to trade with the white men *with nothing*?"

Again the Indians were silent, for they had not an article
to trade about them.

Cameron now felt convinced that this party of Peigans,
into whose hands Joe Blunt and Henri had fallen, were
nothing else than a war party, and that the men now before
him were a scouting party sent out from them, probably
to spy out his own camp, on the trail of which they had
fallen, so he said to them:—

"The Peigans are not wise men; they tell lies to the
traders. I will tell you that you are a war party, and that you
are only a few warriors sent out to spy the traders' camp.
You have also two *Pale-face* prisoners in your camp. You
cannot deceive me. It is useless to try. Now, conduct me

to your camp. My object is not war; it is peace. I will speak with your chiefs about trading with the white men, and we will smoke the pipe of peace. Are my words good?"

Despite their proverbial control of muscle, these Indians could not conceal their astonishment at hearing so much of their affairs thus laid bare; so they said that the Pale-face chief was wise, that he must be a great medicine man, and that what he said was all true except about the white men. They had never seen any Pale-faces, and knew nothing whatever about those he spoke of.

This was a terrible piece of news to poor Dick, and at first his heart fairly sank within him, but by degrees he came to be more hopeful. He concluded that if these men told lies in regard to one thing, they would do it in regard to another, and perhaps they might have some strong reason for denying any knowledge of Joe and Henri.

The Indians now packed up the buffalo robes on which they had slept, and the mouthful of provisions they had taken with them.

"I don't believe a word of what they say about your friends," said Cameron to Dick in a low tone while the Indians were thus engaged. "Depend upon it they hope to hide them till they can send to the settlements and get a ransom, or till they get an opportunity of torturing them to death before their women and children when they get back to their own village. But we'll balk them, my friend, do not fear."

The Indians were soon ready to start, for they were cumbered with marvellously little camp equipage. In less than half-an-hour after their discovery they were running like deer ahead of the cavalcade in the direction of the Peigan camp.

CHAPTER XIX

Adventures with the Peigans—Crusoe does good service as a discoverer—
The savages outwitted—The rescue.

A run of twenty miles brought the travellers to a rugged
defile in the mountains, from which they had a view of a
beautiful valley of considerable extent. During the last
two days a steady thaw had been rapidly melting away the
snow, so that it appeared only here and there in the landscape in dazzling patches. At the distance of about half-a-
mile from where they halted to breathe the horses before
commencing the descent into this vale, several thin wreaths
of smoke were seen rising above the trees.

"Is that your camp?" inquired Cameron, riding up to
the Indian runners, who stood in a group in front, looking
as fresh after their twenty miles' run as though they had
only had a short walk.

To this they answered in the affirmative, adding that
there were about two hundred Peigans there.

It might have been thought that thirty men would have
hesitated to venture to attack so large a number as two
hundred; but it had always been found in the experience
of Indian life that a few resolute white men well armed
were more than a match for ten times their number of
Indians. And this arose not so much from the superior
strength or agility of the Whites over their red foes, as
from that bull-dog courage and utter recklessness of their
lives in combat—qualities which the crafty savage can
neither imitate nor understand. The information was
received with perfect indifference by most of the trappers,
and with contemptuous laughter by some; for a large
number of Cameron's men were wild, evil-disposed fellows,

who would have as gladly taken the life of an Indian as that of a buffalo.

Just as the word was given to resume the march Dick Varley rode up to Cameron and said in a somewhat anxious tone—

" D'ye observe, sir, that one o' the Red-skins has gone off ahead o' his comrades?"

" I see that, Master Dick; and it was a mistake of mine not to have stopped him, but he was gone too far before I observed it, and I thought it better to appear unconcerned. We must push on, though, and give him as short time as possible to talk with his comrades in the camp."

The trappers pressed forward accordingly at a gallop, and were soon in front of the clump of trees amongst which the Peigans were encamped. Their approach had evidently spread great alarm among them, for there was a good deal of bustle and running to and fro; but by the time the trappers had dismounted and advanced in a body on foot, the savages had resumed their usual quiet dignity of appearance, and were seated calmly round their fires with their bows and arrows beside them. There were no tents, no women or children, and the general aspect of the men showed Cameron conclusively that his surmise about their being a war party was correct.

A council was immediately called. The trappers ranged themselves on one side of the council fire and the Indians on the other. Meanwhile, our friend Crusoe had been displaying considerable irritability against the Indians, and he would certainly have attacked the whole two hundred single-handed if he had not been ordered by his master to lie still; but never in his life before had Crusoe obeyed with such a bad grace. He bristled and whined in a low tremulous tone, and looked imploringly at Dick as if for permission to fly at them.

" The Pale-face traders are glad to meet with the Peigans," began Cameron, who determined to make no allusion to his knowledge that they were a war party, " for they wish to be friends with all the children of the woods and prairies. They wish to trade with them—to exchange blankets, and guns, and beads, and other goods which the Peigans require, for furs of animals which the Pale-faces require."

" Ho! ho!" exclaimed the Indians, which expression might be translated, " Hear! hear!"

" But," continued Cameron, " we wish to have no war. We wish to see the hatchet buried, and to see all the Red-men and the White-men smoking the pipe of peace and hunting like brothers."

The " Ho—ho—ing " at this was very emphatic.

" Now," resumed the trader, " the Peigans have got two prisoners—two Pale-faces—in their camp, and as we cannot be on good terms while our brothers are detained, we have come to ask for them, and to *present some gifts* to the Peigans."

To this there was no " Ho " at all, but a prolonged silence, which was at length interrupted by a tall chief stepping forward to address the trappers.

" What the Pale-face chief has said is good," began the Indian. " His words are wise, and his heart is not double. The Red-men are willing to smoke the pipe of peace, and to hunt with all men as brothers, but they cannot do it while many of their scalps are hanging in the lodges of their enemies and fringing the robes of the warriors. The Peigans must have vengeance; then they will make peace."

After a short pause he continued—

" The chief is wrong when he says there are Pale-faces in the Peigan camp. The Peigans are not at war with the Pale-faces; neither have they seen any on their march. The camp is open. Let the Pale-faces look round and see that what we say is true."

The chief waved his hand towards his warriors as he concluded, as if to say, " Search amongst them. There are no Pale-faces there."

Cameron now spoke to Dick in a low tone. " They speak confidently," he said, " and I fear greatly that your poor comrades have either been killed or conveyed away from the camp and hidden among the mountains, in which case,

even though they should not be far off, it would be next
to impossible to find them, especially when such a band of
rascals is near, compelling us to keep together. But I'll
try what a little tempting them with goods will do. At any
rate, we shan't give in without a scuffle."

It now, for the first time, flashed across Dick Varley that
there was something more than he imagined in Crusoe's
restless anxiety, which had not in the least abated, and the
idea of making use of him now occurred to his mind.

"I've a notion that I'll settle this matter in a shorter
time than you think," he said hurriedly, "if you'll agree to
try what *threatening* will do."

The trader looked grave and undecided. "I never resort
to that except as a last hope," he answered; "but I've a
good deal of confidence in your prudence. What would
you advise?"

Dick and the trader whispered a few minutes together,
while some of the men, in order to show the Indians how
perfectly unconcerned they were, and how ready for *anything*, took out their pipes and began to smoke. Both parties
were seated on the ground, and during this interval the
Indians also held eager discussion.

At length Cameron stood up, and said to his men in a
quiet tone, "Be ready, lads, for instant action. When I
give the word 'Up', spring to your feet and cock your
guns; but *don't fire a shot till you get the word*." He then
stepped forward and said—

"The Peigan warriors are double-tongued; they know
that they have hid the Pale-face prisoners. We do not wish
to quarrel, but if they are not delivered up at once the
Pale-faces and the Peigans will not be friends."

Upon this the Indian chief again stood forward and said,
"The Peigans are *not* double-tongued. They have not seen
Pale-faces till to-day. They can say no more."

Without moving hand or foot, Cameron then said in a
firm tone, "The first Peigan that moves shall die! Up,
lads, and ready!"

In the twinkling of an eye the trappers sprang to their

feet, and cocking their rifles stood perfectly motionless, scowling at the savages, who were completely taken by surprise at the unusual suddenness and informality of such a declaration of war. Not a man moved, for, unlike white men, they seldom risk their lives in open fight; and as they looked at the formidable row of muzzles that waited but a word to send instant death into their midst, they felt that discretion was at that time the better part of valour.

"Now," said Cameron, while Dick Varley and Crusoe stepped up beside him, "my young warrior will search for the Pale-face prisoners. If they are found, we will take them and go away. If they are not found, we will ask the Peigans to forgive us, and will give them gifts. But in the meantime, if a Peigan moves from the spot where he sits, or lifts a bow, my young men shall fire, and the Peigans know that the rifle of the Pale-face always kills."

Without waiting for an answer, Dick immediately said, "Seek 'em out, pup," and Crusoe bounded away.

For a few minutes he sprang hither and thither through the camp, quite regardless of the Indians, and snuffed the air several times, whining in an excited tone, as if to relieve his feelings. Then he put his nose to the ground and ran straight forward into the woods. Dick immediately bounded after him like a deer, while the trappers kept silent guard over the savages.

For some time Crusoe ran straight forward. Then he came to a spot where there was a good deal of drifted snow on the ground. Here he seemed to lose the trail for a little, and ran about in all directions, whining in a most piteous tone.

"Seek 'em out, pup," repeated Dick encouragingly, while his own breast heaved with excitement and expectation.

In a few seconds the dog resumed its onward course, and led the way into a wild, dark spot, which was so over-shadowed by trees and precipitous cliffs that the light of the sun scarce found entrance. There were many huge masses of rock scattered over the ground, which had fallen from the cliffs. Behind one of these lay a mound of dried leaves, towards which Crusoe darted and commenced scraping violently.

Trembling with dread that he should find this to be the grave of his murdered companions, Dick rushed forward and hastily cleared away the leaves. The first handful thrown off revealed part of the figure of a man. Dick's heart beat audibly as he cleared the leaves from the face, and he uttered a suppressed cry on beholding the well-known features of Joe Blunt. But they were not those of a dead man. Joe's eyes met his with a scowl of anger, which instantly gave place to one of intense surprise.

"Joe Blunt!" exclaimed Dick in a voice of intense amazement, while Crusoe snuffed round the heap of leaves and whined with excitement. But Joe did not move, neither did he speak a word in reply—for the very good reason that his mouth was tightly bound with a band of leather, his hands and feet were tied, and his whole body was secured in a rigid, immovable position by being bound to a pole of about his own length.

In a moment Dick's knife was out, bands and cords were severed, and Joe Blunt was free.

"Thank God!" exclaimed Joe with a deep, earnest sigh, the instant his lips were loosened, "and thanks to *you*, lad!" he added, endeavouring to rise; but his limbs had become so benumbed in consequence of the cords by which they had been compressed that for some time he could not move.

"I'll rub ye, Joe; I'll soon rub ye into a right state," said Dick, going down on his knees.

"No, no, lad, look sharp and dig up Henri. He's just beside me here."

Dick immediately rose, and pushing aside the heap of leaves, found Henri securely bound in the same fashion. But he could scarce refrain from laughing at the expression of that worthy's face. Hearing the voices of Joe and Dick Varley in conversation, though unable to see their persons, he was filled with such unbounded amazement that his eyes, when uncovered, were found to be at their largest possible stretch, and as for the eyebrows they were gone, utterly lost among the roots of his voluminous hair.

"Henri, friend, I knew I should find ye," said Dick, cutting the thongs that bound him. "Get up if ye can; we haven't much time to lose, an' mayhap we'll have to fight afore we're done wi' the Red-skins. Can ye rise?"

Henri could do nothing but lie on his back and gasp, "Eh! possible! mon frère! Oh, non, non, *not* possible. Oui! my broder Deek!"

Here he attempted to rise, but being unable fell back again, and the whole thing came so suddenly, and made so deep an impression on his impulsive mind, that he incontinently burst into tears; then he burst into a long laugh. Suddenly he paused, and scrambling up to a sitting posture, looked earnestly into Dick's face through his tearful eyes.

"Oh, non, non!" he exclaimed, stretching himself out at full length again, and closing his eyes; "it are too goot to be true. I am dream. I vill wait till I am wake."

Dick roused him out of this resolute sleep, however, somewhat roughly. Meanwhile Joe had rubbed and kicked himself into a state of animation, exclaiming that he felt as if he wos walkin' on a thousand needles and pins, and in a few minutes they were ready to accompany their overjoyed deliverer back to the Peigan camp. Crusoe testified his delight in various elephantine gambols round the persons of his old friends, who were not slow to acknowledge his services.

"They haven't treated us overly well," remarked Joe Blunt, as they strode through the underwood.

"Non, de rascale, vraiment, de am villains. Oui! How de have talk, too, 'bout—oh-o-oo-ooo-wah!—roastin' us alive, an' puttin' our scalp in de vigvam for de poopoose to play wid!"

"Well, niver mind, Henri, we'll be quits wi' them now," said Joe, as they came in sight of the two bands, who remained in precisely the same position in which they had been left, except that one or two of the more reckless of the trappers had lit their pipes and taken to smoking, without, however, laying down their rifles or taking their eyes off the savages.

A loud cheer greeted the arrival of the prisoners, and looks of considerable discomfort began to be evinced by the Indians.

" Glad to see you, friends," said Cameron, as they came up.

" Ve is 'appy ov de same," replied Henri, swaggering up in the joviality of his heart, and seizing the trader's hand in his own enormous fist " Shall ve go to vork an' slay dem all at vounce, or von at a time?"

" We'll consider that afterwards, my lad. Meantime, go you to the rear and get a weapon of some sort."

" Oui. Ah¹ c'est charmant," he cried, going with an immense flounder into the midst of the amused trappers, and slapping those next to him on the back. " Give me veapon, do, mes amis—gun, pistol, anyting—cannon, if you have von."

Meanwhile Cameron and Joe spoke together for a few moments

" You had goods with you, and horses, I believe, when you were captured," said the former.

" Ay, that we had. Yonder stand the horses, under the pine-tree, along wi' the rest o' the Red-skin troop; an' a hard time they've had o't, as their bones may tell without speakin' As for the goods," he continued, glancing round the camp, " I don't know where—ah¹ yes, there they be in the old pack. I see all safe."

Cameron now addressed the Indians.

" The Peigans," he said, " have not done well. Their hearts have not been true to the Pale-faces. Even now I could take your scalps where you sit, but white men do not like war, they do not like revenge. The Peigans may go free '

Considering the fewness of their numbers, this was bold language to use towards the Indians; but the boldest is generally the best policy on such occasions. Moreover, Cameron felt that, being armed with rifles, while the Indians had only bows and arrows, the trappers had a great advantage over them.

The Indian who had spoken before now rose and said he was sorry there should be any cause of difference between them, and added he was sorry for a great many more things besides, but he did not say he was sorry for having told a lie.

"But, before you go, you must deliver up the horses and goods belonging to these men," said Cameron, pointing to Joe and Henri.

This was agreed to. The horses were led out, the two little packs containing Joe's goods were strapped upon them, and then the trappers turned to depart. The Indians did not move until they had mounted; then they rose and advanced in a body to the edge of the wood, to see the Pale-faces go away. Meanwhile Joe spoke a few words to Cameron, and the men were ordered to halt, while the former dismounted and led his horse towards the band of savages.

"Peigans," he said, "you know the object for which I came into this country was to make peace between you and the Pale-faces. I have often told you so when you would not listen, and when you told me that I had a double heart and told lies. You were wrong when you said this; but I do not wonder, for you live among nations who do not fear God, and who think it right to lie. I now repeat to you what I said before. It would be good for the Redmen if they would make peace with the Pale-faces, and if they would make peace with each other. I will now convince you that I am in earnest, and have all along been speaking the truth."

Hereupon Joe Blunt opened his bundle of goods, and presented fully one-half of the gaudy and brilliant contents to the astonished Indians, who seemed quite taken aback by such generous treatment. The result of this was that the two parties separated with mutual expressions of esteem and good-will. The Indians then returned to the forest, and the white men galloped back to their camp among the hills.

CHAPTER XX

New plans—Our travellers join the fur-traders, and see many strange things—A curious fight—A narrow escape, and a prisoner taken.

Not long after the events related in the last chapter, our four friends—Dick, and Joe, and Henri, and Crusoe—agreed to become for a time members of Walter Cameron's band of trappers. Joe joined because one of the objects which the traders had in view was similar to his own mission—namely, the promoting of peace among the various Indian tribes of the mountains and plains to the west. Joe therefore thought it a good opportunity of travelling with a band of men who could secure him a favourable hearing from the Indian tribes they might chance to meet with in the course of their wanderings. Besides, as the traders carried about a large supply of goods with them, he could easily replenish his own nearly exhausted pack by hunting wild animals and exchanging their skins for such articles as he might require.

Dick joined because it afforded him an opportunity of seeing the wild, majestic scenery of the Rocky Mountains, and shooting the big-horned sheep which abounded there, and the grizzly " bars ", as Joe named them, or " Caleb ", as they were more frequently styled by Henri and the other men.

Henri joined because it was agreeable to the inclination of his own rollicking, blundering, floundering, crashing disposition, and because he would have joined anything that had been joined by the other two.

Crusoe's reason for joining was single, simple, easy to be expressed, easy to be understood, and commendable. *He* joined—because Dick did

The very day after the party left the encampment where Dick had shot the grizzly bear and the deer, he had the satisfaction of bringing down a splendid specimen of the big-horned sheep. It came suddenly out from a gorge of the mountain, and stood upon the giddy edge of a tremendous precipice, at a distance of about two hundred and fifty yards.

" *You* could not hit that," said a trapper to Henri, who was rather fond of jeering him about his short-sightedness.

" Non!" cried Henri, who didn't see the animal in the least; " say you dat? ve shall see;" and he let fly with a promptitude that amazed his comrades, and with a result that drew from them peals of laughter.

" Why, you have missed the mountain!"

" Oh, non! dat am eempossoble."

It was true, nevertheless, for his ball had been arrested in its flight by the stem of a tree not twenty yards before him.

While the shot was yet ringing, and before the laugh above referred to had pealed forth, Dick Varley fired, and the animal, springing wildly into the air, fell down the precipice, and was almost dashed to pieces at their feet.

This Rocky Mountain or big-horned sheep was a particularly large and fine one, but being a patriarch of the flock was not well suited for food. It was considerably larger in size than the domestic sheep, and might be described as somewhat resembling a deer in the body and a ram in the head. Its horns were the chief point of interest to Dick; and, truly, they were astounding! Their enormous size was out of all proportion to the animal's body, and they curved backwards and downwards, and then curled up again in a sharp point. These creatures frequent the inaccessible heights of the Rocky Mountains, and are difficult to approach. They have a great fondness for salt, and pay regular visits to the numerous caverns of these mountains, which are encrusted with a saline substance.

Walter Cameron now changed his intention of proceeding to the eastward, as he found the country not so full of beaver at that particular spot as he had anticipated. He therefore turned towards the west, penetrated into the interior of the mountains, and took a considerable sweep through the lovely valleys on their western slopes.

The expedition which this enterprising fur-trader was conducting was one of the first that ever penetrated these wild regions in search of furs. The ground over which they travelled was quite new to them, and having no guide they just moved about at haphazard, encamping on the margin of every stream or river on which signs of the presence of beaver were discovered, and setting their traps.

Beaver skins at this time were worth 25s. apiece in the markets of civilized lands, and in the Snake country, through which our friends were travelling, thousands of them were to be had from the Indians for trinkets and baubles that were scarce worth a farthing. A beaver skin could be procured from the Indians for a brass finger-ring or a penny looking-glass. Horses were also so numerous that one could be procured for an axe or a knife.

Let not the reader, however, hastily conclude that the traders cheated the Indians in this traffic, though the profits were so enormous. The ring or the axe was indeed a trifle to the trader, but the beaver skin and the horse were equally trifles to the savage, who could procure as many of them as he chose with very little trouble, while the ring and the axe were in his estimation of priceless value. Besides, be it remembered, to carry that ring and that axe to the far-distant haunts of the Red-man cost the trader weeks and months of constant toil, trouble, anxiety, and, alas! too frequently cost him his life! The state of trade is utterly different in these regions at the present day. It is not more *justly* conducted, for, in respect of the value of goods given for furs, it was justly conducted *then*, but time and circumstances have tended more to equalize the relative values of articles of trade.

The snow which had prematurely fallen had passed away, and the trappers now found themselves wandering about in a country so beautiful and a season so delightful,

that it would have seemed to them a perfect paradise, but
for the savage tribes who hovered about them, and kept
them ever on the *qui vive*.

They soon passed from the immediate embrace of stupendous heights and dark gorges to a land of sloping ridges,
which divided the country into a hundred luxuriant vales,
composed part of woodland and part of prairie. Through
these, numerous rivers and streams flowed deviously,
beautifying the landscape and enriching the land. There
were also many lakes of all sizes, and these swarmed with
fish, while in some of them were found the much-sought-
after and highly-esteemed beaver. Salt springs and hot
springs of various temperatures abounded here, and many
of the latter were so hot that meat could be boiled in them.
Salt existed in all directions in abundance and of good
quality. A sulphurous spring was also discovered, bubbling
out from the base of a perpendicular rock three hundred
feet high, the waters of which were dark-blue and tasted
like gunpowder. In short, the land presented every variety
of feature calculated to charm the imagination and delight
the eye.

It was a mysterious land, too; for broad rivers burst in
many places from the earth, flowed on for a short space,
and then disappeared as if by magic into the earth from
which they rose. Natural bridges spanned the torrents in
many places, and some of these were so correctly formed
that it was difficult to believe they had not been built by
the hand of man. They often appeared opportunely to our
trappers, and saved them the trouble and danger of fording
rivers. Frequently the whole band would stop in silent
wonder and awe as they listened to the rushing of waters
under their feet, as if another world of streams, and rapids,
and cataracts were flowing below the crust of earth on
which they stood. Some considerable streams were likewise
observed to gush from the faces of precipices, some twenty
or thirty feet from their summits, while on the top no
water was to be seen.

Wild berries of all kinds were found in abundance, and

wild vegetables, besides many nutritious roots. Among other fish, splendid salmon were found in the lakes and rivers, and animal life swarmed on hill and in dale. Woods and valleys, plains and ravines, teemed with it. On every plain the red-deer grazed in herds by the banks of lake and stream. Wherever there were clusters of poplar and elder trees and saplings, the beaver was seen nibbling industriously with his sharp teeth, and committing as much havoc in the forest as if he had been armed with the woodman's axe; others sported in the eddies. Racoons sat in the tree-tops; the marten, the black fox, and the wolf prowled in the woods in quest of prey; mountain sheep and goats browsed on the rocky ridges; and badgers peeped from their holes.

Here, too, the wild horse sprang snorting and dishevelled from his mountain retreats, with flourishing mane and tail, spanking step, and questioning gaze, and thundered away over the plains and valleys, while the rocks echoed back his shrill neigh. The huge, heavy, ungainly elk, or moose-deer, *trotted* away from the travellers with speed equal to that of the mustang: elks seldom gallop; their best speed is attained at the trot. Bears, too,—black, and brown, and grizzly,—roamed about everywhere.

So numerous were all these creatures that on one occasion the hunters of the party brought in six wild horses, three bears, four elks, and thirty red-deer; having shot them all a short distance ahead of the main body, and almost without diverging from the line of march. And this was a matter of everyday occurrence—as it had need to be, considering the number of mouths that had to be filled.

The feathered tribes were not less numerous. Chief among these were eagles and vultures of uncommon size, the wild goose, wild duck, and the majestic swan.

In the midst of such profusion the trappers spent a happy time of it, when not molested by the savages, but they frequently lost a horse or two in consequence of the expertness of these thievish fellows. They often wandered, however, for days at a time without seeing an Indian, and at such times they enjoyed to the full the luxuries with which a bountiful God had blessed these romantic regions.

Dick Varley was almost wild with delight. It was his first excursion into the remote wilderness; he was young, healthy, strong, and romantic; and it is a question whether his or his dog's heart, or that of the noble wild horse he bestrode, bounded most with joy at the glorious sights and sounds and influences by which they were surrounded. It would have been perfection, had it not been for the frequent annoyance and alarms caused by the Indians.

The success of the trappers in procuring beaver here was great. In all sorts of creeks and rivers they were found. One day they came to one of the curious rivers before mentioned, which burst suddenly out of a plain, flowed on for several miles, and then disappeared into the earth as suddenly as it had risen. Even in this strange place beaver were seen, so the traps were set, and a hundred and fifty were caught at the first lift.

The manner in which the party proceeded was as follows: —They marched in a mass in groups or in a long line, according to the nature of the ground over which they travelled. The hunters of the party went forward a mile or two in advance, and scattered through the woods. After them came the advance-guard, being the bravest and most stalwart of the men mounted on their best steeds, and with rifle in hand; immediately behind followed the women and children, also mounted, and the pack-horses with the goods and camp equipage. Another band of trappers formed the rear-guard to this imposing cavalcade. There was no strict regimental order kept, but the people soon came to adopt the arrangements that were most convenient for all parties, and at length fell naturally into their places in the line of march.

Joe Blunt usually was the foremost and always the most successful of the hunters. He was therefore seldom seen on the march except at the hour of starting, and at night when he came back leading his horse, which always groaned under its heavy load of meat. Henri, being a hearty, jovial soul and fond of society, usually kept with the main body.

As for Dick, he was everywhere at once, at least as much
so as it is possible for human nature to be! His horse
never wearied; it seemed to delight in going at full speed;
no other horse in the troop could come near Charlie, and
Dick indulged him by appearing now at the front, now at
the rear, anon in the centre, and frequently *nowhere*!—
having gone off with Crusoe like a flash of lightning after a
buffalo or a deer. Dick soon proved himself to be the best
hunter of the party, and it was not long before he fulfilled
his promise to Crusoe and decorated his neck with a collar
of grizzly bear claws.

Well, when the trappers came to a river where there were
signs of beaver they called a halt, and proceeded to select a
safe and convenient spot, near wood and water, for the
camp. Here the property of the band was securely piled
in such a manner as to form a breast-work or slight for-
tification, and here Walter Cameron established head-
quarters. This was always the post of danger, being exposed
to sudden attack by prowling savages, who often dogged
the footsteps of the party in their journeyings to see what
they could steal. But Cameron was an old hand, and they
found it difficult to escape his vigilant eye.

From this point all the trappers were sent forth in small
parties every morning in various directions, some on foot
and some on horseback, according to the distances they had
to go; but they never went farther than twenty miles, as
they had to return to camp every evening.

Each trapper had ten steel traps allowed him. These he
set every night, and visited every morning, sometimes
oftener when practicable, selecting a spot in the stream
where many trees had been cut down by beavers for the
purpose of damming up the water. In some places as many
as fifty tree stumps were seen in one spot, within the compass of half an acre, all cut through at about eighteen inches
from the root. We may remark, in passing, that the beaver
is very much like a gigantic water-rat, with this marked
difference, that its tail is very broad and flat like a paddle.
The said tail is a greatly-esteemed article of food, as, indeed,

is the whole body at certain seasons of the year. The beaver's fore-legs are very small and short, and it uses its paws as hands to convey food to its mouth, sitting the while in an erect position on its hind legs and tail. Its fur is a dense coat of a greyish-coloured down, concealed by long coarse hair, which lies smooth, and is of a bright chestnut colour. Its teeth and jaws are of enormous power; with them it can cut through the branch of a tree as thick as a walking-stick at one snap, and, as we have said, it gnaws through thick trees themselves.

As soon as a tree falls, the beavers set to work industriously to lop off the branches, which, as well as the smaller trunks, they cut into lengths, according to their weight and thickness. These are then dragged by main force to the water-side, launched, and floated to their destination. Beavers build their houses, or " lodges ", under the banks of rivers and lakes, and always select those of such depth of water that there is no danger of their being frozen to the bottom. When such cannot be found, and they are compelled to build in small rivulets of insufficient depth, these clever little creatures dam up the waters until they are deep enough. The banks thrown up by them across rivulets for this purpose are of great strength, and would do credit to human engineers. Their lodges are built of sticks, mud, and stones, which form a compact mass; this freezes solid in winter, and defies the assaults of that housebreaker, the wolverine, an animal which is the beaver's implacable foe. From this lodge, which is capable often of holding four old and six or eight young ones, a communication is maintained with the water below the ice, so that, should the wolverine succeed in breaking up the lodge, he finds the family " not at home ", they having made good their retreat by the back-door. When man acts the part of housebreaker, however, he cunningly shuts the back-door *first*, by driving stakes through the ice, and thus stopping the passage. Then he enters, and, we almost regret to say, finds the family at home. We regret it, because the beaver is a gentle, peaceable, affectionate, hairy little creature, towards which one feels an irresistible tenderness. But to return from this long digression.

Our trappers, having selected their several localities, set their traps in the water, so that when the beavers roamed about at night they put their feet into them, and were caught and drowned; for although they can swim and dive admirably, they cannot live altogether under water.

Thus the different parties proceeded; and in the mornings the camp was a busy scene indeed, for then the whole were engaged in skinning the animals. The skins were always stretched, dried, folded up with the hair in the inside, and laid by; and the flesh was used for food.

But oftentimes the trappers had to go forth with the gun in one hand and their traps in the other, while they kept a sharp look-out on the bushes to guard against surprise. Despite their utmost efforts, a horse was occasionally stolen before their very eyes, and sometimes even an unfortunate trapper was murdered, and all his traps carried off.

An event of this kind occurred soon after the party had gained the western slopes of the mountains. Three Iroquois Indians, who belonged to the band of trappers, were sent to a stream about ten miles off. Having reached their destination, they all entered the water to set their traps, foolishly neglecting the usual precaution of one remaining on the bank to protect the others. They had scarcely commenced operations when three arrows were discharged into their backs, and a party of Snake Indians rushed upon and slew them, carrying away their traps and horses and scalps. This was not known for several days, when, becoming anxious about their prolonged absence, Cameron sent out a party, which found their mangled bodies affording a loathesome banquet to the wolves and vultures.

After this sad event, the trappers were more careful to go in larger parties, and keep watch.

As long as beaver were taken in abundance, the camp remained stationary; but, whenever the beaver began to grow scarce, the camp was raised, and the party moved on to another valley.

One day Dick Varley came galloping into camp with the news that there were several bears in a valley not far distant, which he was anxious not to disturb until a number of the trappers were collected together to go out and surround them.

On receiving the information, Walter Cameron shook his head.

"We have other things to do, young man," said he, "than go a-hunting after bears. I'm just about making up my mind to send off a party to search out the valley on the other side of the Blue Mountains yonder, and bring back word if there are beaver there; for if not, I mean to strike away direct south. Now, if you've a mind to go with them, you're welcome. I'll warrant you'll find enough in the way of bear-hunting to satisfy you; perhaps a little Indian hunting to boot, for if the Banattees get hold of your horses, you'll have a long hunt before you find them again. Will you go?"

"Ay, right gladly," replied Dick. "When do we start?"

"This afternoon."

Dick went off at once to his own part of the camp to replenish his powder-horn and bullet-pouch, and wipe out his rifle.

That evening the party, under command of a Canadian named Pierre, set out for the Blue Hills. They numbered twenty men, and expected to be absent three days, for they merely went to reconnoitre, not to trap. Neither Joe nor Henri was of this party, both having been out hunting when it was organized; but Crusoe and Charlie were, of course.

Pierre, although a brave and trusty man, was of a sour, angry disposition, and not a favourite with Dick; but the latter resolved to enjoy himself, and disregard his sulky comrade. Being so well mounted, he not unfrequently shot far ahead of his companions, despite their warnings that he ran great risk by so doing. On one of these occasions he and Crusoe witnessed a very singular fight, which is worthy of record.

Dick had felt a little wilder in spirit that morning than

usual, and on coming to a pretty open plain he gave the rein to Charlie, and with an "*Adieu, mes camarades*", he was out of sight in a few minutes. He rode on several miles in advance without checking speed, and then came to a wood where rapid motion was inconvenient; so he pulled up, and, dismounting, tied Charlie to a tree, while he sauntered on a short way on foot.

On coming to the edge of a small plain he observed two large birds engaged in mortal conflict. Crusoe observed them too, and would soon have put an end to the fight had Dick not checked him. Creeping as close to the belligerents as possible, he found that one was a wild turkey-cock, the other a white-headed eagle. These two stood with their heads down and all their feathers bristling for a moment; then they dashed at each other, and struck fiercely with their spurs, as our domestic cocks do, but neither fell, and the fight was continued for about five minutes without apparent advantage on either side.

Dick now observed that, from the uncertainty of its motions, the turkey-cock was blind, a discovery which caused a throb of compunction to enter his breast for standing and looking on, so he ran forward. The eagle saw him instantly, and tried to fly away, but was unable from exhaustion.

"At him, Crusoe," cried Dick, whose sympathies all lay with the other bird.

Crusoe went forward at a bound, and was met by a peck between the eyes that would have turned most dogs; but Crusoe only winked, and the next moment the eagle's career was ended.

Dick found that the turkey-cock was quite blind, the eagle having thrust out both its eyes, so, in mercy, he put an end to its sufferings.

The fight had evidently been a long and severe one, for the grass all round the spot, for about twenty yards, was beaten to the ground, and covered with the blood and feathers of the fierce combatants.

Meditating on the fight which he had just witnessed,

Dick returned towards the spot where he had left Charlie, when he suddenly missed Crusoe from his side.

" Hollo, Crusoe! here, pup! where are you?" he cried.

The only answer to this was a sharp whizzing sound, and an arrow, passing close to his ear, quivered in a tree beyond. Almost at the same moment Crusoe's angry roar was followed by a shriek from some one in fear or agony. Cocking his rifle, the young hunter sprang through the bushes towards his horse, and was just in time to save a Banattee Indian from being strangled by the dog. It had evidently scented out this fellow, and pinned him just as he was in the act of springing on the back of Charlie, for the halter was cut, and the savage lay on the ground close beside him.

Dick called off the dog, and motioned to the Indian to rise, which he did so nimbly that it was quite evident he had sustained no injury beyond the laceration of his neck by Crusoe's teeth, and the surprise.

He was a tall strong Indian for the tribe to which he belonged, so Dick proceeded to secure him at once. Pointing to his rifle and to the Indian's breast, to show what he might expect if he attempted to escape, Dick ordered Crusoe to keep him steady in that position.

The dog planted himself in front of the savage, who began to tremble for his scalp, and gazed up in his face with a look which, to say the least of it, was the reverse of amiable, while Dick went towards his horse for the purpose of procuring a piece of cord to tie him with. The Indian naturally turned his head to see what was going to be done, but a peculiar *gurgle* in Crusoe's throat made him turn it round again very smartly, and he did not venture thereafter to move a muscle.

In a few seconds Dick returned with a piece of leather and tied his hands behind his back. While this was being done the Indian glanced several times at his bow, which lay a few feet away, where it had fallen when the dog caught him; but Crusoe seemed to understand him, for he favoured him with such an additional display of teeth, and such a

low—apparently distant, almost, we might say, subter-
ranean—*rumble*, that he resigned himself to his fate.

His hands secured, a long line was attached to his neck
with a running noose, so that if he ventured to run away
the attempt would effect its own cure by producing stran-
gulation. The other end of this line was given to Crusoe,
who at the word of command marched him off, while Dick
mounted Charlie and brought up the rear.

Great was the laughter and merriment when this appari-
tion met the eyes of the trappers; but when they heard
that he had attempted to shoot Dick their ire was raised,
and a court-martial was held on the spot.

" Hang the reptile !" cried one.

" Burn him !" shouted another.

" No, no," said a third; " don't imitate them villains;
don't be cruel. Let's shoot him."

" Shoot 'im," cried Pierre. " Oui, dat is de ting; it too
goot pour lui, mais it shall be dooed."

" Don't ye think, lads, it would be better to let the poor
wretch off?" said Dick Varley; " he'd p'r'aps give a good
account 'o us to his people."

There was a universal shout of contempt at this mild
proposal. Unfortunately, few of the men sent on this
exploring expedition were imbued with the peace-making
spirit of their chief, and most of them seemed glad to have
a chance of venting their hatred of the poor Indians on this
unhappy wretch, who, although calm, looked sharply from
one speaker to another, to gather hope, if possible, from
the tones of their voices.

Dick was resolved, at the risk of a quarrel with Pierre,
to save the poor man's life, and had made up his mind to
insist on having him conducted to the camp to be tried
by Cameron, when one of the men suggested that they
should take the savage to the top of a hill about three miles
farther on, and there hang him up on a tree as a warning
to all his tribe.

" Agreed, agreed !" cried the men; " come on."

Dick, too, seemed to agree to this proposal, and hastily

ordered Crusoe to run on ahead with the savage; an order
which the dog obeyed so vigorously that, before the men
had done laughing at him, he was a couple of hundred
yards ahead of them.

"Take care that he don't get off!" cried Dick, springing
on Charlie and stretching out at a gallop.

In a moment he was beside the Indian. Scraping together
the little of the Indian language he knew, he stooped down,
and, cutting the thongs that bound him, said—

"Go! white men love the Indians."

The man cast on his deliverer one glance of surprise,
and the next moment bounded aside into the bushes and
was gone.

A loud shout from the party behind showed that this act
had been observed; and Crusoe stood with the end of the
line in his mouth, and an expression on his face that said,
"You're absolutely incomprehensible, Dick! It's all right,
I *know*, but to my feeble capacity it *seems* wrong."

"Fat for you do that?" shouted Pierre in a rage, as he
came up with a menacing look.

Dick confronted him. "The prisoner was mine. I had a
right to do with him as it liked me."

"True, true," cried several of the men who had began
to repent of their resolution, and were glad the savage was
off. "The lad's right. Get along, Pierre."

"You have no right; you vas wrong. Oui, et I have goot
vill to give you one knock on de nose."

Dick looked Pierre in the face, as he said this, in a manner
that cowed him.

"It is time," he said quietly, pointing to the sun, "to
go on. Your bourgeois expects that time won't be wasted."

Pierre muttered something in an angry tone, and wheeling
round his horse, dashed forward at full gallop, followed by
the rest of the men.

The trappers encamped that night on the edge of a wide
grassy plain, which offered such tempting food for the
horses that Pierre resolved to forego his usual cautious plan
of picketing them close to the camp, and set them loose on

the plain, merely hobbling them to prevent their straying far.

Dick remonstrated, but in vain. An insolent answer was all he got for his pains. He determined, however, to keep Charlie close beside him all night, and also made up his mind to keep a sharp look-out on the other horses.

At supper he again remonstrated.

"No 'fraid," said Pierre, whose pipe was beginning to improve his temper. "The red reptiles no dare to come in open plain when de moon so clear."

"Dun know that," said a taciturn trapper, who seldom ventured a remark of any kind; "them varmints 'ud steal the two eyes out o' you' head when they set their hearts on't."

"Dat ar' umposs'ble, for dey have no hearts," said a half-breed; "dey have von hole vere de heart vas be."

This was received with a shout of laughter, in the midst of which an appalling yell was heard, and, as if by magic, four Indians were seen on the backs of four of the best horses, yelling like fiends, and driving all the other horses furiously before them over the plain!

How they got there was a complete mystery, but the men did not wait to consider that point. Catching up their guns they sprang after them with the fury of madmen, and were quickly scattered far and wide. Dick ordered Crusoe to follow and help the men, and turned to spring on the back of Charlie; but at that moment he observed an Indian's head and shoulders rise above the grass, not fifty yards in advance from him, so without hesitation he darted forward, intending to pounce upon him.

Well would it have been for Dick Varley had he at that time possessed a little more experience of the wiles and stratagems of the Banattees. The Snake nation is sub-divided into several tribes, of which those inhabiting the Rocky Mountains, called the Banattees, are the most per-fidious. Indeed, they are confessedly the banditti of the hills, and respect neither friend nor foe, but rob all who come in their way.

Dick reached the spot where the Indian had disappeared in less than a minute, but no savage was to be seen. Thinking he had crept ahead, he ran on a few yards farther, and darted about hither and thither, while his eye glanced from side to side. Suddenly a shout in the camp attracted his attention, and looking back he beheld the savage on Charlie's back turning to fly. Next moment he was off and away far beyond the hope of recovery. Dick had left his rifle in the camp, otherwise the savage would have gone but a short way. As it was, Dick returned, and sitting down on a mound of grass, stared straight before him with a feeling akin to despair. Even Crusoe could not have helped him had he been there, for nothing on four legs, or on two, could keep pace with Charlie.

The Banattee achieved this feat by adopting a stratagem which invariably deceives those who are ignorant of their habits and tactics. When suddenly pursued the Banattee sinks into the grass, and, serpent-like, creeps along with wonderful rapidity, not *from* but *towards* his enemy, taking care, however, to avoid him, so that when the pursuer reaches the spot where the pursued is supposed to be hiding, he hears him shout a yell of defiance far away in the rear.

It was thus that the Banattee eluded Dick and gained the camp almost as soon as the other reached the spot where he had disappeared.

One by one the trappers came back weary, raging and despairing. In a short time they all assembled, and soon began to reproach each other. Ere long one or two had a fight, which resulted in several bloody noses and black eyes, thus adding to the misery which, one would think, had been bad enough without such additions. At last they finished their suppers and their pipes, and then lay down to sleep under the trees till morning, when they arose in a particularly silent and sulky mood, rolled up their blankets, strapped their things on their shoulders, and began to trudge slowly back to the camp on foot.

CHAPTER XXI

Wolves attack the horses, and Cameron circumvents the wolves—A bear-
    hunt, in which Henri shines conspicuous—Joe and the "Natter-
    list"—An alarm—A surprise and a capture.

We must now return to the camp where Walter Cameron
still guarded the goods, and the men pursued their trapping
avocations.

Here seven of the horses had been killed in one night by
wolves while grazing in a plain close to the camp, and on
the night following a horse that had strayed was also torn
to pieces and devoured. The prompt and daring manner
in which this had been done convinced the trader that
white wolves had unfortunately scented them out, and he
set several traps in the hope of capturing them.

White wolves are quite distinct from the ordinary wolves
that prowl through woods and plains in large packs. They
are much larger, weighing sometimes as much as a hundred
and thirty pounds; but they are comparatively scarce, and
move about alone, or in small bands of three or four. Their
strength is enormous, and they are so fierce that they do
not hesitate, upon occasions, to attack man himself. Their
method of killing horses is very deliberate. Two wolves
generally undertake the cold-blooded murder. They approach their victim with the most innocent-looking and
frolicsome gambols, lying down and rolling about, and
frisking presently, until the horse becomes a little accustomed to them. Then one approaches right in front, the
other in rear, still frisking playfully, until they think themselves near enough, when they make a simultaneous rush.
The wolf which approaches in rear is the true assailant;
the rush of the other is a mere feint. Then both fasten on

the poor horse's haunches, and never let go till the sinews are cut and he is rolling on his side.

The horse makes comparatively little struggle in this deadly assault; he seems paralysed, and soon falls to rise no more.

Cameron set his traps towards evening in a circle with a bait in the centre, and then retired to rest. Next morning he called Joe Blunt, and the two went off together.

" It is strange that these rascally white wolves should be so bold when the smaller kinds are so cowardly," remarked Cameron, as they walked along.

" So 'tis," replied Joe; " but I've seed them other chaps bold enough too in the prairie when they were in large packs and starvin'."

" I believe the small wolves follow the big fellows, and help them to eat what they kill, though they generally sit round and look on at the killing."

" Hist!" exclaimed Joe, cocking his gun; " there he is, an' no mistake."

There he was, undoubtedly. A wolf of the largest size with one of his feet in the trap. He was a terrible-looking object, for, besides his immense size and naturally ferocious aspect, his white hair bristled on end and was all covered with streaks and spots of blood from his bloody jaws. In his efforts to escape he had bitten the trap until he had broken his teeth and lacerated his gums, so that his appearance was hideous in the extreme. And when the two men came up he struggled with all his might to fly at them.

Cameron and Joe stood looking at him in a sort of wondering admiration.

" We'd better put a ball in him," suggested Joe after a time. " Mayhap the chain won't stand sich tugs long."

" True, Joe; if it break, we might get an ugly nip before we killed him."

So saying, Cameron fired into the wolf's head and killed it. It was found, on examination, that four wolves had been in the traps, but the rest had escaped. Two of them had gnawed off their paws and left them lying in the traps.

After this the big wolves did not trouble them again. The same afternoon a bear-hunt was undertaken, which well-nigh cost one of the Iroquois his life. It happened thus:—

While Cameron and Joe were away after the white wolves, Henri came floundering into camp tossing his arms like a maniac, and shouting that "seven bars wos be down in de bush close by"! It chanced that this was an idle day with most of the men, so they all leaped on their horses, and taking guns and knives sallied forth to give battle to the bears.

Arrived at the scene of action, they found the seven bears busily engaged in digging up roots, so the men separated in order to surround them, and then closed in. The place was partly open and partly covered with thick bushes into which a horseman could not penetrate. The moment the bears got wind of what was going forward they made off as fast as possible, and then commenced a scene of firing, galloping and yelling that defies description! Four out of the seven were shot before they gained the bushes; the other three were wounded, but made good their retreat. As their places of shelter, however, were like islands in the plain, they had no chance of escaping.

The horsemen now dismounted and dashed recklessly into the bushes, where they soon discovered and killed two of the bears; the third was not found for some time. At last an Iroquois came upon it so suddenly that he had not time to point his gun before the bear sprang upon him and struck him to the earth, where it held him down.

Instantly the place was surrounded by eager men; but the bushes were so thick, and the fallen trees among which the bear stood were so numerous, that they could not use their guns without running the risk of shooting their companions. Most of them drew their knives and seemed about to rush on the bear with these; but the monster's aspect, as it glared around, was so terrible that they held back for a moment in hesitation.

At this moment Henri, who had been at some distance engaged in the killing of one of the other bears, came rushing forward after his own peculiar manner.

" Ah! fat is eet—hay? de bar no go under yit?"

Just then his eye fell on the wounded Iroquois with the bear above him, and he uttered a yell so intense in tone that the bear himself seemed to feel that something decisive was about to be done at last. Henri did not pause, but with a flying dash he sprang like a spread eagle, arms and legs extended, right into the bear's bosom. At the same moment he sent his long hunting-knife down into its heart. But Bruin is proverbially hard to kill, and although mortally wounded, he had strength enough to open his jaws and close them on Henri's neck.

There was a cry of horror, and at the same moment a volley was fired at the bear's head; for the trappers felt that it was better to risk shooting their comrades than see them killed before their eyes. Fortunately the bullets took effect, and tumbled him over at once without doing damage to either of the men, although several of the balls just grazed Henri's temple and carried off his cap.

Although uninjured by the shot, the poor Iroquois had not escaped scathless from the paw of the bear. His scalp was torn almost off, and hung down over his eyes, while blood streamed down his face. He was conveyed by his comrades to the camp, where he lay two days in a state of insensibility, at the end of which time he revived and recovered daily. Afterwards when the camp moved he had to be carried; but in the course of two months he was as well as ever, and quite as fond of bear-hunting!

Among other trophies of this hunt there were two deer and a buffalo, which last had probably strayed from the herd. Four or five Iroquois were round this animal whetting their knives for the purpose of cutting it up when Henri passed, so he turned aside to watch them perform the operation, quite regardless of the fact that his neck and face were covered with blood which flowed from one or two small punctures made by the bear.

The Indians began by taking off the skin, which certainly did not occupy them more than five minutes. Then they cut up the meat and made a pack of it, and cut out the tongue, which is somewhat troublesome, as that member requires to be cut out from under the jaw of the animal, and not through the natural opening of the mouth. One of the fore legs was cut off at the knee joint, and this was used as a hammer with which to break the skull for the purpose of taking out the brains, these being used in the process of dressing and softening the animal's skin. An axe would have been of advantage to break the skull, but in the hurry of rushing to the attack the Indians had forgotten their axes; so they adopted the common fashion of using the buffalo's hoof as a hammer, the shank being the handle. The whole operation of flaying, cutting up, and packing the meat did not occupy more than twenty minutes. Before leaving the ground these expert butchers treated themselves to a little of the marrow and warm liver in a raw state!

Cameron and Joe walked up to the group while they were indulging in this little feast.

" Well, I've often seen that eaten, but I never could do it myself," remarked the former.

" No!" cried Joe in surprise; "now that's oncommon cur'us. I've *lived* on raw liver an' marrow-bones for two or three days at a time, when we wos chased by the Camanchee Injuns an' didn't dare to make a fire; an' it's ra'al good, it is. Won't ye try it *now*?"

Cameron shook his head.

" No, thankee; I'll not refuse when I can't help it, but until then I'll remain in happy ignorance of how good it is."

" Well, it *is* strange how some folk can't abide anything in the meat way they ha'n't bin used to. D'ye know I've actually knowed men from the cities as wouldn't eat a bit o' horseflesh for love or money. Would ye believe it?"

" I can well believe that, Joe, for I have met with such persons myself; in fact, they are rather numerous. What are you chuckling at, Joe?"

" Chucklin'? If ye mean be that ' larfin' in to myself ', it's because I'm thinkin' o' a chap as once comed out to the prairies."

" Let us walk back to the camp, Joe, and you can tell me about him as we go along."

" I think," continued Joe, " he comed from Washington, but I never could make out right whether he wos a Government man or not. Anyhow, he wos a pheelosopher—a natter-list I think he call his-self——"

" A naturalist," suggested Cameron.

" Ay, that wos more like it. Well, he wos about six feet two in his moccasins, an' as thin as a ramrod, an' as blind as a bat—leastways he had weak eyes an' wore green spectacles. He had on a grey shootin' coat an' trousers an' vest an' cap, with rid whiskers an' a long nose as rid at the point as the whiskers wos.

" Well, this gentleman engaged me an' another hunter to go a trip with him into the prairies, so off we sot one fine day on three hosses, with our blankets at our backs—we wos to depend on the rifle for victuals. At first I thought the natter-list one o' the cruellest beggars as iver went on two legs, for he used to go about everywhere pokin' pins through all the beetles an' flies an' creepin' things he could sot eyes on, an' stuck them in a box. But he told me he comed here a-purpose to git as many o' them as he could; so says I, ' If that's it, I'll fill yer box in no time.'

" ' Will ye?' says he, quite pleased like.

" ' I will,' says I, an' galloped off to a place as was filled wi' all sorts o' crawlin' things. So I sets to work, an' whenever I seed a thing crawlin' I sot my fut on it an' crushed it, an' soon filled my breast pocket. I cotched a lot o' butterflies too, an' stuffed them into my shot-pouch, an' went back in an hour or two an' showed him the lot. He put on his green spectacles an' looked at them as if he'd seen a rattlesnake.

" ' My good man,' says he, ' you've crushed them all to pieces!'

" ' They'll taste as good for all that,' says I; for somehow I'd taken't in me head that he'd heard o' the way the Injuns make soup o' the grasshoppers, an' wos wantin' to try his hand at a new dish!

" He laughed when I said this, an' told me he wos col-
lectin' them to take home to be *looked* at. But that's not
wot I was goin' to tell ye about him," continued Joe; " I
wos goin' to tell ye how we made him eat horseflesh. He
carried a revolver, too, this natter-list did, to load wi' shot
as small as dust a'most, an' shoot little birds with. I've
seed him miss birds only three feet away with it. An' one
day he drew it all of a suddent an' let fly at a big bum-bee
that wos passin', yellin' out that it wos the finest wot he
had iver seed. He missed the bee, of coorse, 'cause it wos
a flyin' shot, he said, but he sent the whole charge right into
Martin's back—Martin was my comrade's name. By good
luck Martin had on a thick leather coat, so the shot niver
got the length o' his skin.

" One day I noticed that the natter-list had stuffed small
corks into the muzzles of all the six barrels of his revolver.
I wondered what they wos for, but he wos al'ays doin' sich
queer things that I soon forgot it. ' Maybe,' thought I, jist
before it went out o' my mind—' maybe he thinks that'll
stop the pistol from goin' off by accident '; for ye must
know he'd let it off three times the first day by accident,
an' well-nigh blowed off his leg the last time, only the shot
lodged in the back o' a big toad he'd jist stuffed into his
breeches pocket. Well, soon after we shot a buffalo bull,
so when it fell, off he jumps from his horse an' runs up to it.
So did I, for I wasn't sure the beast was dead, an' I had
jist got up when it rose an' rushed at the natter-list.

" ' Out o' the way,' I yelled, for my rifle was empty; but
he didn't move, so I rushed for'ard an' drew the pistol out
o' his belt and let fly in the bull's ribs jist as it ran the poor
man down. Martin came up that moment an' put a ball
through its heart, an' then we went to pick up the natter-
list. He came to in a little, an' the first thing he said was,
' Where's my revolver?' When I gave it to him he looked
at it, an' said with a solemcholy shake o' the head, ' There's
a whole barrel-full lost!' It turned out that he had taken
to usin' the barrels for bottles to hold things in, but he
forgot to draw the charges, so sure enough I had fired a

charge o' bum-bees an' beetles an' small shot into the buffalo!

"But that's not what I wos goin' to tell ye yit. We comed to a part o' the plains where we wos well-nigh starved for want o' game, an' the natter-list got so thin that ye could a'most see through him, so I offered to kill my horse, an' cut it up for meat; but you niver saw sich a face he made. 'I'd rather die first,' says he, 'than eat it;' so we didn't kill it. But that very day Martin got a shot at a wild horse an' killed it. The natter-list was down in the bed o' a creek at the time gropin' for creepers, an' he didn't see it.

"'He'll niver eat it,' says Martin.

"'That's true,' says I.

"'Let's tell him it's a buffalo,' says he.

"'That would be tellin' a lie,' says I.

"So we stood lookin' at each other, not knowin' what to do.

"'I'll tell ye what,' cries Martin; 'we'll cut it up, and take the meat into camp an' cook it without sayin' a word.'

"'Done,' says I, 'that's it'; for ye must know the poor critter wos no judge o' meat. He couldn't tell one kind from another, an' he niver axed questions. In fact he niver a'most spoke to us all the trip. Well, we cut up the horse, an' carried the flesh an' marrow-bones into camp, takin' care to leave the hoofs and skin behind, an' sot to work an' roasted steaks an' marrow-bones.

"When the natter-list came back ye should ha' seen the joyful face he put on when he smelt the grub, for he was all but starved out, poor critter.

"'What have we got here?' cried he, rubbin' his hands an' sittin' down.

"'Steaks an' marrow-bones,' says Martin.

"'Capital!' says he. 'I'm so hungry.'

"So he fell to work like a wolf. I niver seed a man pitch into anything like as that natter-list did into that horseflesh.

"'These are first-rate marrow-bones,' says he, squintin'

with one eye down the shin-bone o' the hind leg to see if
it was quite empty.

" ' Yes, sir, they is,' answered Martin, as grave as a
judge.

" ' Take another, sir,' says I.

" ' No, thankee,' says he with a sigh, for he didn't like
to leave off.

" Well, we lived for a week on horseflesh, an' first-rate
livin' it wos; then we fell in with buffalo, an' niver ran
short again till we got to the settlements, when he paid us
our money an' shook hands, sayin' we'd had a nice trip,
an' he wished us well. Jist as we wos partin' I said, says I,
' D'ye know what it wos we lived on for a week arter we
wos well-nigh starved in the prairies?'

" ' What,' says he, ' when we got yon capital marrow-
bones?'

" ' The same,' says I. ' Yon was *horse*flesh,' says I; ' an'
I think ye'll surely niver say again that it isn't first-rate
livin'.'

" ' Ye're jokin',' says he, turnin' pale.

" ' It's true, sir; as true as ye're standin' there.'

" Well, would ye believe it, he turned—that natter-list
did—as sick as a dog on the spot wot he wos standin' on,
an' didn't taste meat again for three days!"

Shortly after the conclusion of Joe's story they reached
the camp, and here they found the women and children
flying about in a state of terror, and the few men who had
been left in charge arming themselves in the greatest haste.

" Hollo! something wrong here," cried Cameron, hasten-
ing forward, followed by Joe. " What has happened, eh?"

" Injuns comin', monsieur; look dere," answered a
trapper, pointing down the valley.

" Arm and mount at once, and come to the front of the
camp," cried Cameron, in a tone of voice that silenced every
other, and turned confusion into order.

The cause of all this outcry was a cloud of dust seen far
down the valley, which was raised by a band of mounted
Indians who approached the camp at full speed. Their

numbers could not be made out, but they were a sufficiently formidable band to cause much anxiety to Cameron, whose men, at the time, were scattered to the various trapping-grounds, and only ten chanced to be within call of the camp. However, with these ten he determined to show a bold front to the savages, whether they came as friends or foes. He therefore ordered the women and children within the citadel formed of the goods and packs of furs piled upon each other, which point of retreat was to be defended to the last extremity. Then galloping to the front he collected his men and swept down the valley at full speed. In a few minutes they were near enough to observe that the enemy only numbered four Indians, who were driving a band of about a hundred horses before them, and so busy were they in keeping the troop together that Cameron and his men were close upon them before they were observed.

It was too late to escape. Joe Blunt and Henri had already swept round and cut off their retreat. In this extremity the Indians slipped from the backs of their steeds and darted into the bushes, where they were safe from pursuit, at least on horseback, while the trappers got behind the horses and drove them towards the camp.

At this moment one of the horses sprang ahead of the others and made for the mountain, with its mane and tail flying wildly in the breeze.

"Marrow-bones and buttons!" shouted one of the men, "there goes Dick Varley's horse."

"So it am!" cried Henri, and dashed off in pursuit, followed by Joe and two others.

"Why, these are our own horses," said Cameron in surprise, as they drove them into a corner of the hills from which they could not escape.

This was true, but it was only half the truth, for, besides their own horses, they had secured upwards of seventy Indian steeds; a most acceptable addition to their stud, which, owing to casualties and wolves, had been diminishing too much of late. The fact was that the Indians who had captured the horses belonging to Pierre and his party were

a small band of robbers who had travelled, as was afterwards learned, a considerable distance from the south,
stealing horses from various tribes as they went along. As
we have seen, in an evil hour they fell in with Pierre's
party and carried off their steeds, which they drove to a
pass leading from one valley to the other. Here they
united them with the main band of their ill-gotten gains,
and while the greater number of the robbers descended
farther into the plains in search of more booty, four of
them were sent into the mountains with the horses already
procured. These four, utterly ignorant of the presence of
white men in the valley, drove their charge, as we have
seen, almost into the camp.

Cameron immediately organized a party to go out in
search of Pierre and his companions, about whose fate he
became intensely anxious, and in the course of half an
hour as many men as he could spare with safety were
dispatched in the direction of the Blue Mountains.

CHAPTER XXII

Charlie's adventures with savages and bears—Trapping life.

It is one thing to chase a horse: it is another thing to catch it. Little consideration and less sagacity are required to convince us of the truth of that fact.

The reader may perhaps venture to think this rather a trifling fact. We are not so sure of that. In this world of fancies, to have *any* fact incontestably proved and established is a comfort, and whatever is a source of comfort to mankind is worthy of notice. Surely our reader won't deny that! Perhaps he will, so we can only console ourself with the remark that there are people in this world who would deny *anything*—who would deny that there was a nose on their face if you said there was!

Well, to return to the point, which was the chase of a horse in the abstract; from which we will rapidly diverge to the chase of Dick Varley's horse in particular. This noble charger, having been ridden by savages until all his old fire and blood and mettle were worked up to a red heat, no sooner discovered that he was pursued than he gave a snort of defiance, which he accompanied with a frantic shake of his mane and a fling of contempt in addition to a magnificent wave of his tail. Then he thundered up the valley at a pace which would speedily have left Joe Blunt and Henri out of sight behind if—ay! that's the word, *if*! What a word that *if* is! what a world of *if's* we live in! There never was anything that wouldn't have been something else *if* something hadn't intervened to prevent it! Yes, we repeat, Charlie would have left his two friends miles and miles behind in what is called " no time ", *if* he had not run straight into a gorge which was surrounded by inaccessible precipices, and out of which there was no exit except by the entrance, which was immediately barred by Henri, while Joe advanced to catch the runaway.

For two hours at least did Joe Blunt essay to catch Charlie, and during that space of time he utterly failed. The horse seemed to have made up his mind for what is vulgarly termed "a lark"

"It won't do, Henri," said Joe, advancing towards his companion, and wiping his forehead with the cuff of his leathern coat; "I can't catch him. The wind's a'most blowed out o' me body."

"Dat am vexatiable," replied Henri, in a tone of commiseration. "S'pose I wos make try?"

"In that case I s'pose ye would fail. But go ahead, an' do what ye can. I'll hold yer horse."

So Henri began by a rush and a flourish of legs and arms that nearly frightened the horse out of his wits. For half an hour he went through all the complications of running and twisting of which he was capable, without success, when Joe Blunt suddenly uttered a stentorian yell that rooted him to the spot on which he stood.

To account for this, we must explain that in the heights of the Rocky Mountains vast accumulations of snow take place among the crevices and gorges during winter. Such of these masses as form on steep slopes are loosened by occasional thaws, and are precipitated in the form of avalanches into the valleys below, carrying trees and stones along with them in their thundering descent. In the gloomy gorge where Dick's horse had taken refuge the precipices were so steep that many avalanches had occurred, as was evident from the mounds of heaped snow that lay at the foot of most of them. Neither stones nor trees were carried down here, however, for the cliffs were nearly perpendicular, and the snow slipping over their edges had fallen on the grass below. Such an avalanche was now about to take place, and it was this that caused Joe to utter his cry of alarm and warning.

Henri and the horse were directly under the cliff over

which it was about to be hurled, the latter close to the wall of rock, the other at some distance away from it.

Joe cried again, "Back, Henri! back *vite*!" when the mass *flowed over* and fell with a roar like prolonged thunder. Henri sprang back in time to save his life, though he was knocked down and almost stunned; but poor Charlie was completely buried under the avalanche, which now presented the appearance of a *hill* of snow.

The instant Henri recovered sufficiently, Joe and he mounted their horses and galloped back to the camp as fast as possible.

Meanwhile, another spectator stepped forward upon the scene they had left, and surveyed the snow hill with a critical eye. This was no less than a grizzly bear, which had, unobserved, been a spectator, and which immediately proceeded to dig into the mound, with the purpose, no doubt, of disentombing the carcass of the horse for purposes of his own.

While he was thus actively engaged, the two hunters reached the camp, where they found that Pierre and his party had just arrived. The men sent out in search of them had scarcely advanced a mile when they found them trudging back to the camp in a very disconsolate manner. But all their sorrows were put to flight on hearing of the curious way in which the horses had been returned to them with interest.

Scarcely had Dick Varley, however, congratulated himself on the recovery of his gallant steed, when he was thrown into despair by the sudden arrival of Joe with the tidings of the catastrophe we have just related.

Of course there was a general rush to the rescue. Only a few men were ordered to remain to guard the camp, while the remainder mounted their horses and galloped towards the gorge where Charlie had been entombed. On arriving, they found that Bruin had worked with such laudable zeal that nothing but the tip of his tail was seen sticking out of the hole which he had dug. The hunters could not refrain from laughing as they sprang to the ground, and standing in a semicircle in front of the hole, prepared to fire. But Crusoe resolved to have the honour of leading the assault. He seized fast hold of Bruin's flank, and caused his teeth to meet therein. Caleb backed out at once and turned round, but before he could recover from his surprise a dozen bullets pierced his heart and brain.

" Now, lads," cried Cameron, setting to work with a large wooden shovel, " work like niggers. If there's any life left in the horse, it'll soon be smothered out unless we set him free."

The men needed no urging, however. They worked as if their lives depended on their exertions. Dick Varley, in particular, laboured like a young Hercules, and Henri hurled masses of snow about in a most surprising manner. Crusoe, too, entered heartily into the spirit of the work, and, scraping with his forepaws, sent such a continuous shower of snow behind him that he was speedily lost to view in a hole of his own excavating. In the course of half an hour a cavern was dug in the mound almost close up to the cliff, and the men were beginning to look about for the crushed body of Dick's steed, when an exclamation from Henri attracted their attention.

" Ha ! mes ami, here am be one hole."

The truth of this could not be doubted, for the eccentric trapper had thrust his shovel through the wall of snow into what appeared to be a cavern beyond, and immediately followed up his remark by thrusting in his head and shoulders. He drew them out in a few seconds, with a look of intense amazement.

" Voilà ! Joe Blunt. Look in dere, and you shall see fat you vill behold."

" Why, it's the horse, I do b'lieve !" cried Joe. " Go ahead, lads !"

So saying, he resumed his shovelling vigorously, and in a few minutes the hole was opened up sufficiently to enable a man to enter. Dick sprang in, and there stood Charlie close beside the cliff, looking as sedate and unconcerned as if all that had been going on had no reference to him whatever.

The cause of his safety was simple enough. The precipice beside which he stood when the avalanche occurred over-hung its base at that point considerably, so that when the snow descended a clear space of several feet wide was left all along its base. Here Charlie had remained in perfect comfort until his friends dug him out.

Congratulating themselves not a little on having saved the charger and bagged a grizzly bear, the trappers re-mounted, and returned to the camp.

For some time after this nothing worthy of particular note occurred. The trapping operations went on prosperously and without interruption from the Indians, who seemed to have left the locality altogether. During this period, Dick, and Crusoe, and Charlie had many excursions together, and the silver rifle full many a time sent death to the heart of bear, and elk, and buffalo; while, indirectly, it sent joy to the heart of man, woman, and child in camp, in the shape of juicy steaks and marrow-bones. Joe and Henri devoted themselves almost exclusively to trapping beaver, in which pursuit they were so successful that they speedily became wealthy men, according to backwood notions of wealth. With the beaver that they caught they purchased from Cameron's store powder and shot enough for a long hunting expedition, and a couple of spare horses to carry their packs. They also purchased a large assortment of such goods and trinkets as would prove acceptable to Indians, and supplied themselves with new blankets, and a few pairs of strong moccasins, of which they stood much in need.

Thus they went on from day to day, until symptoms of the approach of winter warned them that it was time to return to the Mustang Valley. About this time an event occurred which totally changed the aspect of affairs in these remote valleys of the Rocky Mountains, and pre-cipitated the departure of our four friends, Dick, Joe, Henri, and Crusoe. This was the sudden arrival of a whole tribe of Indians. As their advent was somewhat remarkable, we shall devote to it the commencement of a new chapter.

CHAPTER XXIII

One day Dick Varley was out on a solitary hunting expedition near the rocky gorge where his horse had received temporary burial a week or two before. Crusoe was with him, of course. Dick had tied Charlie to a tree, and was sunning himself on the edge of a cliff, from the top of which he had a fine view of the valley and the rugged precipices that hemmed it in.

Just in front of the spot on which he sat, the precipices on the opposite side of the gorge rose to a considerable height above him, so that their ragged outlines were drawn sharply across the clear sky. Dick was gazing in dreamy silence at the jutting rocks and dark caverns, and speculating on the probable number of bears that dwelt there, when a slight degree of restlessness on the part of Crusoe attracted him.

" What is't, pup?" said he, laying his hand on the dog's broad back.

Crusoe looked the answer, " I don't know, Dick, but it's *something*, you may depend upon it, else I would not have disturbed you."

Dick lifted his rifle from the ground, and laid it in the hollow of his left arm.

" There must be something in the wind," remarked Dick.

As wind is known to be composed of two distinct gases, Crusoe felt perfectly safe in replying " Yes " with his tail. Immediately after he added " Hollo! did you hear that?" with his ears.

Dick did hear it, and sprang hastily to his feet, as a sound like, yet unlike, distant thunder came faintly down upon the breeze. In a few seconds the sound increased to a roar in which was mingled the wild cries of men. Neither Dick nor Crusoe moved, for the sounds came from behind the heights in front of them, and they felt that the only way to solve the question, "What can the sounds be?" was to wait till the sounds should solve it themselves.

Suddenly the muffled sounds gave place to the distinct bellowing of cattle, the clatter of innumerable hoofs, and the yells of savage men, while at the same moment the edges of the opposite cliffs became alive with Indians and buffaloes rushing about in frantic haste—the former almost mad with savage excitement, the latter with blind rage and terror.

On reaching the edge of the dizzy precipice, the buffaloes turned abruptly and tossed their ponderous heads as they coursed along the edge. Yet a few of them, unable to check their headlong course, fell over, and were dashed to pieces on the rocks below. Such falls, Dick observed, were hailed with shouts of delight by the Indians, whose sole object evidently was to enjoy the sport of driving the terrified animals over the precipice. The wily savages had chosen their ground well for this purpose.

The cliff immediately opposite to Dick Varley was a huge projection from the precipice that hemmed in the gorge— a species of cape or promontory several hundred yards wide at the base, and narrowing abruptly to a point. The sides of this wedge-shaped projection were quite perpendicular,— indeed, in some places the top overhung the base,—and they were at least three hundred feet high. Broken and jagged rocks, of that peculiarly chaotic character which probably suggested the name to this part of the great American chain, projected from and were scattered all round the cliffs. Over these the Indians, whose numbers increased every moment, strove to drive the luckless herd of buffaloes that had chanced to fall in their way. The task was easy. The unsuspecting animals, of which there were hundreds, rushed in a dense mass upon the cape referred to. On they came with irresistible impetuosity, bellowing furiously, while their hoofs thundered on the turf with the muffled continuous roar of a distant but mighty cataract; the Indians, meanwhile, urging them on by hideous yells and frantic gestures.

The advance-guard came bounding madly to the edge of the precipice. Here they stopped short, and gazed affrighted at the gulf below. It was but for a moment. The irresistible momentum of the flying mass behind pushed them over. Down they came, absolutely a living cataract, upon the rocks below. Some struck on the projecting rocks in the descent, and their bodies were dashed almost in pieces, while their blood spurted out in showers. Others leaped from rock to rock with awful bounds, until, losing their foot-hold, they fell headlong; while others descended sheer down into the sweltering mass that lay shattered at the base of the cliffs.

Dick Varley and his dog remained rooted to the rock, as they gazed at the sickening sight, as if petrified. Scarce fifty of that noble herd of buffaloes escaped the awful leap, but they escaped only to fall before the arrows of their ruthless pursuers. Dick had often heard of this tendency of the Indians, where buffaloes were very numerous, to drive them over precipices in mere wanton sport and cruelty, but he had never seen it until now, and the sight filled his soul with horror. It was not until the din and tumult of the perishing herd and the shrill yells of the Indians had almost died away that he turned to quit the spot. But the instant he did so another shout was raised. The savages had observed him, and were seen galloping along the cliffs towards the head of the gorge, with the obvious intention of gaining the other side and capturing him. Dick sprang on Charlie's back, and the next instant was flying down the valley towards the camp.

He did not, however, fear being overtaken, for the gorge could not be crossed, and the way round the head of it was long and rugged; but he was anxious to alarm the camp as quickly as possible, so that they might have time to call in the more distant trappers and make preparations for defence.

"Where away now, youngster?" inquired Cameron, emerging from his tent as Dick, taking the brook that flowed in front at a flying leap, came crashing through the bushes into the midst of the fur-packs at full speed.

"Injuns!" ejaculated Dick, reining up, and vaulting out of the saddle. "Hundreds of 'em. Fiends incarnate every one!"

"Are they near?"

"Yes; an hour'll bring them down on us. Are Joe and Henri far from camp to-day?"

"At Ten-mile Creek," replied Cameron with an expression of bitterness, as he caught up his gun and shouted to several men, who hurried up on seeing our hero burst into camp.

"Ten-mile Creek!" muttered Dick. "I'll bring 'em in, though," he continued, glancing at several of the camp horses that grazed close at hand.

In another moment he was on Charlie's back, the line of one of the best horses was in his hand, and almost before Cameron knew what he was about he was flying down the valley like the wind. Charlie often stretched out at full speed to please his young master, but seldom had he been urged forward as he was upon this occasion. The led horse, being light and wild, kept well up, and in a marvellously short space of time they were at Ten-mile Creek.

"Hollo, Dick, wot's to do?" inquired Joe Blunt, who was up to his knees in the water setting a trap at the moment his friend galloped up.

"Injuns! Where's Henri?" demanded Dick.

"At the head o' the dam there."

Dick was off in a moment, and almost instantly returned with Henri galloping beside him.

No word was spoken. In time of action these men did not waste words. During Dick's momentary absence, Joe Blunt had caught up his rifle and examined the priming, so that when Dick pulled up beside him he merely laid his hand on the saddle, saying, "All right!" as he vaulted on Charlie's back behind his young companion. In another moment they were away at full speed. The mustang seemed to feel that unwonted exertions were required of him. Double weighted though he was, he kept well up with the other horse, and in less than two hours after Dick's leaving the camp the three hunters came in sight of it.

Meanwhile Cameron had collected nearly all his forces and put his camp in a state of defence before the Indians arrived, which they did suddenly, and, as usual, at full gallop, to the amount of at least two hundred. They did not at first seem disposed to hold friendly intercourse with the trappers, but assembled in a semicircle round the camp in a menacing attitude, while one of their chiefs stepped forward to hold a palaver. For some time the conversation on both sides was polite enough, but by degrees the Indian chief assumed an imperious tone, and demanded gifts from the trappers, taking care to enforce his request by hinting that thousands of his countrymen were not far distant. Cameron stoutly refused, and the palaver threatened to come to an abrupt and unpleasant termination just at the time that Dick and his friends appeared on the scene of action.

The brook was cleared at a bound; the three hunters leaped from their steeds and sprang to the front with a degree of energy that had a visible effect on the savages; and Cameron, seizing the moment, proposed that the two parties should smoke a pipe and hold a council. The Indians agreed, and in a few minutes they were engaged in animated and friendly intercourse. The speeches were long, and the compliments paid on either side were inflated, and, we fear, undeserved; but the result of the interview was, that Cameron made the Indians a present of tobacco and a few trinkets, and sent them back to their friends to tell them that he was willing to trade with them.

Next day the whole tribe arrived in the valley, and pitched their deer-skin tents on the plain opposite to the camp of the white men. Their numbers far exceeded

Cameron's expectation, and it was with some anxiety that he proceeded to strengthen his fortifications as much as circumstances and the nature of the ground would admit.

The Indian camp, which numbered upwards of a thousand souls, was arranged with great regularity, and was divided into three distinct sections, each section being composed of a separate tribe. The Great Snake nation at that time embraced three tribes or divisions—namely, the Shirry-dikas, or dog-eaters; the War-are-ree-kas, or fish-eaters; and the Banattees, or robbers. These were the most numerous and powerful Indians on the west side of the Rocky Mountains. The Shirry-dikas dwelt in the plains, and hunted the buffaloes; dressed well; were cleanly; rich in horses; bold, independent, and good warriors. The War-are-ree-kas lived chiefly by fishing, and were found on the banks of the rivers and lakes throughout the country. They were more corpulent, slovenly, and indolent than the Shirry-dikas, and more peaceful. The Banattees, as we have before mentioned, were the robbers of the mountains. They were a wild and contemptible race, and at enmity with every one. In summer they went about nearly naked. In winter they clothed themselves in the skins of rabbits and wolves. Being excellent mimics, they could imitate the howling of wolves, the neighing of horses, and the cries of birds, by which means they could approach travellers, rob them, and then fly to their rocky fastnesses in the mountains, where pursuit was vain.

Such were the men who now assembled in front of the camp of the fur-traders, and Cameron soon found that the news of his presence in the country had spread far and wide among the natives, bringing them to the neighbourhood of his camp in immense crowds, so that during the next few days their numbers increased to thousands.

Several long palavers quickly ensued between the Red-men and the White, and the two great chiefs who seemed to hold despotic rule over the assembled tribes were extremely favourable to the idea of universal peace which was propounded to them. In several set speeches of great length and very considerable power, these natural orators explained their willingness to enter into amicable relations with all the surrounding nations, as well as with the white men.

"But," said Pee-eye-em, the chief of the Shirry-dikas, a man above six feet high, and of immense muscular strength —"but my tribe cannot answer for the Banattees, who are robbers, and cannot be punished, because they dwell in scattered families among the mountains. The Banattees are bad; they cannot be trusted."

None of the Banattees were present at the council when this was said; and if they had been it would have mattered little, for they were neither fierce nor courageous, although bold enough in their own haunts to murder and rob the unwary.

The second chief did not quite agree with Pee-eye-em. He said that it was impossible for them to make peace with their natural enemies, the Peigans and the Blackfeet on the east side of the mountains. It was very desirable, he admitted; but neither of these tribes would consent to it, he felt sure.

Upon this Joe Blunt rose and said, "The great chief of the War-are-ree-kas is wise, and knows that enemies cannot be reconciled unless deputies are sent to make proposals of peace."

"The Pale-face does not know the Blackfeet," answered the chief. "Who will go into the lands of the Blackfeet? My young men have been sent once and again, and their scalps are now fringes to the leggings of their enemies. The War-are-ree-kas do not cross the mountains but for the purpose of making war."

"The chief speaks truth," returned Joe; "yet there are three men round the council fire who will go to the Blackfeet and the Peigans with messages of peace from the Snakes if they wish it."

Joe pointed to himself, Henri, and Dick as he spoke, and added, "We three do not belong to the camp of the fur-traders; we only lodge with them for a time. The Great Chief of the White men has sent us to make peace with the Red-men, and to tell them that he desires to trade with them—to exchange hatchets, and guns, and blankets for furs."

This declaration interested the two chiefs greatly, and after a good deal of discussion they agreed to take advantage of Joe Blunt's offer, and appoint him as a deputy to the court of their enemies. Having arranged these matters to their satisfaction, Cameron bestowed a red flag and a blue surtout with brass buttons on each of the chiefs, and a variety of smaller articles on the other members of the council, and sent them away in a particularly amiable frame of mind.

Pee-eye-em burst the blue surtout at the shoulders and elbows putting it on, as it was much too small for his gigantic frame; but never having seen such an article of apparel before, he either regarded this as the natural and proper consequence of putting it on, or was totally indifferent to it, for he merely looked at the rents with a smile of satisfaction, while his squaw surreptitiously cut off the two back buttons and thrust them into her bosom.

By the time the council closed the night was far advanced, and a bright moon was shedding a flood of soft light over the picturesque and busy scene.

" I'll go to the Injun camp," said Joe to Walter Cameron, as the chiefs rose to depart. " The season's far enough advanced already; it's time to be off; and if I'm to speak for the Red-skins in the Blackfeet Council, I'd need to know what to say "

" Please yourself, Master Blunt," answered Cameron. " I like your company and that of your friends, and if it suited you I would be glad to take you along with us to the coast of the Pacific; but your mission among the Indians is a good one, and I'll help it on all I can.—I suppose you will go also?" he added, turning to Dick Varley, who was still seated beside the council fire caressing Crusoe.

" Wherever Joe goes, I go," answered Dick.

Crusoe's tail, ears, and eyes demonstrated high approval of the sentiment involved in this speech.

" And your friend Henri?"

" He goes too," answered Joe. " It's as well that the
Red-skins should see the three o' us before we start for the
east side o' the mountains.—Ho, Henri! come here, lad."

Henri obeyed, and in a few seconds the three friends
crossed the brook to the Indian camp, and were guided to
the principal lodge by Pee-eye-em. Here a great council
was held, and the proposed attempt at negotiations for
peace with their ancient enemies fully discussed. While they
were thus engaged, and just as Pee-eye-em had, in the
energy of an enthusiastic peroration, burst the blue surtout
almost up to the collar, a distant rushing sound was heard,
which caused every man to spring to his feet, run out of the
tent, and seize his weapons.

" What can it be, Joe?" whispered Dick as they stood
at the tent door leaning on their rifles, and listening intently.

" Dun'no'," answered Joe shortly.

Most of the numerous fires of the camp had gone out,
but the bright moon revealed the dusky forms of thousands
of Indians, whom the unwonted sound had startled, moving
rapidly about.

The mystery was soon explained. The Indian camp was
pitched on an open plain of several miles in extent, which
took a sudden bend half-a-mile distant, where a spur of the
mountains shut out the farther end of the valley from view.
From beyond this point the dull rumbling sound proceeded.
Suddenly there was a roar as if a mighty cataract had been
let loose upon the scene. At the same moment a countless
herd of wild horses came thundering round the base of the
mountain and swept over the plain straight towards the
Indian camp.

" A stampede!" cried Joe, springing to the assistance of
Pee-eye-em, whose favourite horses were picketed near the
tent.

On they came like a living torrent, and the thunder of a
thousand hoofs was soon mingled with the howling of
hundreds of dogs in the camp, and the yelling of Indians,
as they vainly endeavoured to restrain the rising excitement

of their steeds. Henri and Dick stood rooted to the ground, gazing in silent wonder at the fierce and uncontrollable gallop of the thousands of panic-stricken horses that bore down upon the camp with the tumultuous violence of a mighty cataract.

As the maddened troop drew nigh, the camp horses began to snort.and tremble violently, and when the rush of the wild steeds was almost upon them, they became ungovernable with terror, broke their halters and hobbles, and dashed wildly about. To add to the confusion at that moment, a cloud passed over the moon and threw the whole scene into deep obscurity. Blind with terror, which was probably increased by the din of their own mad flight, the galloping troop came on, and with a sound like the continuous roar of thunder that for an instant drowned the yell of dog and man they burst upon the camp, trampling over packs and skins, and dried meat, etc., in their headlong speed, and overturning several of the smaller tents. In another moment they swept out upon the plain beyond, and were soon lost in the darkness of the night, while the yelping of dogs, as they vainly pursued them, mingled and gradually died away with the distant thunder of their retreat.

This was a *stampede*, one of the most extraordinary scenes that can be witnessed in the western wilderness.

" Lend a hand, Henri," shouted Joe, who was struggling with a powerful horse. ' Wot's comed over yer brains, man? This brute'll git off if you don't look sharp."

Dick and Henri both answered to the summons, and they succeeded in throwing the struggling animal on its side and holding it down until its excitement was somewhat abated. Pee-eye-em had also been successful in securing his favourite hunter; but nearly every other horse belonging to the camp had broken loose and joined the whirlwind gallop. But they gradually dropped out, and before morning the most of them were secured by their owners. As there were at least two thousand horses and an equal number of dogs in the part of the Indian camp which had been thus overrun by the wild mustangs, the turmoil, as may be imagined, was prodigious! Yet, strange to say, no accident of a serious nature occurred beyond the loss of several chargers.

In the midst of this exciting scene there was one heart which beat with a nervous vehemence that well-nigh burst it. This was the heart of Dick Varley's horse, Charlie. Well known to him was that distant rumbling sound that floated on the night air into the fur-trader's camp, where he was picketed close to Cameron's tent. Many a time had he heard the approach of such a wild troop, and often, in days not long gone by, had his shrill neigh rung out as he joined and led the panic-stricken band. He was first to hear the sound, and by his restive actions to draw the attention of the fur-traders to it. As a precautionary measure they all sprang up and stood by their horses to soothe them; but as a brook with a belt of bushes and a quarter of a mile of plain intervened between their camp and the mustangs as they flew past, they had little or no trouble in restraining them. Not so, however, with Charlie. At the very moment that his master was congratulating himself on the supposed security of his position, he wrenched the halter from the hand of him who held it, burst through the barrier of felled trees that had been thrown round the camp, cleared the brook at a bound, and with a wild hilarious neigh resumed his old place in the ranks of the free-born mustangs of the prairie.

Little did Dick think, when the flood of horses swept past him, that his own good steed was there, rejoicing in his recovered liberty. But Crusoe knew it. Ay, the wind had borne down the information to his acute nose before the living storm burst upon the camp; and when Charlie rushed past, with the long tough halter trailing at his heels, Crusoe sprang to his side, seized the end of the halter with his teeth, and galloped off along with him.

It was a long gallop and a tough one, but Crusoe held on, for it was a settled principle in his mind *never* to give in. At first the check upon Charlie's speed was imperceptible, but by degrees the weight of the gigantic dog began to

tell, and after a time they fell a little to the rear; then by
good fortune the troop passed through a mass of underwood,
and the line getting entangled brought their mad career
forcibly to a close; the mustangs passed on, and the two
friends were left to keep each other company in the dark.

How long they would have remained thus is uncertain,
for neither of them had sagacity enough to undo a com-
plicated entanglement. Fortunately, however, in his energetic tugs at the line, Crusoe's sharp teeth partially severed
it, and a sudden start on the part of Charlie caused it to
part. Before he could escape, Crusoe again seized the end
of it, and led him slowly but steadily back to the Indian
camp, never halting or turning aside until he had placed
the line in Dick Varley's hand.

"Hollo, pup! where have ye bin? How did ye bring
him here?" exclaimed Dick, as he gazed in amazement at
his foam-covered horse.

Crusoe wagged his tail, as if to say, "Be thankful that
you've got him, Dick, my boy, and don't ask questions
that you know I can't answer."

"He must ha' broke loose and jined the stampede,"
remarked Joe, coming out of the chief's tent at the moment;
"but tie him up, Dick, and come in, for we want to settle
about startin' to-morrow or nixt day."

Having fastened Charlie to a stake, and ordered Crusoe
to watch him, Dick re-entered the tent where the council
had re-assembled, and where Pee-eye-em—having, in the
recent struggle, split the blue surtout completely up to the
collar, so that his backbone was visible throughout the
greater part of its length—was holding forth in eloquent
strains on the subject of peace in general and peace with
the Blackfeet, the ancient enemies of the Shirry-dikas, in
particular.

CHAPTER XXIV

On the following day the Indians gave themselves up to
unlimited feasting, in consequence of the arrival of a large
body of hunters with an immense supply of buffalo meat.
It was a regular day of rejoicing. Upwards of six hundred
buffaloes had been killed, and as the supply of meat before
their arrival had been ample, the camp was now overflowing with plenty. Feasts were given by the chiefs, and
the medicine men went about the camp uttering loud cries,
which were meant to express gratitude to the Great Spirit
for the bountiful supply of food. They also carried a portion
of meat to the aged and infirm who were unable to hunt
for themselves, and had no young men in their family circle
to hunt for them.

This arrival of the hunters was a fortunate circumstance,
as it put the Indians in great good-humour, and inclined
them to hold friendly intercourse with the trappers, who for
some time continued to drive a brisk trade in furs. Having
no market for the disposal of their furs, the Indians of
course had more than they knew what to do with, and
were therefore glad to exchange those of the most beautiful
and valuable kind for a mere trifle, so that the trappers
laid aside their traps for a time and devoted themselves to
traffic.

Meanwhile Joe Blunt and his friends made preparations
for their return journey.

" Ye see," remarked Joe to Henri and Dick, as they sat
beside the fire in Pee-eye-em's lodge, and feasted on a potful
of grasshopper soup, which the great chief's squaw had just
placed before them—" ye see, my calc'lations is as follows.

Wot with trappin' beavers and huntin', we three ha' made enough to sot us up, an it likes us, in the Mustang Valley——"

"Ha!" interrupted Dick, remitting for a few seconds the use of his teeth in order to exercise his tongue—"ha! Joe, but it don't like *me*! What, give up a hunter's life and become a farmer? I should think not!"

"Bon!" ejaculated Henri, but whether the remark had reference to the grasshopper soup or the sentiment we cannot tell.

"Well," continued Joe, commencing to devour a large buffalo steak with a hunter's appetite, "ye'll please yourselves, lads, as to that; but as I wos sayin', we've got a powerful lot o' furs, an' a big pack o' odds and ends for the Injuns we chance to meet with by the way, an' powder and lead to last us a twelvemonth, besides five good horses to carry us an' our packs over the plains; so if it's agreeable to you, I mean to make a bee-line for the Mustang Valley. We're pretty sure to meet with Blackfeet on the way, and if we do we'll try to make peace between them an' the Snakes. I 'xpect it'll be pretty well on for six weeks afore we git to home, so we'll start to-morrow."

"Dat is fat vill do ver' vell," said Henri; "vill you please donnez me one petit morsel of steak."

"I'm ready for anything, Joe," cried Dick; "you are leader. Just point the way, and I'll answer for two o' us followin' ye—eh! won't we, Crusoe?"

"We will," remarked the dog quietly.

"How comes it," inquired Dick, "that these Indians don't care for our tobacco?"

"They like their own better, I s'pose," answered Joe; "most all the western Injuns do. They make it o' the dried leaves o' the shumack and the inner bark o' the red-willow, chopped very small an' mixed together. They call this stuff *kinnekinnik*; but they like to mix about a fourth o' our tobacco with it, so Pee-eye-em tells me, an' he's a good judge. The amount that red-skinned mortal smokes *is* oncommon."

"What are they doin' yonder?" inquired Dick, pointing

to a group of men who had been feasting for some time past in front of a tent within sight of our trio.

" Goin' to sing, I think," replied Joe.

As he spoke six young warriors were seen to work their bodies about in a very remarkable way, and give utterance to still more remarkable sounds, which gradually increased until the singers burst out into that terrific yell, or war-whoop, for which American savages have long been famous. Its effect would have been appalling to unaccustomed ears. Then they allowed their voices to die away in soft, plain-tive tones, while their action corresponded thereto. Sud-denly the furious style was revived, and the men wrought themselves into a condition little short of madness, while their yells rang wildly through the camp. This was too much for ordinary canine nature to withstand, so all the dogs in the neighbourhood joined in the horrible chorus.

Crusoe had long since learned to treat the eccentricities of Indians and their curs with dignified contempt. He paid no attention to this serenade, but lay sleeping by the fire until Dick and his companions rose to take leave of their host and return to the camp of the fur-traders. The re-mainder of that night was spent in making preparations for setting forth on the morrow; and when, at grey dawn, Dick and Crusoe lay down to snatch a few hours' repose, the yells and howling in the Snake camp were going on as vigorously as ever.

The sun had arisen, and his beams were just tipping the summits of the Rocky Mountains, causing the snowy peaks to glitter like flame, and the deep ravines and gorges to look sombre and mysterious by contrast, when Dick and Joe and Henri mounted their gallant steeds, and, with Crusoe gambolling before, and the two packhorses trotting by their side, turned their faces eastward, and bade adieu to the Indian camp.

Crusoe was in great spirits. He was perfectly well aware that he and his companions were on their way home, and testified his satisfaction by bursts of scampering over the hills and valleys. Doubtless he thought of Dick Varley's cottage, and of Dick's mild, kind-hearted mother. Undoubtedly, too, he thought of his own mother, Fan, and felt a glow of filial affection as he did so. Of this we feel quite certain. He would have been unworthy the title of hero if he hadn't. Perchance he thought of Grumps, but of this we are not quite so sure. We rather think, upon the whole, that he did.

Dick, too, let his thoughts run away in the direction of *home*. Sweet word! Those who have never left it cannot, by any effort of imagination, realize the full import of the word "home". Dick was a bold hunter; but he was young, and this was his first long expedition. Oftentimes, when sleeping under the trees and gazing dreamily up through the branches at the stars, had he thought of home, until his longing heart began to yearn to return. He repelled such tender feelings, however, when they became too strong, deeming them unmanly, and sought to turn his mind to the excitements of the chase; but latterly his efforts were in vain. He became thoroughly home-sick, and while admitting the fact to himself, he endeavoured to conceal it from his comrades. He thought that he was successful in this attempt. Poor Dick Varley! As yet he was sadly ignorant of human nature. Henri knew it, and Joe Blunt knew it. Even Crusoe knew that something was wrong with his master, although he could not exactly make out what it was. But Crusoe made memoranda in the note-book of his memory. He jotted down the peculiar phases of his master's new disease with the care and minute exactness of a physician, and, we doubt not, ultimately added the knowledge of the symptoms of home-sickness to his already well-filled stores of erudition.

It was not till they had set out on their homeward journey that Dick Varley's spirits revived, and it was not till they reached the beautiful prairies on the eastern slopes of the Rocky Mountains, and galloped over the greensward towards the Mustang Valley, that Dick ventured to tell Joe Blunt what his feelings had been.

"D'ye know, Joe," he said confidentially, reining up his

gallant steed after a sharp gallop—"d'ye know I've bin feelin' awful low for some time past."

"I know it, lad," answered Joe, with a quiet smile, in which there was a dash of something that implied he knew more than he chose to express.

Dick felt surprised, but he continued, "I wonder what it could have bin. I never felt so before."

"'Twas home-sickness, boy," returned Joe.

"How d'ye know that?"

"The same way as how I know most things—by experience an' observation. I've bin home-sick myself once, but it was long, long agone."

Dick felt much relieved at this candid confession by such a bronzed veteran, and, the chords of sympathy having been struck, he opened up his heart at once, to the evident delight of Henri, who, among other curious partialities, was extremely fond of listening to and taking part in conversations that bordered on the metaphysical, and were hard to be understood. Most conversations that were not connected with eating and hunting were of this nature to Henri.

"Hom'-sik," he cried, "veech mean bein' sik of hom'! Hah! dat is fat I am always be, ven I goes hout on de expedition. Oui, vraiment."

"I always packs up," continued Joe, paying no attention to Henri's remark—"I always packs up an' sots off for home when I gits home-sick. It's the best cure; an' when hunters are young like you, Dick, it's the only cure. I've knowed fellers a'most die o' home-sickness, an' I'm told they *do* go under altogether sometimes."

"Go onder!" exclaimed Henri; "oui, I vas all but die myself ven I fust try to git away from hom'. If I have not git away, I not be here to-day."

Henri's idea of home-sickness was so totally opposed to theirs that his comrades only laughed, and refrained from attempting to set him right.

"The fust time I wos took bad with it wos in a country somethin' like that," said Joe, pointing to the wide stretch of undulating prairie, dotted with clusters of trees and meandering streamlets, that lay before them. " I had bin out about two months, an' was makin' a good thing of it, for game wos plenty, when I began to think somehow more than usual o' home. My mother wos alive then."

Joe's voice sank to a deep, solemn tone as he said this, and for a few minutes he rode on in silence.

" Well, it grew worse and worse. I dreamed o' home all night an' thought of it all day, till I began to shoot bad, an' my comrades wos gittin' tired o' me; so says I to them one night, says I, ' I give out, lads; I'll make tracks for the settlement to-morrow. They tried to laugh me out of it at first, but it was no go, so I packed up, bid them good-day, an' sot off alone on a trip o' five hundred miles. The very first mile o' the way back I began to mend, and before two days I wos all right again."

Joe was interrupted at this point by the sudden appearance of a solitary horseman on the brow of an eminence not half-a-mile distant. The three friends instantly drove their pack-horses behind a clump of trees, but not in time to escape the vigilant eye of the Red-man, who uttered a loud shout, which brought up a band of his comrades at full gallop.

"Remember, Henri," cried Joe Blunt, " our errand is one of *peace*."

The caution was needed, for in the confusion of the moment Henri was making preparation to sell his life as dearly as possible. Before another word could be uttered, they were surrounded by a troop of about twenty yelling Blackfeet Indians. They were, fortunately, not a war party, and, still more fortunately, they were peaceably disposed, and listened to the preliminary address of Joe Blunt with exemplary patience; after which the two parties encamped on the spot, the council fire was lighted, and every preparation made for a long palaver.

We will not trouble the reader with the details of what was said on this occasion. The party of Indians was a small one, and no chief of any importance was attached to it. Suffice it to say that the pacific overtures made by Joe were well received, the trifling gifts made thereafter were still better received, and they separated with mutual expressions of goodwill.

Several other bands which were afterwards met with were equally friendly, and only one war party was seen. Joe's quick eye observed it in time to enable them to retire unseen behind the shelter of some trees, where they remained until the Indian warriors were out of sight.

The next party they met with, however, were more difficult to manage, and, unfortunately, blood was shed on both sides before our travellers escaped.

It was at the close of a beautiful day that a war party of Blackfeet were seen riding along a ridge on the horizon. It chanced that the prairie at this place was almost destitute of trees or shrubs large enough to conceal the horses. By dashing down the grassy wave into the hollow between the two undulations, and dismounting, Joe hoped to elude the savages, so he gave the word; but at the same moment a shout from the Indians told that they were discovered.

"Look sharp, lads! throw down the packs on the highest point of the ridge," cried Joe, undoing the lashings, seizing one of the bales of goods, and hurrying to the top of the undulation with it; "we must keep them at arm's-length, boys—be alive! War parties are not to be trusted."

Dick and Henri seconded Joe's efforts so ably that in the course of two minutes the horses were unloaded, the packs piled in the form of a wall in front of a broken piece of ground, the horses picketed close beside them, and our three travellers peeping over the edge, with their rifles cocked, while the savages—about thirty in number—came sweeping down towards them.

"I'll try to git them to palaver," said Joe Blunt; "but keep yer eye on 'em, Dick, an' if they behave ill, shoot the *horse* o' the leadin' chief. I'll throw up my left hand as a signal. Mind, lad, don't hit human flesh till my second signal is given, and see that Henri don't draw till I git back to ye."

So saying, Joe sprang lightly over the slight parapet of their little fortress, and ran swiftly out, unarmed, towards the Indians. In a few seconds he was close up with them, and in another moment was surrounded. At first the savages brandished their spears and rode round the solitary man, yelling like fiends, as if they wished to intimidate him; but as Joe stood like a statue, with his arms crossed, and a grave expression of contempt on his countenance, they quickly desisted, and, drawing near, asked him where he came from, and what he was doing there.

Joe's story was soon told; but instead of replying, they began to shout vociferously, and evidently meant mischief.

" If the Blackfeet are afraid to speak to the Pale-face, he will go back to his braves," said Joe, passing suddenly between two of the warriors and taking a few steps towards the camp.

Instantly every bow was bent, and it seemed as if our bold hunter were about to be pierced by a score of arrows, when he turned round and cried—

" The Blackfeet must not advance a single step. The first that moves his *horse* shall die. The second that moves *himself* shall die."

To this the Blackfeet chief replied scornfully. " The Pale-face talks with a big mouth. We do not believe his words. The Snakes are liars; we will make no peace with them."

While he was yet speaking, Joe threw up his hand; there was a loud report; and the noble horse of the savage chief lay struggling in death agony on the ground.

The use of the rifle, as we have before hinted, was little known at this period among the Indians of the far west, and many had never heard the dreaded report before, although all were aware, from hearsay, of its fatal power. The fall of the chief's horse, therefore, quite paralysed them for a few moments, and they had not recovered from their surprise when a second report was heard, a bullet whistled past, and a second horse fell. At the same moment there was a loud explosion in the camp of the Pale-faces, a white cloud enveloped it, and from the midst of this a loud shriek was heard, as Dick, Henri, and Crusoe bounded over the packs with frantic gestures.

At this the gaping savages wheeled their steeds round, the dismounted horsemen sprang on behind two of their comrades, and the whole band dashed away over the plains as if they were chased by evil spirits.

Meanwhile Joe hastened towards his comrades in a state of great anxiety, for he knew at once that one of the powder-horns must have been accidentally blown up.

" No damage done, boys, I hope?" he cried on coming up.

" Damage!" cried Henri, holding his hands tight over his face. " Oh! oui, great damage—moche damage; me two eyes be blowed out of dere holes."

"'Not quite so bad as that, I hope," said Dick, who was very slightly singed, and forgot his own hurts in anxiety about his comrade. " Let me see."

" My eye!" exclaimed Joe Blunt, while a broad grin overspread his countenance, " ye've not improved yer looks, Henri."

This was true. The worthy hunter's hair was singed to such an extent that his entire countenance presented the appearance of a universal frizzle. Fortunately the skin, although much blackened, was quite uninjured—a fact which, when he ascertained it beyond a doubt, afforded so much satisfaction to Henri that he capered about shouting with delight, as if some piece of good fortune had befallen him.

The accident had happened in consequence of Henri having omitted to replace the stopper of his powder-horn, and when, in his anxiety for Joe, he fired at random amongst the Indians, despite Dick's entreaties to wait, a spark communicated with the powder-horn and blew him up. Dick and Crusoe were only a little singed, but the former was not disposed to quarrel with an accident which had sent their enemies so promptly to the right-about.

This band followed them for some nights, in the hope of being able to steal their horses while they slept; but they were not brave enough to venture a second time within range of the death-dealing rifle.

CHAPTER XXV

Dangers of the prairie—Our travellers attacked by Indians, and
delivered in a remarkable manner.

There are periods in the life of almost all men when
misfortunes seem to crowd upon them in rapid succession,
when they escape from one danger only to encounter
another, and when, to use a well-known expression, they
succeed in leaping out of the frying-pan at the expense of
plunging into the fire.

So was it with our three friends upon this occasion. They
were scarcely rid of the Blackfeet, who found them too
watchful to be caught napping, when, about daybreak one
morning, they encountered a roving band of Camanchee
Indians, who wore such a warlike aspect that Joe deemed
it prudent to avoid them if possible.

" They don't see us yit, I guess," said Joe, as he and his
companions drove the horses into a hollow between the
grassy waves of the prairie, " an' if we only can escape their
sharp eyes till we're in yonder clump o' willows, we're safe
enough."

" But why don't you ride up to them, Joe," inquired
Dick, " and make peace between them and the Pale-faces,
as you ha' done with other bands?"

" Because it's o' no use to risk our scalps for the chance
o' makin' peace wi' a rovin' war party. Keep yer head
down, Henri! If they git only a sight o' the top o' yer cap,
they'll be down on us like a breeze o' wind."

" Ha! let dem come!" said Henri.

" They'll come without askin' yer leave," remarked Joe,
dryly.

Notwithstanding his defiant expression, Henri had sufficient prudence to induce him to bend his head and shoulders, and in a few minutes they reached the shelter of the willows unseen by the savages. At least so thought Henri, Joe was not quite sure about it, and Dick hoped for the best.

In the course of half an hour the last of the Camanchees was seen to hover for a second on the horizon, like a speck of black against the sky, and then to disappear.

Immediately the three hunters vaulted on their steeds and resumed their journey; but before that evening closed they had sad evidence of the savage nature of the band from which they had escaped. On passing the brow of a slight eminence, Dick, who rode first, observed that Crusoe stopped 'and snuffed the breeze in an anxious, inquiring manner.

" What is't, pup?" said Dick, drawing up, for he knew that his faithful dog never gave a false alarm.

Crusoe replied by a short, uncertain bark, and then, bounding forward, disappeared behind a little wooded knoll. In another moment a long, dismal howl floated over the plains. There was a mystery about the dog's conduct which, coupled with his melancholy cry, struck the travellers with a superstitious feeling of dread, as they sat looking at each other in surprise.

" Come, let's clear it up," cried Joe Blunt, shaking the reins of his steed, and galloping forward. A few strides brought them to the other side of the knoll, where, scattered upon the torn and bloody turf, they discovered the scalped and mangled remains of about twenty or thirty human beings. Their skulls had been cleft by the tomahawk and their breasts pierced by the scalping-knife, and from the position in which many of them lay it was evident that they had been slain while asleep.

Joe's brow flushed and his lips became tightly compressed as he muttered between his set teeth, " Their skins are white."

A short examination sufficed to show that the men who had thus been barbarously murdered while they slept had been a band of trappers or hunters, but what their errand had been, or whence they came, they could not discover.

Everything of value had been carried off, and all the scalps had been taken. Most of the bodies, although much mutilated, lay in a posture that led our hunters to believe they had been killed while asleep, but one or two were cut almost to pieces, and from the blood-bespattered and trampled sward around, it seemed as if they had struggled long and fiercely for life. Whether or not any of the savages had been slain, it was impossible to tell, for if such had been the case, their comrades, doubtless, had carried away their bodies. That they had been slaughtered by the party of Camanchees who had been seen at daybreak was quite clear to Joe; but his burning desire to revenge the death of the white men had to be stifled, as his party was so small.

Long afterwards it was discovered that this was a band of trappers who, like those mentioned at the beginning of this volume, had set out to avenge the death of a comrade; but God, who has retained the right of vengeance in His own hand, saw fit to frustrate their purpose, by giving them into the hands of the savages whom they had set forth to slay.

As it was impossible to bury so many bodies, the travellers resumed their journey, and left them to bleach there in the wilderness; but they rode the whole of that day almost without uttering a word.

Meanwhile the Camanchees, who had observed the trio, and had ridden away at first for the purpose of deceiving them into the belief that they had passed unobserved, doubled on their track, and took a long sweep in order to keep out of sight until they could approach under the shelter of a belt of woodland towards which the travellers now approached.

The Indians adopted this course instead of the easier method of simply pursuing so weak a party, because the plains at this part were bordered by a long stretch of forest

into which the hunters could have plunged, and rendered
pursuit more difficult, if not almost useless. The detour
thus taken was so extensive that the shades of evening were
beginning to descend before they could put their plan into
execution. The forest lay about a mile to the right of our
hunters, like some dark mainland, of which the prairie was
the sea and the scattered clumps of wood the islands.

"There's no lack o' game here," said Dick Varley,
pointing to a herd of buffaloes which rose at their approach
and fled away towards the wood.

"I think we'll ha' thunder soon," remarked Joe. "I
never feel it onnatteral hot like this without lookin' out for
a plump."

"Ha! den ve better look hout for one goot tree to get
b'low," suggested Henri. "Voilà!" he added, pointing
with his finger towards the plain; "dere am a lot of wild
hosses."

A troop of about thirty wild horses appeared, as he spoke,
on the brow of a ridge, and advanced slowly towards
them.

"Hist!" exclaimed Joe, reining up; "hold on, lads.
Wild horses! my rifle to a pop-gun there's wilder men on
t'other side o' them."

"What mean you, Joe?" inquired Dick, riding close up

"D'ye see the little lumps on the shoulder o' each
horse?" said Joe. "Them's Injun's *feet*; an' if we don't
want to lose our scalps we'd better make for the forest."

Joe proved himself to be in earnest by wheeling round
and making straight for the thick wood as fast as his horse
could run. The others followed, driving the pack-horses
before them.

The effect of this sudden movement on the so-called
"wild horses" was very remarkable, and to one un-
acquainted with the habits of the Camanchee Indians must
have appeared almost supernatural. In the twinkling of an
eye every steed had a rider on its back, and before the
hunters had taken five strides in the direction of the forest,
the whole band were in hot pursuit, yelling like furies.

The manner in which these Indians accomplish this feat is very singular, and implies great activity and strength of muscle on the part of the savages.

The Camanchees are low in stature, and usually are rather corpulent. In their movements on foot they are heavy and ungraceful, and they are, on the whole, a slovenly and unattractive race of men. But the instant they mount their horses they seem to be entirely changed, and surprise the spectator with the ease and elegance of their movements. Their great and distinctive peculiarity as horsemen is the power they have acquired of throwing themselves suddenly on either side of their horse's body, and clinging on in such a way that no part of them is visible from the other side save the foot by which they cling. In this manner they approach their enemies at full gallop, and, without rising again to the saddle, discharge their arrows at them over the horses' backs, or even under their necks.

This apparently magical feat is accomplished by means of a halter of horse-hair, which is passed round under the neck of the horse, and both ends braided into the mane, on the withers, thus forming a loop which hangs under the neck and against the breast. This being caught by the hand, makes a sling, into which the elbow falls, taking the weight of the body on the middle of the upper arm. Into this loop the rider drops suddenly and fearlessly, leaving his heel to hang over the horse's back to steady him, and also to restore him to his seat when desired.

By this stratagem the Indians had approached on the present occasion almost within rifle range before they were discovered, and it required the utmost speed of the hunters' horses to enable them to avoid being overtaken. One of the Indians, who was better mounted than his fellows, gained on the fugitives so much that he came within arrow range, but reserved his shaft until they were close on the margin of the wood, when, being almost alongside of Henri, he fitted an arrow to his bow. Henri's eye was upon him, however. Letting go the line of the pack-horse which he was leading, he threw forward his rifle; but at the same moment the savage disappeared behind his horse, and an arrow whizzed past the hunter's ear.

Henri fired at the horse, which dropped instantly, hurling the astonished Camanchee upon the ground, where he lay for some time insensible. In a few seconds pursued and pursuers entered the wood, where both had to advance with caution, in order to avoid being swept off by the overhanging branches of the trees.

Meanwhile the sultry heat of which Joe had formerly spoken increased considerably, and a rumbling noise, as if of distant thunder, was heard; but the flying hunters paid no attention to it, for the led horses gave them so much trouble, and retarded their flight so much, that the Indians were gradually and visibly gaining on them.

"We'll ha' to let the packs go," said Joe, somewhat bitterly, as he looked over his shoulder. "Our scalps 'll pay for't, if we don't."

Henri uttered a peculiar and significant *hiss* between his teeth, as he said, "P'r'aps ve better stop and fight!"

Dick said nothing, being resolved to do exactly what Joe Blunt bid him; and Crusoe, for reasons best known to himself, also said nothing, but bounded along beside his master's horse, casting an occasional glance upwards to catch any signal that might be given.

They had passed over a considerable space of ground, and were forcing their way at the imminent hazard of their necks through a densely-clothed part of the wood, when the sound above referred to increased, attracting the attention of both parties. In a few seconds the air was filled with a steady and continuous rumbling sound, like the noise of a distant cataract. Pursuers and fugitives drew reign instinctively, and came to a dead stand; while the rumbling increased to a roar, and evidently approached them rapidly, though as yet nothing to cause it could be seen, except that there was a dense, dark cloud overspreading the sky to the southward. The air was oppressively still and hot.

"What can it be?" inquired Dick, looking at Joe, who

was gazing with an expression of wonder, not unmixed with concern, at the southern sky.

"Dun'no', boy. I've bin more in the woods than in the clearin' in my day, but I niver heerd the likes o' that."

"It am like t'ondre," said Henri; "mais it nevair do stop."

This was true. The sound was similar to continuous, un-interrupted thunder. On it came with a magnificent roar that shook the very earth, and revealed itself at last in the shape of a mighty whirlwind. In a moment the distant woods bent before it, and fell like grass before the scythe. It was a whirling hurricane, accompanied by a deluge of rain such as none of the party had ever before witnessed. Steadily, fiercely, irresistibly it bore down upon them, while the crash of falling, snapping, and uprooting trees mingled with the dire artillery of that sweeping storm like the musketry on a battle-field.

"Follow me, lads!" shouted Joe, turning his horse and dashing at full speed towards a rocky eminence that offered shelter. But shelter was not needed. The storm was clearly defined. Its limits were as distinctly marked as if it had been a living intelligence sent forth to put a belt of desola-tion round the world; and, although the edge of devastation was not five hundred yards from the rock behind which the hunters were stationed, only a few drops of ice-cold rain fell upon them.

It passed directly between the Camanchee Indians and their intended victims, placing between them a barrier which it would have taken days to cut through. The storm blew for an hour, then it travelled onward in its might, and was lost in the distance. Whence it came and whither it went none could tell, but far as the eye could see on either hand an avenue a quarter of a mile wide was cut through the forest. It had levelled everything with the dust; the very grass was beaten flat; the trees were torn, shivered, snapped across, and crushed; and the earth itself in many places was ploughed up and furrowed with deep scars. The chaos was indescribable, and it is probable that centuries will not quite obliterate the work of that single hour.

While it lasted, Joe and his comrades remained speechless and awe-stricken. When it passed, no Indians were to be, seen. So our hunters remounted their steeds, and, with feelings of gratitude to God for having delivered them alike from savage foes and from the destructive power of the whirlwind, resumed their journey towards the Mustang Valley.

CHAPTER XXVI

One fine afternoon, a few weeks after the storm of which we have given an account in the last chapter, old Mrs. Varley was seated beside her own chimney corner in the little cottage by the lake, gazing at the glowing logs with the earnest expression of one whose thoughts were far away. Her kind face was paler than usual, and her hands rested idly on her knee, grasping the knitting-wires to which was attached a half-finished stocking.

On a stool near to her sat young Marston, the lad to whom, on the day of the shooting-match, Dick Varley had given his old rifle. The boy had an anxious look about him, as he lifted his eyes from time to time to the widow's face.

" Did ye say, my boy, that they were *all* killed?" inquired Mrs. Varley, awaking from her reverie with a deep sigh.

" Every one," replied Marston. " Jim Scraggs, who brought the news, said they wos all lying dead with their scalps off. They wos a party o' white men."

Mrs. Varley sighed again, and her face assumed an expression of anxious pain as she thought of her son Dick being exposed to a similar fate. Mrs. Varley was not given to nervous fears, but as she listened to the boy's recital of the slaughter of a party of white men, news of which had just reached the valley, her heart sank, and she prayed inwardly to Him who is the husband of the widow that her dear one might be protected from the ruthless hand of the savage.

After a short pause, during which young Marston fidgeted

about and looked concerned, as if he had something to say which he would fain leave unsaid, Mrs. Varley continued—

" Was it far off where the bloody deed was done?"

" Yes; three weeks off, I believe. And Jim Scraggs said that he found a knife that looked like the one wot belonged to—to—" the lad hesitated.

" To whom, my boy? Why don't ye go on?"

" To your son Dick."

The widow's hands dropped by her side, and she would have fallen had not Marston caught her.

" Oh, mother dear, don't take on like that!" he cried, smoothing down the widow's hair as her head rested on his breast.

For some time Mrs. Varley suffered the boy to fondle her in silence, while her breast laboured with anxious dread

" Tell me all," she said at last, recovering a little. " Did Jim see—Dick?"

" No," answered the boy. " He looked at all the bodies, but did not find his; so he sent me over here to tell ye that p'r'aps he's escaped."

Mrs. Varley breathed more freely, and earnestly thanked God; but her fears soon returned when she thought of his being a prisoner, and recalled the tales of terrible cruelty often related of the savages.

While she was still engaged in closely questioning the lad, Jim Scraggs himself entered the cottage, and endeavoured in a gruff sort of way to reassure the widow.

" Ye see, mistress," he said, " Dick is an uncommon tough customer, an' if he could only git fifty yards' start, there's not an Injun in the West as could git hold o' him agin; so don't be takin' on."

" But what if he's been taken prisoner?" said the widow.

" Ay, that's jest wot I've comed about. Ye see, it's not onlikely he's bin took; so about thirty o' the lads o' the valley are ready jest now to start away and give the red reptiles chase, an' I come to tell ye; so keep up heart, mistress."

With this parting word of comfort, Jim withdrew, and

Marston soon followed, leaving the widow to weep and pray in solitude.

Meanwhile an animated scene was going on near the block-house. Here thirty of the young hunters of the Mustang Valley were assembled, actively engaged in supplying themselves with powder and lead, and tightening their girths, preparatory to setting out in pursuit of the Indians who had murdered the white men; while hundreds of boys and girls, and not a few matrons, crowded round and listened to the conversation, and to the deep threats of vengeance that were uttered ever and anon by the younger men.

Major Hope, too, was among them. The worthy major, unable to restrain his roving propensities, determined to revisit the Mustang Valley, and had arrived only two days before.

Backwoodsmen's preparations are usually of the shortest and simplest. In a few minutes the cavalcade was ready, and away they went towards the prairies, with the bold major at their head. But their journey was destined to come to an abrupt and unexpected close. A couple of hours' gallop brought them to the edge of one of those open plains which sometimes break up the woodland near the verge of the great prairies. It stretched out like a green lake towards the horizon, on which, just as the band of horsemen reached it, the sun was descending in a blaze of glory

With a shout of enthusiasm, several of the younger members of the party sprang forward into the plain at a gallop; but the shout was mingled with one of a different tone from the older men.

"Hist!—hollo!—hold on, ye catamounts! There's Injuns ahead!"

The whole band came to a sudden halt at this cry, and watched eagerly, and for some time in silence, the motions of a small party of horsemen who were seen in the far distance, like black specks on the golden sky

"They come this way, I think," said Major Hope, after gazing steadfastly at them for some minutes.

Several of the old hands signified their assent to this suggestion by a grunt, although to unaccustomed eyes the objects in question looked more like crows than horsemen, and their motion was for some time scarcely perceptible.

"I sees pack-horses among them," cried young Marston in an excited tone; "an' there's three riders; but there's som'thin' else, only wot it be I can't tell."

"Ye've sharp eyes, younker," remarked one of the men, "an' I do believe ye're right."

Presently the horsemen approached, and soon there was a brisk fire of guessing as to who they could be. It was evident that the strangers observed the cavalcade of white men, and regarded them as friends, for they did not check the headlong speed at which they approached. In a few minutes they were clearly made out to be a party of three horsemen driving pack-horses before them, and *somethin'* which some of the hunters guessed was a buffalo calf.

Young Marston guessed too, but his guess was different. Moreover, it was uttered with a yell that would have done credit to the fiercest of all the savages. "Crusoe!" he shouted, while at the same moment he brought his whip heavily down on the flank of his little horse, and sprang over the prairie like an arrow.

One of the approaching horsemen was far ahead of his comrades, and seemed as if encircled with the flying and voluminous mane of his magnificent horse.

"Ha! ho!" gasped Marston in a low tone to himself, as he flew along. "Crusoe! I'd know ye, dog, among a thousand! A buffalo calf! Ha! git on with ye!"

This last part of the remark was added to his horse, and was followed by a whack that increased the pace considerably.

The pace between two such riders was soon devoured.

"Hollo! Dick—Dick Varley!"

"Eh! why, Marston, my boy!"

The friends reined up so suddenly that one might have fancied they had met like the knights of old in the shock of mortal conflict.

" Is't yerself, Dick Varley?"

Dick held out his hand, and his eyes glistened, but he could not find words.

Marston seized it, and, pushing his horse close up, vaulted nimbly off and alighted on Charlie's back behind his friend.

" Off ye go, Dick! I'll take ye to yer mother."

Without reply, Dick shook the reins, and in another minute was in the midst of the hunters.

To the numberless questions that were put to him he only waited to shout aloud, " We're all safe! They'll tell ye all about it," he added, pointing to his comrades, who were now close at hand; and then, dashing onward, made straight for home, with little Marston clinging to his waist like a monkey.

Charlie was fresh, and so was Crusoe, so you may be sure it was not long before they all drew up opposite the door of the widow's cottage. Before Dick could dismount Marston had slipped off, and was already in the kitchen.

" Here's Dick, mother!"

The boy was an orphan, and loved the widow so much that he had come at last to call her mother.

Before another word could be uttered, Dick Varley was in the room. Marston immediately stepped out and softly shut the door. Reader—we shall not open it!

Having shut the door, as we have said, Marston ran down to the edge of the lake and yelled with delight—usually terminating each paroxysm with the Indian war-whoop, with which he was well acquainted. Then he danced, and then he sat down on a rock, and became suddenly aware that there were other hearts there, close beside him, as glad as his own. Another mother of the Mustang Valley was rejoicing over a long-lost son.

Crusoe and his mother Fan were scampering round each other in a manner that evinced powerfully the strength of their mutual affection.

Talk of holding converse! Every hair on Crusoe's body—every motion of his limbs—was eloquent with silent language. He gazed into his mother's mild eyes as if he would read her inmost soul (supposing that she had one). He turned his head to every possible angle, and cocked his ears to every conceivable elevation, and rubbed his nose against Fan's and barked softly, in every imaginable degree of modulation, and varied these proceedings by bounding away at full speed over the rocks of the beach, and in among the bushes and out again, but always circling round and round Fan, and keeping her in view!

It was a sight worth seeing, and young Marston sat down on a rock, deliberately and enthusiastically, to gloat over it. But perhaps the most remarkable part of it has not yet been referred to. There was yet another heart there that was glad—exceeding glad that day. It was a little one too, but it was big for the body that held it. Grumps was there, and all that Grumps did was to sit on his haunches and stare at Fan and Crusoe, and wag his tail as well as he could in so awkward a position! Grumps was evidently bewildered with delight, and had lost nearly all power to express it. Crusoe's conduct towards him, too, was not calculated to clear his faculties. Every time he chanced to pass near Grumps in his elephantine gambols he gave him a passing touch with his nose, which always knocked him head over heels; whereat Grumps invariably got up quickly and wagged his tail with additional energy. Before the feelings of those canine friends were calmed, they were all three ruffled into a state of comparative exhaustion.

Then young Marston called Crusoe to him, and Crusoe, obedient to the voice of friendship, went.

"Are you happy, my dog?"

"You're a stupid fellow to ask such question; however, it's an amiable one. Yes, I am."

"What do *you* want, ye small bundle o' hair?"

This was addressed to Grumps, who came forward innocently, and sat down to listen to the conversation.

On being thus sternly questioned the little dog put down its ears flat, and hung its head, looking up at the same time with a deprecatory look, as if to say, " Oh dear, I beg pardon. I—I only want to sit near Crusoe, please; but if you wish it, I'll go away, sad and lonely, with my tail *very* much between my legs; indeed I will—only say the word, but—but I'd *rather* stay if I might."

"Poor bundle!" said Marston, patting its head, " you can stay, then. Hooray! Crusoe, are you happy, I say? Does your heart bound in you like a cannon-ball that wants to find its way out, and can't, eh?"

Crusoe put his snout against Marston's cheek, and in the excess of his joy the lad threw his arms round the dog's neck and hugged it vigorously—a piece of impulsive affection which that noble animal bore with characteristic meekness, and which Grumps regarded with idiotic satisfaction.

CHAPTER XXVII

Rejoicings—The feast at the block-house—Grumps and Crusoe come out
strong—The closing scene.

The day of Dick's arrival with his companions was a
great day in the annals of the Mustang Valley, and Major
Hope resolved to celebrate it by an impromptu festival at
the old block-house; for many hearts in the valley had
been made glad that day, and he knew full well that, under
such circumstances, some safety-valve must be devised for
the escape of overflowing excitement.

A messenger was sent round to invite the population to
assemble without delay in front of the block-house. With
backwoods-like celerity the summons was obeyed; men,
women, and children hurried towards the central point,
wondering, yet more than half suspecting, what was the
major's object in calling them together.

They were not long in doubt. The first sight that presented itself, as they came trooping up the slope in front of
the log-hut, was an ox roasting whole before a gigantic
bonfire. Tables were being extemporized on the broad level
plot in front of the gate. Other fires there were, of smaller
dimensions, on which sundry steaming pots were placed,
and various joints of wild horse, bear, and venison roasted,
and sent forth a savoury odour as well as a pleasant hissing
noise. The inhabitants of the block-house were self-taught
brewers, and the result of their recent labours now stood
displayed in a row of goodly casks of beer—the only beverage with which the dwellers in these far-off regions were
wont to regale themselves.

The whole scene, as the cooks moved actively about upon
the lawn, and children romped round the fires, and settlers
came flocking through the forests, might have recalled the

revelry of merry England in the olden time, though the costumes of the far west were perhaps somewhat different from those of old England.

No one of all the band assembled there on that day of rejoicing required to ask what it was all about. Had any one been in doubt for a moment, a glance at the centre of the crowd assembled round the gate of the western fortress would have quickly enlightened him. For there stood Dick Varley, and his mild-looking mother, and his loving dog Crusoe. There, too, stood Joe Blunt, like a bronzed warrior returned from the fight, turning from one to another as question poured in upon question almost too rapidly to permit of a reply. There, too, stood Henri, making enthusiastic speeches to whoever chose to listen to him—now glaring at the crowd with clenched fists and growling voice, as he told of how Joe and he had been tied hand and foot, and lashed to poles, and buried in leaves, and threatened with a slow death by torture; at other times bursting into a hilarious laugh as he held forth on the predicament of Mahtawa, when that wily chief was treed by Crusoe in the prairie.

Young Marston was there, too, hanging about Dick, whom he loved as a brother and regarded as a perfect hero. Grumps, too, was there, and Fan. Do you think, reader, that Grumps looked at any one but Crusoe? If you do, you are mistaken. Grumps on that day became a regular, an incorrigible, utter, and perfect nuisance to everybody—not excepting himself, poor beast! Grumps was a dog of one idea, and that idea was Crusoe. Out of that great idea there grew one little secondary idea, and that idea was that the only joy on earth worth mentioning was to sit on his haunches, exactly six inches from Crusoe's nose, and gaze steadfastly into his face. Wherever Crusoe went Grumps went. If Crusoe stopped, Grumps was down before him in an instant. If Crusoe bounded away, which in the exuberance of his spirits he often did, Grumps was after him like a bundle of mad hair. He was in everybody's way, in Crusoe's way, and being, so to speak, " beside

himself ", was also in his own way. If people trod upon
him accidentally, which they often did, Grumps uttered a
solitary heart-rending yell proportioned in intensity to the
excruciating nature of the torture he endured, then instantly
resumed his position and his fascinated stare. Crusoe
generally held his head up, and gazed over his little friend
at what was going on around him; but if for a moment he
permitted his eye to rest on the countenance of Grumps,
that creature's tail became suddenly imbued with an
amount of wriggling vitality that seemed to threaten its
separation from the body.

It was really quite interesting to watch this unblushing,
and disinterested, and utterly reckless display of affection
on the part of Grumps, and the amiable way in which
Crusoe put up with it. We say put up with it advisedly,
because it must have been a very great inconvenience to
him, seeing that if he attempted to move, his satellite
moved in front of him, so that his only way of escaping
temporarily was by jumping over Grumps's head.

Grumps was everywhere all day. Nobody, almost,
escaped trampling on part of him. He tumbled over everything, into everything, and against everything. He knocked
himself, singed himself, and scalded himself, and in fact
forgot himself altogether; and when, late that night, Crusoe
went with Dick into his mother's cottage, and the door was
shut, Grumps stretched his ruffled, battered, ill-used, and
dishevelled little body down on the door-step, thrust his
nose against the opening below the door, and lay in humble
contentment all night, for he knew that Crusoe was there.

Of course such an occasion could not pass without a
shooting-match. Rifles were brought out after the feast
was over, just before the sun went down into its bed on the
western prairies, and " the nail " was soon surrounded by
bullets, tipped by Joe Blunt and Jim Scraggs, and of course
driven home by Dick Varley, whose " silver rifle " had now
become in its owner's hand a never-failing weapon. Races,
too, were started, and here again Dick stood pre-eminent;
and when night spread her dark mantle over the scene,

the two best fiddlers in the settlement were placed on empty beer-casks, and some danced by the light of the monster fires, while others listened to Joe Blunt as he recounted their adventures on the prairies and among the Rocky Mountains.

There were sweethearts, and wives, and lovers at the feast; but we question if any heart there was so full of love, and admiration, and gratitude, as that of the Widow Varley as she watched her son Dick throughout that merry evening.

.   .   .   .

Years rolled by, and the Mustang Valley prospered. One sad blow fell on the Widow Varley's heart. Her only brother, Daniel Hood, was murdered by the Indians. Deeply and long she mourned, and it required all Dick's efforts to comfort her.

Joe Blunt and Henri became leading men in the councils of the Mustang Valley; but Dick Varley preferred the woods, although, as long as his mother lived, he hovered round her cottage—going off sometimes for a day, sometimes for a week, but never longer. After her head was laid in the dust, Dick took altogether to the woods, with Crusoe and Charlie, the wild horse, as his only companions. And soon Dick, the bold hunter, and his dog Crusoe became renowned in the frontier settlements from the banks of the Yellowstone River to the Gulf of Mexico.

Many a grizzly bear did the famous " silver rifle " lay low, and many a wild, exciting chase and adventure did Dick go through; but during his occasional visits to the Mustang Valley he was wont to say to Joe Blunt and Henri—with whom he always sojourned—that " nothin' he ever felt or saw came up to his *first* grand dash over the western prairies into the heart of the Rocky Mountains ". And in saying this, with enthusiasm in his eye and voice, Dick invariably appealed to, and received a ready affirmative glance from, his early companion and his faithful loving friend, the dog Crusoe.

PRINTED IN ROMANIA

Abbey